Rogue States and Nuclear Outlaws

ROGUE STATES

America's Search for a

AND NUCLEAR

New Foreign Policy

OUTLAWS

MICHAEL KLARE

HILL AND WANG • *New York*

A division of Farrar, Straus & Giroux

LIBRARY OF CONGRESS CATALOGING-IN-PUBLICATION DATA
Klare, Michael.
Rogue states and nuclear outlaws : America's search for a new
foreign policy / Michael Klare.—1st ed.
p.   cm.
Includes bibliographical references and index.
1. Nuclear weapons—Government policy—United States. 2. United
States—Defenses. 3. Nuclear weapons—Developing countries.
4. World politics—1989–   I. Title.
UA23.K627   1994   355.02'07'0973—dc20   94–45267   CIP

To my father, Charles Klare,
and my son, Alexander (Sasha) Klare-Ayvazian,
with the hope that Sasha will live in a world as
safe and decent as the one my father tried to make for me

Acknowledgments

A BOOK PROJECT on this scale, which took three years of long nights and many weekends to complete, could not have been realized without considerable help from a great number of people. Throughout this enterprise, I relied on my family, friends, colleagues, my editors, and professional acquaintances far and wide for encouragement, support, advice, and assistance. I am deeply indebted to each and every one of them for their kind and generous contributions to the success of this effort.

My first and most vigorous expression of gratitude is due to my family, notably my partner Andrea Ayvazian and my son Alexander (Sasha) Klare-Ayvazian. From the beginning of this project to its completion, they supported my work, helped me in an infinite number of ways, and put up with my frequent disappearances to the writing table. Although this project must have seemed endless at times, and they missed my company on many evenings and weekends, they always rallied when I needed them, and I will be grateful to them always.

Many friends also provided advice and support during the length of this project, making my job that much easier. I regret that I cannot name them all, but I would like to give a special vote of thanks to Fred, Gina, and Gloria Ayvazian, Meg Gage, Andrew Janiak, David Leech, Jim Levey, Deborah Lubar, Lucy Mathiak, David Morrison, Daniel Thomas, Daniel Volman, and Cora Weiss. Special thanks are also due to three people who were especially supportive: my father, Charles Klare; my brother, Karl Klare; and my sister, Jane Klare.

While working on this book, I served as director of the Five College Program in Peace and World Security Studies (PAWSS), and I owe an enormous debt of gratitude to my colleagues at PAWSS and the Five Colleges, Inc. Not only did they encourage me to undertake this endeavor, but also provided invaluable support, advice, and assistance at every step along the way. My deep appreciation to Adi Bemak, Yogesh Chandrani, and Linda Harris of the PAWSS staff, and to Lorna Peterson, Elizabeth Loudon, and their wonderful colleagues at the Five College Center. Thanks also to Gregory Prince, the president of Hampshire College (where PAWSS is housed) and a strong supporter of PAWSS's work.

I also benefited enormously from my collegial ties with other faculty members at the Five Colleges (Amherst, Hampshire, Mount Holyoke, and Smith colleges, and the University of Massachusetts at Amherst). Many of the ideas presented in this book were first tested out—and often revised as a result—during conversations with colleagues at seminars, workshops, and lunch and dinner meetings. I regret that I cannot recall all these conversations, but I would like to pay special tribute to Eqbal Ahmad, Carollee Bengelsdorf, Margaret Cerullo, and Allan Krass of Hampshire, Pavel Machala, Bill Taubman, and Ron Tiersky of Amherst, Vinnie Ferraro of Mount Holyoke, Tom Riddell of Smith, and James Der Derian, Eric Einhorn, and George Levinger of the University of Massachusetts.

A project of this sort entails the collection of vast amounts of documents and information—a task that I could not have completed without the help of many fine individuals at key centers in Washington. We are fortunate in this country to possess a large network of non-profit, public-interest organizations that support research and otherwise contribute to informed public discussion of critical policy issues. I am especially indebted in this regard to Lee Feinstein and Jon Wolfstahl of the Arms Control Association, Natalie Goldring of the British-American Security Information Council (BASIC), Lora Lumpe and Paul Pineo of the Federation of American Scientists, Richard Barnet of the Institute for Policy Studies, and Peter Kornbluh of the National Security Archive.

Many friends and colleagues made helpful suggestions at various stages in this project, but one person, Tom Engelhardt, provided exceptional assistance far beyond the call of duty. Tom read several drafts of the entire manuscript, made innumerable suggestions for its improvement, and encouraged me to stick with the project during those difficult months when my enthusiasm was at its lowest ebb. I am enormously grateful for his support and assistance.

Finally, I want to pay special tribute to my editor, Sara Bershtel, and to all the other wonderful people at Hill and Wang / Farrar, Straus and Giroux. Sara did a terrific job of editing and, more than that, had a vision of this book's importance that helped sustain me through three years of difficult and sometimes frustrating labor. And I have nothing but respect for her colleagues and associates: Thank you all for everything you have done to make this book a reality.

—Michael Klare
Northampton, Mass.
October 1994

Contents

Rogue States and Nuclear Outlaws

Chapter One

IN PURSUIT OF ENEMIES

The Remaking of

U. S. Military Strategy

IF THE COLD War had ended in combat, the fall of the Berlin Wall on November 8, 1989, would have been its Normandy—the day on which enemy defenses started to fragment and the ultimate triumph of the United States became inevitable. The Soviet Union itself would survive for two more years, and large numbers of Soviet and American forces would continue to eye each other warily across the East-West divide in Europe, but from that day onward, there was never any doubt about the ultimate demise of the Soviet empire. Within days of the Wall's collapse, East Germany and Czechoslovakia discarded their Communist leaders, and reformist parties in Hungary and Bulgaria began a drive for power. By the end of 1989, the Warsaw Treaty Organization had ceased to exist as a functioning military alliance, and Soviet forces had begun their withdrawal to decrepit and unwelcoming bases in the crumbling imperial heartland.

At long last, official Washington could anticipate victory in its forty-year struggle to encircle, weaken and ultimately dismember the Communist bloc. For America's leaders, many of whom had devoted a lifetime to orchestrating the "containment" of Soviet power, this was a moment to be cheered and savored. "This is a remarkable event," Secretary of State James Baker declared. "It is the most significant event in terms of the East-West relationship since the end of the [Second World] War."[1] Cheer as they might, however, these leaders could not entirely conceal from themselves the fact that the Soviet collapse spelled significant hardship for the American military establishment, no less than the Russian.

Throughout the Cold War era, the U.S. war machine had been trained and equipped for one all-consuming mission: to deter Soviet aggression in Europe while blocking Soviet inroads into contested Third World areas. To sustain this mission, a bipartisan consensus in Congress had allocated some $11.5 trillion in military appropriations between 1947 and 1989, plus billions of dollars on such related activities as nuclear weapons fabrication, foreign military assistance, intelligence collection, civil defense preparation, and military-related research. In further support, Congress had approved a peacetime draft, the formation of numerous military alliances, and the permanent deployment of hundreds of thousands of American troops at bases and garrisons abroad.

The Soviet threat also governed the shape and orientation of America's military forces. Every officer, NCO, and soldier was trained and equipped to fight against Soviet combat units, while the defense establishment as a whole was configured for high-intensity conflict with the Warsaw Pact. Every American weapon was designed with Soviet capabilities in mind. "It would be really impossible to overstate the degree to which our defense planning focused on the Soviet Union," Secretary of Defense Les Aspin later acknowledged. "It determined the size of the defense budget, the kinds of divisions we had, how we organized our forces . . . even how we designed [our] weapons."[2]

Furthermore, the Cold War provided a mental map for military and civilian strategists—a cognitive system for dividing the world into friends and enemies, shaping a response to overseas crises, and providing a rationale for periodic military intervention abroad. As historian Gaddis Smith suggested, "American leaders during this period were confident that they had discovered a grand historical pattern that showed what the role of the United States in the world must be." No matter the nature of the challenge to America's global interests, these leaders determined their response by defining the problem in terms of U.S.–Soviet competition.[3]

Although reluctant to admit it even to themselves, U.S. military leaders understood that for nearly half a century, they had lived in what amounted to a symbiotic relationship with the Soviet military. When the Soviet war machine grew in strength and vitality, American forces would be bolstered accordingly, with each increase in Soviet manpower matched by a corresponding increase in U.S. firepower, and each increase in Soviet firepower countered by fresh advances in U.S. technology. So long as the public perceived a significant national security threat from Soviet forces, Congress was ready to finance almost every weapon, program, or combat unit deemed necessary by U.S. strategists.

Because Soviet strength was still thought to be increasing in the late 1970s and early 1980s, most Americans favored President Ronald Reagan's proposals for a sizeable increase in military power. Pentagon spending rose from $143.9 billion in fiscal year 1980 to $294.7 billion in fiscal 1985, and new Army divisions, fighter squadrons, and naval units were added to the American military lineup. The Reagan administration also initiated the systematic modernization of U.S. nuclear forces, including the production and deployment of the B-1 bomber, the M-X intercontinental ballistic missile, and the Trident-II submarine-launched ballistic missile.

At the time of the Berlin Wall's collapse, the U.S. military establishment consisted of 2,124,900 active-duty personnel, of whom 766,500 served in the Army, 583,900 in the Navy, 579,200 in the Air Force, and 195,300 in the Marine Corps. In terms of basic combat units, this force comprised eighteen Army divisions, fourteen aircraft carrier battle groups, twenty-five tactical fighter wings, and three Marine Corps divisions.[4] The Pentagon lineup also encompassed a wide range of specialized military commands, including nuclear weapons forces, logistical brigades, intelligence units, and communications teams. Each of these units, moreover, was linked to a supporting network of think-tanks, research organizations, industrial firms, and trade associations. At the close of the Cold War, this network encompassed some 30,000 large and small firms, employed some 3.3 million American workers, and divided up some $175 billion per year in military contracts. These firms conducted scientific research, designed and built major weapons, fed U.S. troops at home and abroad, and managed the paperwork of the world's largest bureaucracy. The entire apparatus—scientific, technical, educational, and industrial—was dependent on a substantial Soviet threat for its continued health and vitality.

Not surprisingly, then, the end of the Cold War provided an enormous shock for American military leaders. Not only did it deprive them of an enemy against which to train and equip their forces, but it also eradicated the mental map that hitherto had explained world events and governed U.S. policymaking. "No longer could the question, 'Which course will most contribute to frustrating the Kremlin design?' be asked at every turn and be seen to yield the definitive answer on where the United States must go," observed Smith.[5]

For policymakers at the Department of State, this lack of a clear strategic template proved awkward and inconvenient, but not incapacitating. In lieu of a coherent grand strategy, senior officials simply improvised when faced with overseas crises. For planners at the Department of Defense, however, the end of the Cold War proved devastating. Without the Soviet threat to guard against, they had no basis on which to develop contingency plans, train troops, design weapons, or test their combat skills. As MIT professor and former Pentagon adviser William W. Kaufmann observed at the time, American military officers plunged into a severe "identity crisis," leaving the Defense Department mentally "rudderless" at this critical juncture in its history.[6]

"For almost all of my adult life," admitted General Colin Powell, the nation's highest-ranking military officer, "I worried, in one way or another, about World War III." This meant planning for a war with "an empire that had worldwide ambitions, a worldwide strategy, and the ability to project power around the world." Suddenly, it was all "gone," said Powell; the empire that had appeared so menacing for so many years, and that had governed the lives and careers of all those who now commanded U.S. forces, had ceased to exist.[7]

Aside from its psychological effects, the collapse of the Warsaw Pact posed some very immediate practical problems for senior military officials. With the Soviet Union in disarray, public support for a large military establishment began to diminish, and every program in the defense budget came under intense scrutiny. Like all U.S. government agencies, the Department of Defense must obtain Congressional approval for its budgetary allocations on a year-by-year basis, justifying its spending plans anew each January. Unless a new rationale for these programs could be found, the Pentagon would soon encounter great difficulty in securing the funds needed to preserve them.

But no such rationale was at hand. Despite the billions of dollars that had been spent over the years to monitor Soviet activities and plan for all conceivable crises and contingencies, the Department of Defense had never given serious thought to the possibility of a world unmenaced by the Soviet Union. While lip service had been paid to the eventual resolution—through combat or otherwise—of the U.S.–Soviet rivalry, no strategic plans had been devised for a post–Cold War period. As a result, no justification had been developed for the continued existence of a large military establishment. Military officials who had always been ready to offer a variety of rationales for the pursuit of one or another anti-Soviet program now found themselves at a loss to describe their long-range strategic vision.

In fact, during the preceding decade, the only people who had given any thought to the orientation and structure of the U.S. military-industrial enterprise in a post–Cold War period were the Pentagon's critics. From the late 1970s on, a vociferous antinuclear movement had called for a U.S.–Soviet freeze in nuclear weapons production, to be followed by the gradual elimination of all such weapons. With the ascendancy in Moscow of Mikhail Gorbachev and the subsequent signing of new U.S.–Soviet arms control agreements, the antinuclear movement began to subside; however, other critics began to stress the negative economic consequences of pumped-up military budgets and to call for the reallocation of military funds to the civilian sector. Together, these two strains of thought represented a formidable challenge to the Cold-War-as-usual thinking that pervaded the military leadership.

In the late 1980s, as Gorbachev began to promote his policies of perestroika, a number of economists in the United States spoke of an urgent need for "reinvestment," "reindustrialization," and the "revitalization" of the faltering American economy. To accomplish this transformation, they argued, more funds would have to be invested in America's domestic infrastructure—schools, roads, universities, and so on—and less in military forces and installations.[8] This argument received further credibility from the 1987 publication of Yale professor Paul Kennedy's *The Rise and Fall of the Great Powers*. Comparing America's current political and economic status to that of other great empires in decline, Kennedy argued that the United States could not avert irreversible decay unless it shed some of its overseas military commitments and channeled additional resources into the reconstruction of its domestic industrial infrastructure.[9]

The publication of Kennedy's book ignited a major debate in the United States over the tradeoffs between a costly, far-flung military establishment and a deteriorating infrastructure at home.[10] Some pundits sought to ridicule the notion of a United States in decline, but many policymakers began to look closely at the potential economic benefits of a shift in emphasis from military preparedness to economic reconstruction.[11] Even such former military leaders as Robert S. McNamara, the Secretary of Defense in the Kennedy and Johnson administrations, and Lawrence J. Korb, an Assistant Secretary of Defense in the Reagan administration, began to call for a significant decrease in military spending linked to fresh investment in America's health, education, and transportation systems.[12]

When the Berlin Wall fell in November 1989, these critics, unlike

U.S. military leaders, were already prepared to unveil sweeping alternatives to the nation's Cold War–oriented strategic posture. On December 11, 1989, McNamara and Korb told the Senate Budget Committee that U.S. military spending could safely be cut in half over the next five years, freeing hundreds of billions of dollars for domestic reconstruction. "By such a shift," McNamara testified, "we should be able to enhance global stability, strengthen our own security, and, at the same time, produce the resources to support a much-needed restructuring of the economy."[13]

Although most members of Congress were not willing to approve an immediate fifty percent cut in military spending, many were ready to consider a series of smaller, but nonetheless significant, reductions in Pentagon appropriations. "For the first time in a long time," House Budget Committee chairman Leon E. Panetta noted in early 1990, a major military spending cut "is on the table in a big way."[14] Panetta's counterpart in the Senate, Jim Sasser of Tennessee, drew up a long list of military programs for possible cancellation or reduction, including the B-2 Stealth bomber, the mobile M-X missile, the C-17 cargo plane, and the Reagan administration's much-vaunted Strategic Defense Initiative (popularly known as "Star Wars").[15] Other members of Congress, including such prominent Republicans as Senator John W. Warner of Virginia, also began compiling lists of possible program cuts.[16]

These disparate plans and proposals, which together fell under the rubric of a "peace dividend," left the Pentagon's leaders in an unaccustomed defensive position. With neither an obvious enemy nor a coherent post–Cold War blueprint of their own to fall back on, they faced the dismaying prospect of cuts in troop strength, weapons procurement, and the officer corps, on a scale not seen since the end of World War II. It had become clear that only one "enemy" was truly capable of wounding them: the supporters of the so-called peace dividend, who threatened to capture public opinion and overrun Congress.

In response, some military officials chose to engage in what psychologists would characterize as "denial," a systematic refusal to face

up to the facts. Prominent among these officials was Secretary of
Defense Dick Cheney, who continued to identify the Soviet Union
as the principal threat to American security. "While cooperative aspects of the U.S. relationship with the Soviet Union are growing,"
he observed in late 1989, "the United States must be prepared to
remain in long-term competition with the Soviet Union."[17] Even in
1990, with the Warsaw Pact in ruins, Cheney continued to emphasize
the threat posed by Soviet expansionism. "Fundamental Soviet objectives in the Third World do not appear to have changed," he told
U.S. commanders that February.[18]

Other senior officers, who could not hide from themselves the
ominous implications of the Warsaw Pact's collapse, chose instead
to engage in another time-honored response to budget cuts: interservice wrangling over the disposition of available funds. Suspecting
that the defense establishment as a whole would be downsized significantly in the years ahead, these officers sought to ensure that *their*
service—be it the Army, the Navy, the Air Force, or the Marine
Corps—would be subjected to smaller cutbacks than the others. In
particular, the Army fought with the Marine Corps over which service should be assigned the primary interventionary role in the post–
Cold War era, and the Navy and the Air Force fought over which
service could best project power to distant conflict zones.[19]

But, while many officers joined Cheney in focusing on Soviet
threat, or plunged into interservice disputes over roles and missions,
some senior officials responded by seeking to invent a new *raison
d'être* for the military establishment. Recognizing that Congress and
the public would no longer support a Soviet-oriented military posture
at a time of diminishing Soviet strength, these officers, led by General
George Lee Butler of the J-5 (Strategic Plans and Policy) Directorate
of the Joint Staff, set out to develop an alternative strategic outlook
based on non-Soviet threats to U.S. security. In essence, they sought
to reconstruct military strategy around a new guiding principle that
would prove as reliable in the post–Cold War era as containment
had during the Cold War period.[20]

The quest for a new strategic posture gained momentum in November 1990 under the leadership of General Powell, the newly appointed Chairman of the Joint Chiefs of Staff. A long-term Army career officer who had risen through the ranks, Powell was no stranger to Washington policymaking circles. From 1983 to 1986, he had served as Defense Secretary Caspar Weinberger's personal military assistant, and then had worked for two years in the White House as National Security Adviser to President Reagan. After returning to the Army as head of the Forces Command (the headquarters unit responsible for all U.S.–based land forces), Powell had taken over as Chairman on October 1, 1989, just five weeks before the Berlin Wall's collapse.

In the preceding years, Powell had become increasingly skeptical about the long-term prospects for a Soviet-oriented military posture. Now, with the disintegration of the Soviet bloc, he was determined to find an alternative. Invoking his authority as the nation's highest military officer, Powell ordered General Butler and his associates on the Joint Staff (the multiservice command team responsible for the development and execution of U.S. war plans) to devise a new posture that focused on threats other than those posed by the former Soviet bloc and that allowed for the preservation of a large military establishment.[21]

General Powell's formal instructions to the Joint Staff have never been made public. One point, however, remains certain: his insistence that the United States remain a global superpower, whatever military posture was ultimately devised.[22] "We have to put a shingle outside our door saying, 'Superpower Lives Here,' no matter what the Soviets do, even if they evacuate from Eastern Europe," he declared.[23] According to Powell, this would require the maintenance of a powerful, high-tech military establishment equipped with a full range of modern combat systems. Although this establishment might prove smaller than that fielded during the peak years of the Cold War era, it must, he insisted, be similar to it in its basic structure and capabilities.[24]

IN SEARCH OF THE PERFECT ENEMY

In attempting to satisfy Powell's requirements, the Joint Staff soon ran into a major problem: the absence of clearly identifiable enemies of a stature that would justify the retention of a large military establishment. The Soviet Union was in terminal decay, and none of its constituent parts appeared destined, at least in the short run, to serve as a suitable replacement. All other major powers were either allies of the United States, or linked to it through trade and politics. While a number of smaller states, even some guerrilla bands, could be described as potential enemies, none possessed sufficient strength for the Pentagon's strategic purposes.

One possible response to this dilemma was to describe all of these minor threats as components of a large systemwide threat to global stability—and, on this basis, to reconfigure U.S. forces to fight an infinite number of police-type, low-intensity conflicts in the Third World. As General A. M. Gray of the Marine Corps suggested in 1990, the many insurgencies then smoldering around the world "jeopardize regional stability and our access to vital economic and military resources." To defend these resources, he argued, the United States must "maintain within our active force structure a credible military power projection capability with the flexibility to respond to conflict across the spectrum of violence throughout the globe."[25]

Such an approach, if adopted by General Powell, could have built upon the Pentagon's historic interest in guerrilla warfare and the strategy and tactics of counterinsurgency. After all, from the 1960s on, counterinsurgency in Third World areas had been viewed as the natural complement to containment in Europe. To resist what was seen as a growing Soviet presence in the developing world, the United States had adopted new strategies for fighting revolutionary movements in remote and inaccessible areas, and had employed these strategies in a score of countries, culminating with the 1965 U.S. intervention in South Vietnam. Though counterinsurgency had lost some of its prominence after the U.S. defeat in Vietnam, it had returned to favor during the Reagan administration under the rubric of "low-intensity conflict" (LIC). In its new guise, LIC included not only counterguerrilla warfare as seen in Vietnam and elsewhere, but also "pro-insurgency" (covert support for anticommunist guerrillas seeking the overthrow of Soviet-backed regimes), antidrug and antiterrorist operations, and other police-type activities.[26]

But while an LIC-based strategy might have appeared sensible to some officers, it was anathema to Powell—partly because it was likely to provoke resistance from those in Congress who found a "global policeman" role increasingly repugnant, but more critically, because it entailed no significant role for the high-tech forces that long had constituted the backbone of the U.S. military establishment. No conceivable assortment of guerrilla conflicts and overseas police missions could justify anything resembling the Cold War military-industrial apparatus.

Another possible approach was to dispense with the issue of enemies altogether, and adopt a military posture aimed at the "unknown." This approach was attractive precisely because it did not require the existence of an identifiable enemy (or group of enemies); rather, it allowed U.S. strategists, already experiencing difficulty in locating genuine enemies, to affirm the future emergence of unspecified security threats. "Faced with political instability and uncertainty in important regions of the globe," General Larry D. Welch of the Air Force suggested in early 1990, "the United States must provide forces capable of dealing with the full spectrum of potential conflicts, from nuclear war to the fight against illegal drugs."[27]

But this argument also failed to win General Powell's support, because it left U.S. forces without a clear-cut strategic mission. As a longtime Washington player, Powell understood that American lawmakers would seek a detailed justification—based on specific enemy threats—for every item in the military budget. A clearly identifiable and sufficiently menacing enemy would have the added benefit of isolating Congressional "doves" who were seeking to reduce military spending in pursuit of a substantial peace dividend.

Any doubt about the need for an identifiable enemy was firmly put to rest in March 1990 by Senator Sam Nunn, chairman of the

Senate Armed Services Committee and an acknowledged ally of the military establishment. In a blistering attack on the Soviet-oriented military posture still officially embraced by Defense Secretary Cheney, Nunn charged that the Pentagon's proposed spending plans were rendered worthless by a glaring "threat blank"—an unrealistic and unconvincing analysis of future adversaries. "The basic assessment of the overall threat to our national security on which this budget is based is rooted in the past," he told fellow senators. If the Department of Defense hoped to obtain Senate approval of its proposed budget, Nunn warned, it would have to fill in the "threat blank" with a more plausible assessment of future security risks.[28]

To satisfy Nunn's concerns, military planners would have to produce a plausible array of enemies. But, while it was certainly possible to identify many countries with imposing military capabilities, and some with possible motives for picking a fight with the United States, none was nearly so powerful as even a weakened Russia, and all were either allies of the United States or sufficiently wary of American power to refrain from overtly provocative behavior. In fact, it would have been hard to imagine a global security environment in which the United States might appear less threatened by external enemies. To fill in the "threat blank" identified by Nunn, the Pentagon had little choice but to find a way to elevate some previously neglected potential threats into major adversaries.

But what countries could be selected to perform this role? Virtually the entire membership of the "Second World"—the original Soviet bloc—was seeking Western aid and advice and, in some cases, inclusion in the North Atlantic Treaty Organization. That left the two other major camps in the original Cold War triad: the First World, consisting of the advanced capitalist powers, and the Third World, the underdeveloped states of Africa, Asia, and Latin America.

While the First World contained a number of potential candidates, including Germany and Japan, no senior U.S. official was prepared to say in public that our allies might someday become our adversaries. Although it was possible to imagine a future in which the United States stood at the brink of war with either (or both) of these industrial giants, and many Americans might even be prepared to entertain such a distant possibility, it was politically inconceivable that Congress would accept such a prospect as the basis on which to maintain a large military establishment. By default, then, the Pentagon was forced to select its hypothetical enemies from among Third World nations.

The United States had, of course, experienced serious conflicts with Third World nations before. Throughout the Cold War period, Washington had clashed with Third World states whose leaders were seen as allies of, or surrogates for, the Soviet Union. In most cases, these encounters had involved the delivery of military aid and training to neighboring, pro–U.S. countries, or the deployment of military advisory teams. On several occasions, however, the United States had engaged in direct military action to resist or disable such regimes: in Korea (1950–53), Vietnam (1965–73), the Dominican Republic (1965), and Grenada (1983). But if the terrain in these encounters was the Third World, the enemy, in Washington's eyes, had remained the Second World.

American involvement in Third World conflicts reached a new stage in the 1980s, when, under the aegis of the "Reagan Doctrine," the United States provided covert assistance to anticommunist insurgents seeking the overthrow of pro-Soviet regimes in Afghanistan, Angola, Cambodia, Libya, and Nicaragua. In each of these cases, the target state involved was characterized in official rhetoric as an adversary of the United States. But, here again, as in other instances of American involvement, the real target was Moscow. According to then Secretary of State George Shultz, the ultimate goal of the Reagan Doctrine was to knock out Soviet "surrogates" in the Third World and thereby shift the global "correlation of forces" in America's favor.[29]

Washington had independent reasons for targeting certain Third World states that it considered Moscow's allies. Some were suspected of supporting insurgent movements directed against allies of the United States; others had engaged in economic experiments considered injurious to American business interests. In all these cases, however, the military threat potential of these states—their ability to attack the United States and its principal allies—was said to be derived from their association with the Soviet Union. Left to themselves, these regimes might have been viewed as serious nuisances, but not as significant military actors. Thus, with the demise of the Soviet empire, states like Angola, Cuba, and Vietnam could hardly be viewed as major military threats to the United States.

If U.S. strategists were to identify any Third World countries as major enemies of the United States, they would have to establish a new basis—unrelated to Soviet power—on which to calculate the threat they posed. Fortunately for American military planners, the 1980s had witnessed the emergence of a new class of regional Third World powers—states with large military forces and the inclination to dominate other, weaker states in their immediate vicinity. It was this class of rising Third World powers that was chosen to replace the fading Soviet empire in Pentagon analyses of the global threat environment.

EMERGING REGIONAL POWERS

Members of this new class of states—Argentina, Brazil, China, Egypt, India, Iran, Iraq, Israel, Libya, Pakistan, South Africa, Syria, Taiwan, Turkey, and the two Koreas—professed allegiance to a wide range of political and economic philosophies, but all had sought to acquire large arsenals of modern weapons and/or to produce weapons of mass destruction. Moreover, most had come to see themselves as threatened by other rising powers in their vicinity, and as needing in response to expand their own military capabilities. Some of these states sought to accomplish this by aligning with the West, some with the East, still others by playing one bloc off against the other, but all enjoyed some sort of arms-supply relationship with one or more of the major industrial powers.

Throughout the 1980s, as these states turned to the arms trade to build up their military capabilities, American strategists had viewed them not as autonomous threats to U.S. security, but rather as pawns in the Cold War struggle for power and influence in vital Third World areas. So long as these states were seen as potential allies in the global competition with Moscow, Washington sought to strengthen rather than limit their growing military capabilities. From 1950 to 1990, under the Foreign Military Sales and Military Assistance programs, the United States sold or gave some $168 billion worth of arms and military equipment to Third World states. Most of this largesse went to such favored allies as Egypt, Israel, Pakistan, Saudi Arabia, South Korea, Taiwan, and Turkey.[30] The military (and associated contractors) also provided these states with the technology and equipment to produce sophisticated weapons on their own, and trained their personnel to operate and maintain modern military systems. In some cases, Washington even chose to overlook these countries' nuclear and chemical weapons programs rather than combat such activities and thereby run the risk of weakening their ties with the United States.[31]

As a result of this U.S. aid and comparable efforts on the part of the Soviet Union, the rising powers of the Third World ended the 1980s in a far more powerful military position than that with which they had started it. Between 1975 and 1990, Iraq increased its supply of tanks from 1,900 to 5,500. Israel's tank force grew from 1,900 to 3,800; India's from 1,700 to 3,150; and Syria's from 1,600 to 4,050. Pakistan increased its air fleet from 283 combat planes to 451; South Korea, from 210 to 447.[32] Several of these countries also acquired nuclear and/or chemical weapons during this period, or added to existing stockpiles of such munitions.

So long as U.S. military planners focused on the threat posed by Soviet and Warsaw Pact forces, few of the above developments were noted in the annual threat assessments prepared for Congress by the Department of Defense. Mention was made of Soviet arms transfers to the Third World insofar as they contributed to the net military power of the Soviet bloc, but this was seen as a peripheral problem compared to the continuing buildup of Soviet strength in Europe and at sea. Nowhere in these assessments was there a serious discussion of the growing military power of such friendly states as Egypt, India, Israel, Pakistan, South Korea, and Taiwan, or of the possibility that such states might someday serve as potential adversaries of the United States.

APPROPRIATING THE PROLIFERATION PERIL

While military strategists were paying little heed to the growing strength of these emerging regional powers, other analysts outside of the U.S. military establishment (and sometimes critical of it) were paving the way for a new, post-Soviet vision of an all-encompassing enemy, based on the growing threat of weapons proliferation among Third World powers.

Measures to curb the "horizontal proliferation" of nuclear, chemical, and biological weapons to weapons-seeking states were first proposed by arms control advocates in the 1960s as a natural complement to efforts to cap the "vertical proliferation" (increased production) of such weapons by the major powers. So long as the United States and the Soviet Union were continually adding to their arsenals of nuclear weapons and delivery systems, putting a stop to vertical proliferation had seemed by far the more critical of these tasks. However, with the signing of the Strategic Arms Limitation Treaty (SALT-I) in 1972 and the prospect of follow-on agreements, arms control experts began to turn their attention to the challenge of weapons proliferation in Third World areas. India's test of a nuclear explosive device in 1974 gave added impetus to this concern.

The new emphasis on horizontal proliferation became further evident in the 1980s, with the publication of a series of books by Leonard S. Spector of the Carnegie Endowment for International Peace on the nuclear weapons programs of such developing nations as Argentina, Brazil, India, Iraq, Israel, North Korea, Pakistan, South Africa, and Taiwan.[33] Similar studies by the Arms Control Association, the Stockholm International Peace Research Institute, and other such groups provided additional information on nuclear and chemical proliferation in Third World areas. But while these studies began to attract considerable interest on Capitol Hill, they had little immediate impact on military policy.

In the late 1980s, however, concern over the spread of advanced military capabilities began to grow in Pentagon-affiliated think-tanks and the U.S. intelligence community. The first significant expression of this concern appeared in *Discriminate Deterrence*, a January 1988 report by the U.S. Commission on Integrated Long-Term Strategy. The Commission, whose members included thirteen handpicked senior policymakers (among them former Secretary of State Henry Kissinger), had been established by the Reagan administration in 1986 to develop a long-term strategic blueprint for the United States.

Although the Commission focused most of its attention on strategies for countering what its members still saw as the growing military power of the USSR, it nonetheless devoted surprising attention to rising Third World powers. "In the years ahead," the report noted, "weapons production will be much more widely diffused, [and] many lesser powers will have sizeable arsenals" brimming with high-tech conventional arms, ballistic missiles, and chemical and nuclear munitions.[34] These developments, the Commission claimed, would pose significant new threats to American security and complicate future U.S. military operations in Third World areas:

> The [expanding] arsenals of the lesser powers will make it riskier and more difficult for the superpowers to intervene in regional wars. The U.S. ability to support its allies around the world will increasingly be called into question. Where American intervention seems necessary, it will [be necessary to] use our most sophisticated weaponry, even though this could compromise its effectiveness in a U.S.–Soviet war.[35]

In this and similar passages, a new theme was introduced to American strategic thinking: the prospect of high-tech, all-out war against rising Third World powers not necessarily affiliated with the Soviet Union.

The Future Security Environment, a 1988 backup report produced by the Commission, reinforced such thinking. Its goal was to identify potential threats to U.S. security in the late 1990s and the early years of the twenty-first century. Not surprisingly, the report predicted that the Soviet Union would grow in power, remaining America's preeminent enemy for the indefinite future. But it also predicted that the economic and industrial might of certain rising powers—particularly China, India, South Korea, Taiwan, Turkey, and Egypt—would grow rapidly, investing these countries with significant military power.[36] Even more significant, the report predicted that the most advanced Third World countries were likely to make impressive strides in military technology, enabling them to manufacture increasingly sophisticated munitions and delivery systems. "Along with increases in their military capital stocks," the report noted, "these developing countries will acquire a growing capacity to produce and export a wide range of weapons, featuring all but the most advanced technologies."[37]

The report concluded with an urgent plea that American strategists and policymakers devote more resources and energy to the study of rising Third World powers equipped with modern weapons. "A number of countries that will become increasingly important to the security environment are relatively neglected by U.S. analysts, certainly in comparison to the attention devoted to the Soviet Union," the report asserted. "Programs are needed to recruit young analysts and provide them with the language training and the opportunity to develop knowledge of Japan, China, Brazil, India, and other future regional powers." Such knowledge, it was argued, would prove essential to U.S. security in the years ahead.[38]

A similar outlook was articulated at that time by a study group convened by the Center for Strategic and International Studies (CSIS), a conservative, Washington-based think-tank. This group, which included such figures as former Army Chief of Staff General Edward C. Meyer and former Chief of Naval Operations Admiral

Thomas Moorer, published its findings in a 1988 CSIS report, *Meeting the Mavericks: Regional Challenges for the Next President.* According to the report's authors, the "mavericks" of the title, a new class of Third World powers equipped with modern weapons and hegemonic ambitions, would "inevitably create new dilemmas for the conduct of U.S. foreign policy and pose new risks to U.S. national security."[39] By acquiring large stockpiles of modern weapons, moreover, they would constrain greatly U.S. military options in the Third World. "More potent arsenals in the Third World will vastly complicate the problem of projecting power abroad, casting doubt on the ability of any power center to obtain satisfaction cheaply."[40]

At the same time, another group of analysts—senior officials in the U.S. intelligence community—began to speak out on the military dangers inherent in the emergence of well-equipped Third World powers. These officials joined their counterparts in the arms control and think-tank communities in highlighting the growing accumulation of modern weapons by Third World powers and warning of their accelerating progress in the nuclear, chemical, and missile fields. The first and most influential of these statements was a December 1988 speech by CIA director William H. Webster to the Council on Foreign Relations in Washington, D.C. Predictably, Webster focused mainly on recent military developments in the USSR, but he surprised his listeners by noting that "the Soviet Union is certainly not our only focus." Another major concern was "the proliferation of advanced weapons," particularly ballistic missiles and weapons of mass destruction. "By the year 2000, at least fifteen developing countries will either have produced or be able to produce their own ballistic missiles," Webster noted. He also said that an even larger group of countries—twenty in all—was producing chemical weapons, and, in some cases, developing chemical warheads for ballistic missiles.[41]

Three months later, in a speech in Los Angeles, Webster broadened his discussion of proliferation threats to include nuclear weapons and biological warfare agents. He noted that in addition to the five declared nuclear powers, "several countries either possess a nuclear device or can fabricate and assemble one on short notice," while a number of other countries were "developing key nuclear technology that could later be used for a nuclear explosive." Furthermore, he claimed that at least ten countries were working to produce biological weapons.[42] Webster did not provide any specifics to back up these allegations, and much doubt has since emerged as to the accuracy of some of his assertions. Nevertheless, his statements, and those of other intelligence officials, added a new and frightening theme to public discussion of national security affairs.

Webster and his colleagues found a receptive audience for their concerns on Capitol Hill. Beginning in 1988, several Congressional committees held extensive hearings on proliferation issues. At a February 1989 hearing, Judge Webster spoke at length on the dangers of chemical weapons proliferation; at another, in July 1989, the Carnegie Endowment's Leonard Spector testified on the spread of ballistic missiles and nuclear weapons. These hearings attracted considerable attention from prominent members of Congress, many of whom, including Senator Nunn, delivered ringing denunciations of nuclear and chemical weapons proliferation.[43]

By the end of 1989, Pentagon officials desperate to identify a credible military threat to American security had at least these warnings to draw on for ammunition in the fight for Congressional funding. Although concern over the proliferation of weapons of mass destruction (or WMD, as they were increasingly termed by U.S. strategists) to Third World countries had developed originally as a complement to deeper worries about U.S. and Soviet weapons programs, it now took on a life of its own, as military planners came to the realization that they could gain support for a large military establishment by lending their own weight to Congressional warnings. Once largely indifferent to the problem of WMD-equipped Third World powers, they now picked up the proliferation issue and made it the centerpiece of their new strategic outlook.

In early 1990, Pentagon officials began to substitute the threat of Third World proliferation for the Soviet threat in their statements on global security. Just as communism once had been described as a sinister, alien ideology that inevitably would provoke conflict between East and West, proliferation now was described as an insidious and growing threat to national and international stability. "The increased lethality of weaponry and the proliferation of force in the developing world make regional conflicts more rather than less likely," Army Secretary Michael P. W. Stone declared in January 1990. "As more developing countries gain significant military capabilities, they may resort more readily to force in settling local disputes."[44]

From such analyses, military planners posited a new enemy type: aggressively-minded Third World powers armed with nuclear and/ or chemical weapons and the means of delivering them to distant lands. In place of the now discredited Soviet threat, military officials began to speak of "well-equipped regional powers" and Third World countries "armed with 'First World' weapons."[45] While none of these states by itself could be said to pose a Soviet-style global threat, a group of such states might be described as doing so, especially when their growing arsenals of nuclear and chemical weapons were thrown into the equation.

In April 1990, the first, and in many ways most articulate, expression of this outlook appeared in *Sea Power* magazine. Writing on "the strategic army in the 1990s and beyond," Army Chief of Staff General Carl E. Vuono began:

> Because the United States is a global power with vital interests that must be protected throughout an increasingly turbulent world, we must look beyond the European continent and consider other threats to our national security. The proliferation of military power in what is often called the "Third World" presents a troubling picture. Many Third World nations now possess mounting arsenals of tanks, heavy artillery, ballistic missiles, and chemical weapons. At least a dozen developing countries have more than 1,000 main battle tanks, and portable anti-aircraft and anti-tank missiles are widespread as well. . . .
> The United States cannot ignore the expanding military power

of these countries, and the Army must retain the capability to defeat potential threats wherever they occur. This could mean confronting a well-equipped army in the Third World.[46]

Here, General Vuono touched on all of the main themes in what would become the Pentagon's new strategic concept: the emphasis on future Third World battlefields; the emergence of well-armed Third World powers; the growing pace of WMD proliferation; the risk of conflict with these states; and, of course, the resulting need to retain a large U.S. military establishment.

Vuono was not able to indicate precisely which nations he believed would threaten U.S. interests in the years ahead. However, in this and similar statements, he and other senior officers alluded to the growing power of several prominent Third World countries, including Egypt, India, Iran, Iraq, Israel, Libya, Pakistan, Syria, and the two Koreas. Such states were said by Army officials to "have undergone a dramatic qualitative and quantitative expansion of their military forces," and to have sought nuclear and/or chemical weapons. These developments, they noted, "will make warfare in developing countries a more dangerous proposition."[47]

THE NEW DEMONOLOGY

At first, discussion of this outlook focused largely on the military capabilities of rising Third World powers, particularly their holdings of modern weapons. Before long, however, this discourse came to focus as well on these nations' political character. Several of these states were now described by U.S. strategists as "rogues" or "outlaws" because of their "anti-Western orientation" and their involvement in what was characterized as "illicit proliferation activities"— that is, activities that violated the Nuclear Non-proliferation Treaty and other nonproliferation agreements. Such activities, it was argued, constituted a fundamental threat to U.S. and international security.[48]

American history has a long tradition of demonizing the alien

Other, extending from the vilification of native peoples during the Indian Wars to the anticommunist hysteria of the Cold War period. For decades, the "Communist threat" had been depicted as far more than a distant military challenge: in countless popular venues, the Communist had been given terrifying embodiment as the subverter of public order, the instigator of riots and rebellions, and the enemy of traditional American values. Such images had helped to mobilize public support for a large and potent military establishment, and for periodic U.S. intervention in contested Third World areas. But the demonizing tradition developed over almost a half-century of the Cold War now seemed anachronistic. To insure the survival of a large military, American leaders began constructing a new demonology based on WMD-equipped Third World powers.

Investing Third World states with a high degree of menace did not, in 1990, seem an easy proposition. Many of the states in question, including Argentina, Brazil, Egypt, India, Israel, Pakistan, South Korea, and Taiwan, were allies of the United States or seen as relatively friendly powers; others, including Iran, Iraq, Libya, Syria, and North Korea, were viewed as unfriendly by most Americans, but not as significant threats to U.S. security. None of these countries had a nuclear arsenal even remotely close to that of the Soviet Union, and none possessed bases and naval forces stretching significantly beyond its territory, let alone around the globe. These states were not even linked by a common ideology that could be described—as had Soviet-style communism—as inimical to basic American values.

To secure public backing for their long-range strategic plans, military officials focused increasingly on the most threatening characteristics of the least friendly powers, attempting to portray these nations' military plans as posing a clear and present danger to American security interests. At the same time, they began to ascribe to the leaders of these states violent and immoral intentions of a sort long identified with Soviet leaders. The officials hoped in this fashion to define a strategic environment that would compel legislators to relinquish dreams of a substantial peace dividend in return for enhanced national security.

Out of this process came what might best be termed the Rogue Doctrine—the characterization of hostile (or seemingly hostile) Third World states with large military forces and nascent WMD capabilities as "rogue states" or "nuclear outlaws" bent on sabotaging the prevailing world order. Such regimes were said to harbor aggressive intentions vis-à-vis their less powerful neighbors, to oppose the "spread of democracy," and to be guilty of circumventing international norms against nuclear and chemical proliferation. National Security Adviser Anthony Lake said in 1994 that "these nations exhibit a chronic inability to engage constructively with the outside world," evidenced in their "aggressive and defiant behavior" and their "misguided quest" for weapons of mass destruction.[49]

In constructing this new demonology, U.S. officials drew heavily on the "international terrorism" literature generated during the Reagan era. The early 1980s had witnessed a number of dramatic terrorist actions against American citizens abroad, and the need to combat such violence had become a major theme in President Reagan's foreign policy discourse. In 1984, this rhetoric changed dramatically: instead of focusing on the terrorist organizations considered directly responsible for such incidents, the administration began to focus its opprobrium on "state-sponsored terrorism"—the support of terrorist activities by hostile Third World countries. "States that support and sponsor terrorist actions have managed in recent years to co-opt and manipulate the phenomenon in pursuit of their own strategic goals," Secretary of State George Shultz averred in 1984. These states, he said, sought to use terrorism "to shake the West's self-confidence and sap its will to resist aggression and intimidation."[50]

Shultz did not identify the states in this category, but President Reagan was more forthcoming. In a much-publicized 1985 speech, he named Cuba, Iran, Libya, Nicaragua, and North Korea as the leading members of "a confederation of terrorist states." Most of the terrorists attacking U.S. citizens abroad, he argued, were "being trained, financed, and directly or indirectly controlled" by a core group of "outlaw states" seeking to undermine America's foreign policy objectives.[51]

Reagan's speech provoked much discussion about the nature of terrorism and the appropriate manner of combating it. Some analysts questioned the concept of "state-sponsored terrorism," contending that it diverted attention from the underground organizations directly involved in terrorist activity. Others argued that Reagan's list was constructed for political reasons alone, to provide a rationale for attacking certain states considered hostile by the administration, while ignoring others, such as Iraq and Syria, that were known to be harboring terrorists but were seen by Washington as potential allies.[52] Nevertheless, the concept of "outlaw states" engaged in pernicious anti-American behavior became a familiar theme in administration rhetoric.

As the 1980s drew to a close, U.S. officials began to describe WMD-seeking Third World powers in terms previously applied to terror-sponsoring states. "A dangerous proliferation of high technology has begun," Secretary of State-designate James Baker told the Senate Foreign Relations Committee in early 1989. "Chemical warheads and ballistic missiles have fallen into the hands of governments and groups with proven records of aggression and terrorism." To counter this new peril, he argued, vigorous nonproliferation efforts were needed.[53] From this point on, U.S. leaders increasingly employed "rogue," "outlaw," and "renegade" imagery when speaking of hostile, WMD-equipped Third World powers.[54]

This imagery, although hastily manufactured in response to the sudden collapse of Soviet power, proved surprisingly effective, tapping into American fears of nuclear weapons and malevolent Third World leaders. The Rogue Doctrine played particularly well on Capitol Hill, where several prominent senators, including Sam Nunn of Georgia and William Roth of Delaware, had already begun describing weapons-seeking states in the Third World as an emerging peril. By the spring of 1990, senior Pentagon officials and many members of Congress had begun using a common analysis and terminology to describe the threat posed by a new type of enemy.[55]

From 1990 on, the general model of a "rogue state" ruled by an "outlaw regime" armed with chemical and nuclear weapons became the standard currency of national security discourse. All that was required was the emergence of a specific "demon"—a particular ruler of a specific state—to bring the newly developed doctrine into vivid focus and thereby forestall an even more terrifying enemy, the Congressional advocates of a peace dividend, from launching a full-scale attack on the U.S. military establishment.

THE TWO-WAR STRATEGY

Having filled in the "threat blank" identified by Senator Nunn in early 1990, senior Pentagon officials began to develop a strategic blueprint to guide the development of military policy and justify the preservation of a near–Cold War military apparatus. Hoping to have a new strategic blueprint completed and ready for public airing by the early summer of 1990, Powell's staff worked throughout the winter and spring of that year to produce the necessary plans and concepts.[56]

The Pentagon's new strategic plan now rested on the assumption that in the absence of a significant Soviet threat, the greatest danger to U.S. security would be posed by well-equipped Third World hegemons. It was further assumed that some of these countries would be tempted to attack fundamental U.S. interests in the years ahead, and that the military would be called upon to engage and defeat such states in combat. The only tasks remaining were to determine the nature and scale of the threat posed by these countries and calculate the type and number of U.S. forces that would be needed to overcome them.

From the perspective of U.S. strategists, many of the rising Third World powers bore considerable resemblance to the pre-1990 Warsaw Pact countries of Eastern Europe in that they possessed fairly large armies with substantial numbers of serviceable (if not always very sophisticated) tanks, artillery pieces, and combat planes. (See Table 1.1.) Many of these states also possessed ballistic missiles of one type or another, along with chemical and/or nuclear weapons. This was heartening news for American military officials, as it could be used to justify the retention of heavy tank units, artillery brigades, fighter squadrons, and other high-tech forces in the U.S. military lineup. It also provided a rationale for the preservation of a nuclear arsenal and the application of "Star Wars" technology to defenses against future Third World ballistic missile attacks.

TABLE 1.1
MILITARY CAPABILITIES OF
THE WARSAW PACT COUNTRIES
AND SELECTED THIRD WORLD POWERS
AS OF 1989–90

(In rank order by total military manpower)

COUNTRY	TOTAL MILITARY MANPOWER	TANKS	ARTILLERY PIECES	COMBAT AIRCRAFT
North Korea	1,040,000	3,200	4,700	650
Iraq	1,000,000	5,500	3,500	513
South Korea	650,000	1,560	4,000	447
Iran	604,500	500	800	121
Pakistan	520,000	1,750	n/a	451
Egypt	448,000	2,425	1,260	517
Poland	412,000	3,300	2,090	565
Taiwan	405,500	309	1,375	469
Syria	404,000	4,050	2,000	499
Czechoslovakia	199,700	4,585	2,100	377
Cuba	180,500	1,100	n/a	206
East Germany	173,100	3,140	1,260	335
Romania	171,000	3,200	1,130	295
Israel	141,000	3,794	1,360	574
Bulgaria	117,500	2,200	830	193
Hungary	91,000	1,435	866	101
Libya	85,000	1,800	1,182	515

Source: International Institute for Strategic Studies, *The Military Balance 1989–1990* (London, 1989).

Not all of the news was equally gratifying. At some point, U.S. officials came to realize that none of these rising powers possessed sufficient military strength to justify the retention of anything close to America's Cold War military establishment. They recognized that even the most powerful of these states could be defeated by a force of under one million U.S. soldiers, or less than half of the existing American force. An American strategy based on preparation for combat with any *one* of these powers would thus entail a military establishment much smaller than that fielded in the Cold War era. As this was unacceptable to Powell and his staff, they came up with a novel solution: they argued that this large field of potential adversaries might someday produce various combinations of paired enemies, and that the new strategy, therefore, would call for a U.S. capability to fight simultaneously against *two* such enemies. This still would not justify a force as big as that needed to defeat the Soviet Union—a force that large would never have won the support of Congressional leaders, anyway—but it would come as close to this as Powell's staff thought politically possible.

So it was decided: American forces would be reconfigured to conduct a continuing series of military engagements with rising Third World powers, whether operating singly or in pairs. This would require the maintenance of a U.S. force about three-quarters the size of that maintained during the Cold War era. In addition, the Pentagon blueprint called for a significant enhancement of America's "power projection" capability, the ability to bring U.S. military power to bear on remote and unfamiliar battlefields.[57]

The Powell plan also incorporated certain assumptions regarding the manner in which U.S. forces would be expected to fight in future clashes with rising Third World powers. Rejecting what senior officers viewed as the incremental approach to the application of force during the Vietnam War, the new strategy called for the rapid concentration of military power and the use of superior firepower to stun and disable enemy forces at the very onset of battle. "One of the essential elements of our national military strategy," Powell explained, "is the ability to rapidly assemble the forces needed to win—the concept of applying decisive force to overwhelm our adversaries and thereby terminate conflicts swiftly." This, in turn, required the continued possession of "technological superiority" in weapons and support systems and a robust capability for "strategic mobility," or the rapid deployment of U.S. forces and equipment to distant battle zones.[58]

On this basis, Powell and his staff began to identify the actual forces theoretically needed to implement such a strategy. Because an individual regional conflict probably would require a U.S. commitment of approximately half to three-quarters of a million soldiers, a war against *two* such powers presumably would require a total commitment of at least one to one and a half million troops. Adding to this the need for specialized nuclear forces and a reservoir of "contingency forces" for unforeseen emergencies, the total manpower requirement arrived at was approximately 1.5 to 1.75 million active-duty personnel—significantly fewer than the 2.1 million soldiers in the existing force, but far more than the numbers envisioned in many of the proposals for a downsized military establishment.

Figuring in this manner, Powell and his staff settled on a plan calling for the conversion of the existing Cold War military apparatus into a "Base Force" of approximately 1.6 million men and women. Included in this force would be 12 active Army divisions (down from 16 in 1990), 12 aircraft carrier battle groups (down from 15), 15 tactical fighter wings (down from 22), and 3 Marine Corps divisions (no change). Also included was a large assortment of "power projection forces"—Marine amphibious groups, Army airborne units, and other mobile forces used to deliver American power to distant battlefields. According to Powell, a military establishment of this size and type would be sufficient to conduct two major regional conflicts simultaneously and to permit simultaneous U.S. participation in isolated peacekeeping or low-intensity operations.[59] (See Table 1.2.)

Although smaller than the Cold War military, the Base Force nevertheless would satisfy Powell's requirement for a superpower-type capability. The plan would leave Washington with a fleet of 435 combat ships, along with a sizeable inventory of combat planes. With twelve aircraft carrier battle groups, moreover, the United States would still be able to project military power to virtually any point on the earth's surface. In addition, the plan allowed for the retention of some of the heavy armored divisions, bomber wings, and other high-tech forces previously intended for all-out combat with the Warsaw Pact.[60]

By retaining a significant array of heavy combat forces, the Powell plan would also insure a need for continued acquisition of new, high-tech weapons systems, thus preserving a significant portion of the military-industrial apparatus built up during the Cold War era.

TABLE 1.2
THE PROPOSED "BASE FORCE"

	ACTUAL 1990 FORCE	PROPOSED BASE FORCE
Army Forces:		
Active divisions	16	12
Reserve divisions	10	6
Navy Forces:		
Combat ships	530	450
Carrier battle groups	15	12
Active naval air wings	13	11
Reserve air wings	2	2
Marine Corps:		
Active divisions	3	3
Reserve divisions	1	1
Air Force:		
Active fighter wings	22	15
Reserve fighter wings	12	11

Source: U.S. Department of Defense, *National Military Strategy of the United States* (1992).

Not every military contractor could be saved in this manner—with twenty-five percent fewer forces, the armed services inevitably would be forced to cancel some weapons programs—but the Base Force would still generate a substantial requirement for new aircraft, missiles, armored vehicles, and so on. Furthermore, to enhance U.S. power projection capabilities, the Department of Defense would need to procure additional cargo planes, amphibious assault vessels, supply ships, and helicopters.

The strategic blueprint adopted by General Powell and his staff in the spring of 1990, known as the "New Strategy" or the "Regional Defense Strategy" in Pentagon documents, was submitted to Secretary of Defense Cheney in May, and then forwarded to President Bush for his inspection.[61] In June, the New Strategy received formal White House approval, and the forthcoming fortieth anniversary celebration of the Aspen Institute (a high-level study group on national security affairs) in Aspen, Colorado, on August 2, was selected as a suitable occasion for announcing the plan to the American public.

In his Aspen speech, Bush reiterated many of the themes expressed in General Vuono's April 1990 article and in other statements by top military officials. "In a world less driven by an immediate threat to Europe and the danger of global war," he noted, "the size of our forces will increasingly be shaped by the needs of regional conflict and peacetime [military] presence [abroad]." In line with this new posture, with its emphasis on regional conflicts beyond Europe, "America must possess forces able to respond to threats in whatever corner of the globe they may occur." To satisfy this need, he argued, "we will have to have air- and sea-lift capacities to get our forces where they are needed, when they are needed."[62]

Bush's speech was meant to provide American citizens with a glossy overview of the Pentagon's new posture. Many additional months would be needed to paint in the fine detail, and it was not until early 1991 that Congress had an opportunity to discuss the plan with senior Pentagon officials. Nevertheless, the broad outlines of the new U.S. strategic posture were in place by the early summer of 1990. As General Vuono later put it, "the second of August 1990 will be remembered for generations to come as a turning point for the United States in its conduct of foreign affairs—the day America announced the end of containment and embarked upon the strategy of power projection."[63]

By an extraordinary coincidence, this was also the day on which the Iraqi forces of Saddam Hussein invaded Kuwait.

Chapter Two

OPERATION DESERT STORM

The Liquidation

of a Rogue

ON JULY 16, 1990, U.S. spy satellites began picking up signs of unusual activity along the Iraq-Kuwait border—the movement of hundreds of Iraqi tanks and armored vehicles into assault positions just north of the Kuwaiti line. In the days that followed, more tanks and vehicles arrived, until some 100,000 Iraqi troops were deployed there, poised for attack. Meanwhile, intelligence analysts in Washington debated the implications of the Iraqi move: was it an enormous bluff intended to pressure Kuwait into making concessions in the oil price dispute then under way between the two countries, or a prelude to invasion? No conclusion had been reached when, on the morning of August 2, Iraqi forces ended all discussion by crossing into Kuwait.[1]

Not only official Washington was surprised by the Iraqi move. Although Kuwaiti forces were, in fact, meager when compared to the million-strong Iraqi army, most Americans were unaware that Iraq was capable of planning and executing an invasion of this magnitude. But not all Americans were caught off guard: at the headquarters of the U.S. Central Command (CENTCOM) in Tampa, Florida, senior officers were already planning for a war with Iraq. At the very moment that Iraqi tanks were gathering in the desert near Kuwait, senior CENTCOM staff were testing their combat plans in a week-long simulated battle—code named "Internal Look '90" —between U.S. and Iraqi forces.[2] As the Pentagon admitted in 1992, "the basic concepts for Operations Desert Shield and Desert Storm were established before a single Iraqi soldier entered Kuwait."[3]

The Department of Defense (DoD) had developed these plans and concepts not because it had advance warning of the Iraqi attack (or even believed that such an invasion was imminent), but because it had decided that rising Third World powers like Iraq would gradually replace the Soviet Union as the primary threat to U.S. security. In line with this assumption, Secretary of Defense Dick Cheney in late 1989 had ordered the Pentagon's regional commands to develop and test contingency plans for conflicts with such powers. For CENTCOM—which exercised command over all U.S. forces sent to the Persian Gulf area—this meant preparing for a war with Iraq.

In March 1990, a team of five hundred military specialists from CENTCOM and other U.S. commands began working at Fort Mc-Pherson, Georgia, to develop a detailed blueprint for a U.S.–Iraqi war in the Kuwait/Saudi Arabia area. Known as Operations Plan (OPLAN) 1002-90, the resulting document, reportedly the size of a large city's Yellow Pages, covered every aspect of a future conflict. The plan "spelled out which [U.S.] divisions would go to Saudi Arabia, what radio frequencies they would use, where they would get their water, how they would treat their casualties, and how they would handle the news media."[4]

Secretary Cheney confirmed in 1992 testimony before the House Foreign Affairs Committee that preparation for such a war had begun in 1989, in response to developments in Eastern Europe, and not in mid-1990, in response to developments in the Gulf. "In late 1989, with the fall of the Berlin Wall and the retrenchment of Soviet power, the Department [of Defense] reassessed threats to key regions. For a decade, DoD planning for Southwest Asia had been primarily concerned with a possible Soviet threat to Iran. But the reassessment in 1989 led us to shift our planning focus to regional threats to the Arabian peninsula, particularly from Iraq."[5]

At that point, Iraq was not viewed as the only, or even the most likely, Third World state to be headed for a showdown with the United States. Other potential adversaries, including Iran, Libya, Pakistan, Syria, and North Korea, were also the subject of such contingency planning. But Iraq was seen as one of the few perfect examples of the *type* of enemy that the Defense Department was betting on: a rising regional power with modern military forces, a large supply of potent weapons, and evident hegemonic aspirations. By early 1990, Iraq, with its million-man army and potent arsenal of modern weapons, had risen to the top of the list of candidate adversaries, figuring more and more prominently in Pentagon statements on the emerging Third World threat.[6]

But while a growing number of military officers were coming to see Saddam Hussein as an ambitious ruler who might give the Rogue Doctrine its missing human face and thus become the archetypal enemy of the post–Cold War era, officials in other government departments were not as yet prepared to view Baghdad in this manner. For eight years, from 1982 to early 1990, American leaders had viewed Iraq as a quasi-ally. Iraq's survival in its ongoing war with Iran had been considered essential to U.S. security. To help strengthen Iraqi defenses, the Reagan and Bush administrations had provided Hussein's regime with economic credits, secret intelligence data, and military-related technology. Even after the 1980–88 Iran-Iraq war ended in an Iraqi victory, the Bush administration continued to aid Iraq in the belief that Baghdad—a longtime Soviet ally in the Middle East—might be drawn further into the Western camp.

As a result, Iraqi leaders preparing for the invasion of Kuwait faced two distinct realities in Washington: a Pentagon increasingly focused on possible conflict with Iraq, and a White House still committed to improved U.S.–Iraqi relations. Though the Pentagon's views were in ascendancy, Hussein must have assumed otherwise. Evidently believing that the Bush administration was seeking to retain friendly ties with Iraq and was prepared to overlook a certain degree of adventurism on Baghdad's part, Hussein planned the invasion of Kuwait with no apparent expectation of a hostile military response.

He was clearly encouraged to proceed on this basis by the U.S. Ambassador to Iraq, April Glaspie. In an extraordinary interview with the Iraqi leader on July 25, 1990, she told Hussein, "I have a direct instruction from the President to seek better relations with Iraq." She also stated that the United States had "no opinion" on inter-Arab disagreements, including Baghdad's border dispute with Kuwait.[7] Hussein, who no doubt was pleased by Glaspie's subservient manner, probably found this sufficient diplomatic inference to conclude that officials at the highest levels in Washington would not object strenuously to an Iraqi takeover of Kuwait (or, at least, some portion thereof).[8]

In the aftermath of the Iraqi invasion, Glaspie's statements were much criticized in Congress. She was, however, merely articulating the prevailing White House view. What Glaspie did not say, and probably did not know, was that a significant segment of opinion in official Washington favored a more belligerent policy toward Iraq, and was even prepared to consider going to war against that country. Had Glaspie communicated that information to Hussein, or had he been informed of it through other channels, it is possible that Iraq might have been deterred from invading Kuwait.

Once the invasion began, however, the last vestiges of pro-Iraqi sentiment evaporated in Washington and the war party took over. Worried that any further conciliatory overtures to Baghdad might be viewed by most Americans as "appeasement," President Bush took the opposite tack. On August 4, he set in motion planning for an all-out military campaign against Hussein, and on August 7 he ordered U.S. forces to prepare for immediate deployment to the Persian Gulf area. At this time, he also took the first diplomatic steps toward assembling the coalition of anti-Iraqi states that would later participate in Operation Desert Storm.

In discussing his response to the Iraqi invasion of Kuwait, Bush found it natural to draw upon the "rogue" imagery. "These are outlaws," he told reporters on August 5, "international outlaws and renegades."[9] Bush's rhetoric continued to escalate; he accused Saddam Hussein of war crimes, and compared him to Adolf Hitler. At the same time, Bush sought to place the Iraqis outside the community of law-abiding nations. "Iraq's invasion was more than a military attack on tiny Kuwait," he remarked on August 20. "It was a ruthless assault on the very essence of international order and civilized ideals."[10] Having been defined by Washington as a rogue regime acting outside acceptable international norms, Iraq could no longer expect to be exempted from appropriate punishment.

The Bush administration couched its initial military moves in wholly defensive terms. "Our military mission is clearcut," Secretary of Defense Cheney informed Congress on September 11. "Specifically, we were told by the President to deploy forces in order to deter further aggression by Iraq against other nations in the region [and] to defend Saudi Arabia and others should deterrence fail."[11] However, we now know that the President had decided on an offensive drive against Iraq at a very early stage in the crisis. At a meeting at the presidential retreat at Camp David on August 4, President Bush, Secretary Cheney, General Powell, and others had already considered the strategy and logistics of an offensive campaign, building on the combat scenarios developed by the CENTCOM staff several months earlier. Shortly thereafter, Bush ordered Powell and Cheney to begin planning for such a campaign while proceeding with Operation Desert Shield, the initial buildup of U.S. forces and equipment in Saudi Arabia.[12]

In taking these steps, the Bush administration turned its back on the Europe-oriented, anti-Soviet strategic doctrine of the Cold War era and embraced the new, Third World-oriented doctrine that General Powell and his staff had been developing. Under the earlier doctrine, Washington would have viewed Kuwait as a secondary theater of operations that could be fought over only if the United States retained sufficient strength to counter Soviet provocations in Europe; now, however, a place like Kuwait could become the center of geostrategic conflict, leaving the President free to deploy there any

U.S. forces he considered necessary. Cold War doctrine would also have required Bush to avoid certain aggressive actions in the Gulf lest he trigger a chain reaction of events leading to World War III; now, he was relieved of any such constraints.

By ordering a military response to the invasion, Bush explicitly endorsed the military concepts incorporated into the new Pentagon strategy. As envisioned by Powell, this was to be a war of "power projection," the mobilization in strength of forces based elsewhere and their transport to the Persian Gulf area. In conducting military operations, moreover, U.S. forces would be governed by the principle of "decisive force," the concentration of overwhelming firepower to stun and disable Iraqi forces with the lowest possible cost in American lives.

The President essentially turned the Gulf conflict into a test of the Rogue Doctrine. It would be, in consequence, a two-front war: against the Iraqis in Kuwait; and against the liberal media and Congressional doves at home. From the Pentagon's perspective, a failure in Kuwait would discredit the whole post–Cold War era approach to military policy and lead to further military cutbacks, while failure in the media and Congress could further diminish public support for a global U.S. military role. Hence, in ordering an all–out offensive against Iraqi forces, Bush and his colleagues were seeking both to "liberate" Kuwait and to secure the best possible military-industrial future at home. It was not surprising, then, that the military deployed a force large enough to destroy quickly and thoroughly not one but two or three "rogue" war machines.

In addition, each of the individual armed services had an interest in contributing to an overwhelming defeat of Saddam Hussein. Fearing that Congress and the American people might have to choose among competing military services and commands in deciding which units to eliminate from the active force structure, each was determined to play as conspicuous a role as possible in the campaign against Iraq. This, too, added to the concentration of military strength in the Persian Gulf.

By invading Kuwait, Saddam Hussein invited a U.S. response far more forceful and violent than he could have imagined. Whatever reaction he may have expected from Washington, it assuredly did not include the deployment within six months of a coalition force of more than 795,000 soldiers, sailors, and airmen (of whom 540,000 were Americans), accompanied by 1,796 modern combat planes and 230 warships (including six aircraft carriers).[13] President Bush's embrace of the plans and concepts advanced by General Powell had set in motion a military response more powerful than any assembled by the United States since the Normandy invasion of June 1944. Unless the Iraqi forces in Kuwait were withdrawn before the onset of Operation Desert Storm, they were doomed.

ASSESSING THE ENEMY

Once General Powell received the President's go-ahead to organize an offensive campaign against Iraq, the military's tasks were clear: intelligence gathering, operations planning, and battle management. The United States enjoyed great advantages in all three of these areas—in its knowledge of the enemy, its ability to dictate the nature and tempo of the fighting, and its capacity to deliver superior combat power on the battlefield—and it employed these advantages to the maximum.

Emulating U.S. war planners in 1990, it makes good sense to turn first to the intelligence-gathering phase of the operation, the assessment of Iraq's military capabilities. At the onset of the Gulf crisis, Iraq possessed one of the largest and most heavily armed military forces in the Third World. According to the International Institute of Strategic Studies, this force consisted of approximately one million military personnel organized into an Army of 955,000, an Air Force of 40,000, and a Navy of 5,000. The Army possessed some 5,500 tanks, 3,500 major artillery pieces, and 8,100 armored personnel carriers; the Air Force possessed 513 combat aircraft (including Soviet-supplied MiG-23s, MiG-25s, MiG-29s, and French Mirage F-1s); while the Navy possessed only a handful of escort ships and smaller vessels.[14] In addition, Iraq had several hundred Soviet-type Scud missiles and domestically produced Scud derivatives, plus a large supply of chemical munitions.[15]

According to U.S. officials, these capabilities endowed Iraq with a very large and formidable military force. The Iraqi ground force, often described as the "world's fourth largest army" (later recalibrated as the "world's sixth largest army"), was depicted as a juggernaut capable of sweeping anything from its path.[16] "These are battle-hardened units," Secretary Cheney said of the Iraqi forces in Kuwait, "with leadership that has demonstrated a proclivity to use any and all forms of warfare, against civilian as well as military targets."[17] These forces were also said to possess an infinite array of modern conventional weapons as well as ballistic missiles and chemical munitions. "Clearly," Cheney noted, we face "a Third World country that presents us with a first-rate military threat with which we have to deal."[18]

This assessment, which went largely unchallenged at the time, was used to justify the deployment of a mammoth U.S. expeditionary force in the Gulf and the commitment of a wide array of America's most advanced aircraft, missiles, and warships. These forces were bolstered by troops, ships, and planes from the NATO countries, along with ground units from a number of Arab states.

As later became apparent, however, the Iraqi war machine possessed a wide range of weaknesses and vulnerabilities that greatly diminished Baghdad's combat capabilities. To begin with, Iraq's million-man army was not composed entirely or even largely of troops "battle-hardened" in its eight-year war with Iran, but rather of a diverse population of combatants, including raw recruits and older men not up to the rigors of high-intensity warfare. It also included representatives of minority groups such as the Kurds and Shiites, who held no love for Saddam Hussein. Many of these soldiers deserted in the early days of battle, or surrendered to Coalition forces at the first opportunity.[19]

Iraq's much-vaunted Air Force lacked a cadre of pilots with the skills and resolve to put up any sort of fight against American air power. While many Iraqi aircraft were equal in quality to those flown by Coalition forces, Iraq lacked the early warning, command-and-control, and target acquisition systems needed to convert a collection of aircraft into an effective, modern fighting force. It is not surprising, therefore, that most Iraqi aircraft were either grounded during the war or sent into "sanctuary" in Iran (only to be impounded by the Iranian government).[20]

Iraq's navy hardly existed. This would not have been a significant deficit had Iraq been threatened by another land power equally lacking in naval capabilities (as in the Iran-Iraq war), but it was a critical liability when the threat was the United States, a major maritime power capable of using the sea to transport supplies and equipment, deliver air and missile strikes against coastal and inland targets, and deny such options to its adversaries. Lacking any capacity to challenge U.S. naval supremacy, Iraq found itself unable to prevent the massive buildup of U.S. strength in the region, or to defend itself against naval attack.[21]

As the Iran-Iraq war of 1980–88 demonstrated, the Iraqis had not fully mastered the organizational and conceptual skills needed to effectively deploy a large fighting force on the modern battlefield. Because Iraq had not faced a significant threat from Iranian air attacks, it had not needed to perfect the anti-air warfare techniques essential in confrontation with a major air power such as the United States. And because the Iranian military had been composed largely of untrained and inexperienced volunteers, the Iraqis had not been forced to merge their infantry, armor, and artillery units into what the Pentagon calls a "combined arms team," and so were unprepared to engage enemy forces that were organized in this fashion.[22]

Finally, Iraq suffered from significant geostrategic vulnerabilities. Unlike North Korea and North Vietnam during their 1950–53 and 1965–73 conflicts with the United States, Iraq did not abut on a friendly power that provided aid and sanctuary, but against hostile states—Iran, Syria, and Turkey—that posed significant threats of opportunistic invasion. To further complicate matters, the Baghdad regime faced potential threats from Kurdish separatists in its northern regions and Shiite insurgents in the southeast. For these reasons, Hussein could not concentrate all of his strength in Kuwait and southern Iraq, where the major American threat was concentrated, but had to divert at least some of his forces to the Iranian, Syrian, and Turkish borders, while retaining others inside the country to protect the regime from internal revolt or possible coup d'état.

Iraqi forces, which had driven through the relatively small and unmotivated Kuwaiti army to conquer that country in a matter of hours, did not pose the sort of overpowering threat that U.S. officials led the American people to expect in the early months of the crisis. Moreover, Saddam Hussein committed one colossal blunder after another as the crisis unfolded, seriously degrading his already vulnerable forces' capacity to fight. Nevertheless, predictions of massive World War II–type tank battles sweeping across the desert, of tens of thousands of American casualties, and of mine-laden "killing fields" on the roads to Kuwait were nurtured by the administration in a highly sophisticated propaganda assault on the media, all meant to justify the deployment of an outsized American force in the Gulf.

———

IN CONTRAST TO the images of strength and cohesion provided by the U.S. media, Iraq was a war-exhausted nation ruled by an unpopular dictator and weakened by rebellious minority populations. What made Iraq's strategic weaknesses less noticeable at the time was Baghdad's reputed threat as a rising power armed with potentially awesome weapons of mass destruction. After offering up a quick succession of explanations for the American deployment in the Gulf—the critical need for access to the region's oil supplies, the obligation to liberate a pro-American emirate, the desire to protect American jobs—the administration settled, two months into the crisis, on the need to prevent Iraq from flexing its WMD muscles and becoming a novice nuclear power.

Throughout the final months of 1990, President Bush and other senior administration officials warned repeatedly of the imminent danger posed by Iraqi weapons programs, and suggested that military action would be needed to eliminate this threat. In a Thanksgiving Day address to U.S. soldiers in Saudi Arabia, Bush solemnly stated, "We understand that we can sacrifice now, or we can pay an even stiffer price later as Saddam moves to multiply his weapons of mass destruction—chemical, biological, and, most ominous, nuclear. And we all know that Saddam Hussein has never possessed a weapon that he hasn't used."[23]

Because claims about Iraq's nuclear, chemical, and missile programs figured so prominently in the Pentagon's public assessments of the Iraqi threat, it is important to examine this issue in some detail, starting with two background issues that require particular attention: Iraq's military behavior during the Iran-Iraq war of 1980–88, and America's role in aiding Hussein during this critical period.

In September 1980, Iraq invaded an unprepared Iran, then ruled by the Ayatollah Ruhollah Khomeini. Iraqi forces, at first victorious, quickly became bogged down in southwestern Iran when Iranian forces stepped up their resistance and the local population (of Arabic rather than Persian origin) failed to rally to Baghdad's side. By 1981, Iran had seized the battlefield initiative and began to push the Iraqis back into their own territory. Using large numbers of youthful volunteers in costly "human wave" attacks, the Iranians crossed into Iraq and began a six-year siege of the southern Iraqi city of Basra.[24] At this point, Iraq initiated the development and production of chemical weapons and ballistic missiles in order to blunt the Iranian offensives and wreak destruction on Iran's interior cities.

Unlike the invasion of Kuwait ten years later, the Iraqi invasion of Iran provoked no cries of outrage in Washington. The Khomeini regime had replaced the pro-American government of Shah Mohammed Reza Pahlavi, and pro-Khomeini students had seized the U.S. embassy and its American occupants in November 1979; and so, in 1980, American leaders shed no tears over the Iraqi occupation of oil-rich southwestern Iran. When the Iranians went on the offensive and threatened Iraq itself, however, Washington rushed to Baghdad's assistance, believing, as one CIA official put it, that "the enemy of our enemy is our friend."[25]

From 1982 to 1988, the United States aided Iraq through a wide variety of channels, overt and covert. Overt forms of assistance included the provision of government-backed credits for the purchase of American foodstuffs, and the sale of supposedly civilian products—trucks, helicopters, computers, and so on—with significant military applications.[26] Covertly, the Reagan administration provided Hussein with sensitive intelligence data on Iranian military positions and counselled his forces on combat tactics.[27] The United States also aided Baghdad by encouraging its European allies, including Britain and France, to sell Hussein a variety of high-tech weapons. It also assured such states as Egypt, Jordan, Kuwait, and Saudi Arabia that if they transferred some of their U.S.–supplied weaponry to Iraq, all such hardware would be replaced with fresh supplies from American stockpiles.[28]

In addition, the United States systematically ignored Iraq's development and use of chemical weapons and ballistic missiles. It was no secret that Saddam Hussein was developing such capabilities; the Iraqis first employed chemical munitions against the Iranians in 1982, and by 1984 were using them regularly to blunt Iranian offensives and slaughter rebellious Kurdish villagers. Although ballistic missiles were not used regularly against Iranian cities until 1987, preparations for such attacks were evident to American intelligence in the early 1980s. In neither case did Washington protest Iraqi actions or impose sanctions of any sort; rather, it turned its back on these activities, continuing to allow or encourage Western firms to provide Iraq with weapons-related technology.[29]

The Bush administration would later seek to portray the Iraqi weapons effort as wholly indigenous, thereby relieving the United States and its European allies of any responsibility. However, while the Iraqis no doubt would have made considerable progress on their own, they could not have advanced as far as they did in the development of chemical agents, ballistic missiles, and nuclear weapons without external assistance.[30]

The Iraqis had begun manufacturing chemical warfare (CW) agents on a large scale in 1982. Using production technology and chemical feedstocks (industrial chemicals used in the manufacture of CW agents) obtained from the West, Baghdad built up an elaborate chemical weapons complex at Samarra, about seventy miles northwest of Baghdad.[31] The Samarra complex evidently was capable of manufacturing large quantities of mustard gas (a poisonous compound first used in World War I), along with the nerve agents Tabun and Sarin (originally developed by German scientists during World War II).[32] The Iraqis continued to manufacture and use chemical munitions throughout the Iran-Iraq war, and to increase the number and sophistication of delivery systems for such munitions. Production did not cease after the war, and, by the onset of Desert Storm, Iraq possessed over 100,000 operable chemical weapons—bombs, rockets, and artillery shells—plus thousands of tons of prepared chemical agents. It had also begun to produce chemical warheads for its growing arsenal of ballistic missiles.[33]

Iraq's possession of large stockpiles of chemical weapons obviously had an impact on U.S. planning for Operation Desert Storm. American troops were supplied with CW protective gear and trained in CW detection and decontamination procedures.[34] But U.S. strategists ultimately concluded that any Iraqi chemical attacks would have only a negligible effect on the battlefield, given American superiority in all other aspects of combat. While "the tempo of the Operation Desert Storm campaign would have been hindered" by the need to wear protective clothing, the Pentagon noted later, "the outcome would have been unaffected."[35]

What was true of chemical weapons proved equally true of ballistic missiles. Iraq began the 1980–88 Gulf war with a small number of 40-mile-range Frog-7 and 190-mile-range Scud-B surface-to-surface missiles (SSMs) that had been acquired over the years from the Soviet Union. With their limited accuracy, these missiles could not be employed against precise military targets, nor could they reach Iran's capital, Teheran, or any of its other interior cities. In 1982, however, the Iraqis began to seek more effective missiles, with sufficient range to hit Teheran.[36]

Initially, Iraq attempted to acquire long-range SS-12 missiles from the Soviet Union; when these efforts proved unsuccessful, Baghdad sought assistance from other countries to produce its own SSMs. Multimillion-dollar contracts were signed with prominent West German companies, including Messerschmitt-Bölkow-Blohm (MBB), to help establish a missile production complex in Iraq.[37] This program initially focused on the manufacture of the 500-mile-range Argentinean-Egyptian Condor-II missile; when this effort, too, ended in failure, the Iraqis (with further West German assistance) began to work on improved versions of the Scud.[38] Finally, in 1987, the Iraqis unveiled the Al-Husayn SSM, a modified Scud with an estimated range of 375 miles—sufficient to hit Teheran and other interior Iranian cities from positions in Iraq.[39]

Even while barraging these cities with the Al-Husayn, the Iraqis proceeded to develop yet more capable missiles. In 1988, they test-fired the Al-Abbas, a modified Scud with a 560-mile range and improved accuracy; in December 1989, they launched the Al-Abid, a multistaged space vehicle that was widely perceived as the prototype for a long-range ballistic missile.[40] In these, as in other such endeavors, the Iraqis relied heavily on Western sources of electronics, test equipment, and special materials.[41]

American war planners gave considerable attention to the threat Iraqi missiles posed to Coalition forces. Several batteries of Patriot missiles were deployed in Saudi Arabia in late 1990 to provide an antimissile defense screen, and U.S. satellites and aircraft were used to pinpoint the location of fixed Iraqi missile launchers for preemptive attacks at the onset of Desert Storm. But U.S. planners knew that the Al-Husayn and Al-Abbas, while useful in terror attacks on civilian populations in neighboring countries, lacked the precision for strategic attacks on U.S. command centers, communications nodes, and other vital military facilities, and thus concluded that these missiles would not affect the outcome of the war.[42]

There was, however, the question of Iraqi nuclear capabilities. In the weeks leading up to Operation Desert Storm, some U.S. officials claimed that the Iraqis were within "months" of acquiring nuclear weapons, others that they were "within a few years" of possessing the bomb.[43] These claims were used to generate domestic support for the idea of a military offensive against Hussein, even though no military planner took seriously an Iraqi nuclear threat to Coalition forces, and no special precautions were taken against possible Iraqi nuclear strikes.

The Iraqis had initiated their nuclear weapons program in the mid-1970s, when they signed a nuclear cooperation agreement with France and, with French assistance, began construction of the Osiraq reactor at Tuwaitha, some twenty miles south of Baghdad. Although the 40-megawatt Osiraq reactor purportedly was intended for peaceful research purposes only, many nuclear experts, particularly those in Israel, suspected it to be the centerpiece for a covert Iraqi weapons program. On June 7, 1981, a lightning attack by Israeli aircraft destroyed the reactor.[44]

This did not, however, put a halt to Baghdad's efforts to acquire nuclear weapons. In the wake of the Israeli attack, senior Iraqi officials simply developed an alternate approach to acquiring the bomb that would diminish the vulnerability of Iraqi facilities to preemptive attack. Instead of concentrating on a single conspicuous project like Osiraq, the Iraqis decided to launch several nuclear weapons programs at once, each with its own facilities, staff, and supporting infrastructure.[45] In the years that followed, Baghdad employed at least three approaches to the manufacture of fissionable materials for a nuclear bomb: plutonium reprocessing from spent nuclear reactor fuel; uranium enrichment using high-speed gas centrifuges; and uranium enrichment using electromagnetic isotope separation. (The first approach was tested on a laboratory scale only, producing very small amounts of plutonium, but the other two were being pursued aggressively when the Gulf War began.)[46]

Gas centrifuge separation and electromagnetic isotope separation were both methods intended to produce bomb-grade material by separating out the fissionable isotope U-235 from the nonfissionable U-238 in natural uranium ore. By early 1991, when the Gulf war began, Iraq had produced only small quantities of U-235 through the electromagnetic separation process, and several more years of effort would probably have been needed to accumulate sufficient material for even a single bomb; as for the centrifuge process, no U-235 had yet been produced, and the Iraqis had not yet even manufactured centrifuges of sufficient quality to operate at the speed and duration needed for effective U-235 separation.[47]

Nonetheless, between 1981 and 1991, the Iraqis had made great strides in their nuclear program. Assuming that they continued to progress at the same rate, they would, in all likelihood, have begun producing bombs by the late 1990s. As in the chemical and missile areas, however, Baghdad had relied on foreign technology in developing nuclear weapons—the centrifuges used in the gas separation operation, for instance, were based on a European design and were being produced with assistance from West German firms—and it would have needed continued foreign assistance to sustain a high rate of progress.[48] It is possible, therefore, that the Iraqi program could have been delayed simply by the imposition of tight economic and trade sanctions.

Finally, Iraq was thought to be developing biological warfare (BW) agents at the time of Operation Desert Storm. Although there was considerable doubt as to whether the Iraqis had as yet developed militarized BW agents (toxic substances packaged for delivery by military systems), American forces were trained and equipped to cope with a possible BW attack. Iraq's known BW facilities were also targeted for early air attack. But again, as in the chemical area, Iraqi BW capabilities were not considered sufficiently threatening to affect the outcome of the war.[49]

In summary, then, the (correct) assumption that Iraq's WMD capabilities would not alter the basic military equation in the Gulf was structured into American planning for Operation Desert Storm. What the prewar alarm over Iraqi nuclear capabilities and aspirations did accomplish, from the Bush administration's point of view, was to cover up the fact that the various Iraqi weapons programs had made their greatest progress during the 1982–90 period, when Washington had drawn closest to the Hussein regime and chosen to allow Iraq to proceed unhindered on its WMD course. Had the U.S. government pursued a vigorous nonproliferation effort aimed at Iraq, taking steps to cut off the flow of external aid, Baghdad would have posed a far less significant chemical warfare threat in 1990, and no nuclear threat until the end of the century, or beyond. In making the destruction of Iraq's known WMD and missile facilities a major strategic objective of Desert Storm, the Bush administration sought to eliminate not only Baghdad's ability to wage future wars of mass destruction, but also the evidence of U.S. and European complicity in the creation of a powerful Iraq with abundant chemical weapons supplies and an emerging nuclear capability.

PLANNING THE OFFENSIVE

In planning for an offensive campaign against Iraq, General Powell and his associates were governed by two fundamental strategic goals: to drive Iraqi forces out of Kuwait, and to destroy Iraq's heavy armored forces (especially the Republican Guards, Hussein's elite armored units) and its military-industrial establishment. Not only was this particular instance of Iraqi aggression to be reversed, but Iraq's ability to launch future aggressions was to be erased. As the Department of Defense noted in 1991, U.S. military operations in the Gulf were intended to "eliminate Iraq's offensive military capability by destroying major portions of [its] military production, infrastructure, and power projection capabilities."[50]

To achieve these objectives, the Pentagon adopted a "multidimensional" strategy designed to disable Iraqi forces with concentrated attacks from the air, sea, and land. "We will use our technical advantages" to the maximum, General Powell told Congress in December 1990. The Iraqis "will not be dealing with 15-year-old Iranians. They will be dealing with a very, very powerful, capable force that is fully up to the task that has been given to us."[51]

In developing this strategy, Powell and his associates drew on a key thread in recent American military thinking, the "lessons of Vietnam" as developed by Pentagon analysts over many years in scores of books, articles, and reports. In essence, this analysis held that the United States had lost the initiative in Vietnam because civilian policymakers in Washington had insisted on pursuing a strategy of "graduated escalation." U.S. power had been brought to bear slowly and incrementally, in the belief that this would encourage the enemy to cease fighting at an early stage of the conflict, rather than face ever-increasing levels of "pain." The Pentagon's analysts argued that such "incrementalism" allowed the North Vietnamese to build up their fighting strength over a period of time, with the result that the United States was never able to deliver a decisive blow against Hanoi, and was drawn into a protracted war of attrition in which American willpower collapsed before that of the Vietnamese.[52]

According to this analysis, the military had been "handcuffed" by civilian leaders who placed certain targets out of bounds (for example, Soviet supply ships in Haiphong harbor) and usurped military authority by "micromanaging" the war from offices in Washington. Had U.S. combat officers been given a freer hand, it was claimed, the armed services would have been able to attack vital enemy targets and bring the war to an end on successful terms.

One could, of course, argue with these various assertions. Whether "gradual" or not, the United States directed enormous firepower against North Vietnam, destroying most major structures and killing hundreds of thousands of Vietnamese. It is difficult to imagine what additional "pain" could have been inflicted on that country without resorting to nuclear annihilation. In addition, blaming civilian policymakers for the U.S. defeat was disingenuous, given the fact that Presidents Kennedy and Johnson had routinely approved Pentagon requests for troop increases.

Of greater importance here, however, is the fact that most senior officers believed the Pentagon's Vietnam analysis. The generals who planned Operation Desert Storm, including Powell, had all fought in Indochina as younger officers, and were determined to avoid the gradualism and political interference that they associated with the Vietnam conflict. "Many of us here [in Saudi Arabia] who are in this position now were in Vietnam, and that war left a profound impact on our feelings about how our nation ought to conduct its business," General Charles A. Horner of the Air Force told the *New York Times* in August 1990. "We will carry out any particular policy [dictated by Washington], but as individuals we think war is a very serious business and it should not be dragged out in an effort to achieve some political objective."[53]

Pentagon officials were determined that from the earliest moments of the campaign, the war against Iraq would entail the maximum application of force. In line with this, U.S. strategists concluded in October 1990 that the 300,000 or so American soldiers committed to the initial, defensive phase of the Gulf operation would be insufficient for a high-speed offensive campaign against Iraqi forces in Kuwait, and that an additional 250,000 troops would be needed to carry out the Pentagon's chosen plan. General H. Norman Schwarzkopf, who commanded U.S. forces in the Gulf, was particularly adamant about the need for extra forces. After several meetings with the President, Secretary of Defense Cheney secured permission for the deployment of these additional forces on October 31, 1990.[54]

The President made no secret of his sympathy for the Pentagon's analysis. "This will not be a protracted, drawn-out war [like Vietnam]," he told reporters in November. If U.S. troops were sent into combat, he affirmed, "we will not permit [them] to have their hands tied behind their backs. . . . If one American soldier has to go into battle, that soldier will have enough force behind him to win, and then get out as soon as possible."[55]

From this conviction came the decision to concentrate U.S. strength in the Gulf and to begin with a crushing, round-the-clock air war. "In order to achieve assigned goals quickly and with minimum Coalition casualties," the Pentagon later reported, "U.S. defense planners applied the principle of decisive force," planning "massive, simultaneous operations throughout the KTO [Kuwaiti Theater of Operations] and Iraq," while eschewing "the incremental, attrition warfare which had characterized U.S. operations in Vietnam."[56]

In planning this campaign, moreover, the Pentagon drew on stra-

tegic concepts developed by the United States and NATO for intensive, non-nuclear operations against Warsaw Pact forces in Europe.
Somewhat misleadingly grouped under the rubric "competitive strategies," these concepts called for the exploitation of Western superiority in intelligence-gathering, surveillance, communications, air
power, and weaponry to detect and engage the Soviet military establishment at its most vulnerable spots. "A competitive strategy
[seeks] to align enduring U.S. strengths against enduring Soviet weaknesses in a move-countermove-countercountermove se-
quence," Secretary of Defense Frank C. Carlucci explained in 1989.[57]
In essence, the "competitive" approach called for war planners to
identify critical flaws in the Soviet war-fighting system and develop
weapons and tactics that would allow NATO forces to leverage these
weaknesses into significant gains for the West.

The competitive approach and the technologies associated with it
had been developed in the early 1980s in reaction to growing
antinuclear sentiment in Western Europe. With millions of peace
activists taking to the streets in England, Holland, and Germany to
protest the deployment of a new generation of nuclear-armed cruise
missiles in Europe, NATO officials had begun to seek alternative
weapons and strategies that would enable them to retain their technological edge over the Warsaw Pact even if they were forced to
reduce their reliance on nuclear munitions. In particular, they sought
strategies and delivery systems that would allow NATO to locate and
destroy critical enemy installations with high-tech conventional
weapons.[58]

NATO strategists concluded that the greatest weakness in the
Soviet war machine was its dependence on highly centralized,
top-down decisionmaking, a mode of command that put great reliance on secure communications to transmit information on enemy
bases, troop dispositions, and so on, from the front to rear-area
headquarters, and to convey battle orders from the rear to front-line
combat units. If this network could be damaged or destroyed, it was
reasoned, Soviet commanders would be "blinded" (that is, deprived
of accurate intelligence data) and their combat forces "decapitated"

(that is, severed from higher command authority), producing inconceivable chaos and confusion and significantly degrading the fighting ability of Warsaw Pact forces.[59]

A second aspect of Soviet combat doctrine that NATO planners sought to address through the competitive strategies approach was its emphasis on the "echeloning" of Warsaw Pact forces in successive waves of offensive armies, each deployed several hundred miles behind the other. NATO planners assumed that in the event of war the first of these waves would pour across the border into West Germany and attempt to puncture allied defense lines; the second and third waves would then be brought up to the front in order to exploit any of the resulting breakthroughs. To counter this strategy, NATO planners adopted a "deep strike" doctrine under which allied planes and missiles would attack the enemy's follow-on forces while still in their original positions or while proceeding to the front. This, it was hoped, would enable NATO's front-line units to contain any initial Warsaw Pact breakthroughs without being hammered by additional waves of enemy attackers.

The competitive approach called for the development of sophisticated weapons systems to locate and destroy critical Soviet command and control centers, communications nodes, and radar stations, while simultaneously engaging the Warsaw Pact's rear-area forces. To accomplish the latter, the strategy called for the development of advanced surveillance systems that could locate and track enemy forces in "real time" (that is, nearly instantaneously), along with bombs and missiles that could be used to attack these targets with a high degree of precision.[60] Out of this effort came a number of major weapons and combat systems that were later to play a critical role in the Persian Gulf conflict, including the Joint Surveillance and Target Attack Radar System (JSTARS), a militarized Boeing 707 with sophisticated radars capable of detecting enemy vehicles while on the move, and the Army Tactical Missile System (ATACMS), an advanced surface-to-surface missile with a range of 100 miles.[61]

Furthermore, to ensure that allied forces could demolish major Warsaw Pact targets like air bases and tank formations without relying on nuclear weapons, the new strategy called for the employment of "wide-area" conventional weapons meant to duplicate the immediate killing power of small nuclear explosives without producing any lingering radioactivity. These "near-nuclear" weapons typically employed "cluster bomb units" (CBUs), or dispenser systems, that popped open over the battlefield and disgorged hundreds of smaller bombs or "submunitions" over a very large area.[62] Weapons of this type had first been used on a significant scale during the Vietnam War to decimate enemy infantry units, and had been further developed after Vietnam to permit attacks on larger, more heavily protected forces. One such system, the Army's Multiple-Launch Rocket System (MLRS), was capable of firing twelve rockets in less than a minute and inundating a thirty-acre area with seven thousand grenadelike submunitions.[63] Other systems, like the Air Force's CBU-87/B Combined Effects Munition, dispensed both antipersonnel and antitank submunitions in order to maximize their destructive potential.[64] These, and other such munitions, had reached a mature stage of development by the time the Persian Gulf crisis erupted in August 1990, and were quickly repositioned and reconfigured for use against Iraqi forces in Kuwait.

In employing these weapons, U.S. war planners were able to take advantage of the fact that Iraqi forces were structured very much like those of the East European members of the Warsaw Pact, with highly centralized command-and-control systems and an inadequate air-defense capability. According to the Department of Defense, critical Iraqi vulnerabilities included "the rigid top-down nature of the command and control system," and "ground forces and logistics vulnerable to air attack."[65] As in the U.S./NATO strategy for combat with the Warsaw Pact, the Pentagon's plan for Desert Storm called for concentrated air and missile attacks against these vulnerabilities at the very onset of battle.

To plan the air campaign against Iraq's military infrastructure, the Department of Defense established a special planning unit at CENTCOM's headquarters in Tampa, Florida. From the very beginning, the unit's leaders envisioned a relentless, day and night assault on Iraqi installations, employing the full strength of American air power. In a conscious effort to distinguish this assault from "Operation Rolling Thunder," the protracted air campaign against North Vietnam initiated by President Johnson in 1965, these officers christened it "Operation Instant Thunder."[66]

Military planners also sought to "decapitate" the Iraqi army by attacking and destroying enemy command bunkers in downtown Baghdad.[67] Although Saddam Hussein was never specifically identified as a target of U.S. air strikes (at least in public testimony), Pentagon officials clearly intended to kill many of his senior lieutenants (assumed to be stationed in these bunkers) and, no doubt, hoped to catch the Iraqi dictator himself in one of these raids on Iraqi command facilities. Even if this did not occur, the Pentagon later noted, these attacks were designed to "neutralize the regime's ability to direct military operations by eroding communications and depriving leaders of secure locations from which to plan and control operations."[68]

EXECUTING THE PLAN

The operational plan for Desert Storm was developed, tested (via computer simulations), and refined in the weeks leading up to the January 15, 1991, U.N. deadline for the Iraqis to abandon Kuwait. As finally configured, the plan incorporated four distinct phases: a strategic air campaign to incapacitate Iraqi command centers and destroy known nuclear, chemical, and missile facilities; a drive to establish air superiority over Iraq and the Kuwaiti Theater of Operations (KTO); an extended air campaign against Iraqi ground units in the KTO; and a ground offensive designed to cut off and destroy Iraqi forces in Kuwait.[69]

To assemble the forces and equipment needed to carry out this plan, the Pentagon conducted its largest logistical operation since World War II. More than 3.2 million tons of cargo were ferried from ports in the United States and Europe to the Gulf area, 112,500 tracked and wheeled vehicles were delivered to the combat zone, $2.5 billion worth of ammunition was supplied to fighting units, and more than $615 million worth of temporary support facilities were constructed in Saudi Arabia.[70] In addition, the Pentagon delivered sufficient food, fuel, and drinking water to supply a combat force of 550,000 men and women in an austere desert environment that could barely sustain human life.

During this entire period, the Iraqi forces in Kuwait remained largely quiescent, building additional trenches and fortifications and stockpiling ammunition. Had they attacked allied port facilities and supply depots in Saudi Arabia during the buildup phase of Desert Shield, when U.S. defenses were still insubstantial, they might have inflicted significant damage and thrown off the schedule for Desert Storm. "One of the great mysteries of the Gulf War," military analyst Jeffrey Record wrote in 1993, "is why [Saddam Hussein] sat by passively for almost six months while the United States and its Coalition partners amassed overwhelming military power in Saudi Arabia."[71] By not attacking at this time, Hussein gave the Coalition an enormous advantage that was to cost him dearly.[72] Even when it was becoming increasingly evident that Coalition forces were planning to go on the offensive, Hussein squandered every remaining opportunity to negotiate his way out of Kuwait and thereby save the bulk of his army.[73]

Phase I of Operation Desert Storm commenced at 3:00 a.m. local time on January 17, 1991 (7:00 p.m. of the sixteenth on the East Coast of the United States). Following nighttime attacks on Iraqi radar sites by AH-64 Apache helicopters, an armada of seven hundred combat aircraft bombed Iraqi bases and facilities in what was described by the Pentagon as the "biggest air strike since World War II."[74] In one of the most dramatic incidents of the war, radar-evading F-117As dropped bombs on the Iraqi Air Force headquarters in downtown Baghdad, triggering an incandescent (but largely ineffective) barrage of antiaircraft artillery fire. At the same time, a total of 116 Tomahawk land-attack cruise missiles were fired at key military targets in the Iraqi capital from U.S. warships in the Red

Sea and Persian Gulf.[75] Air and missile attacks were also mounted against Iraqi nuclear, chemical, and biological weapons facilities, and against known ballistic missile launch sites.[76]

Accompanying this strategic campaign was a systematic effort to destroy Iraq's air defense system. F-4G "Wild Weasel" electronic warfare planes sought out enemy radar sites and attacked them with the AGM-88 High-speed Anti-radiation Missile (HARM), an air-to-surface weapon that homes in on the electronic signals given off by operating radar emitters. Allied aircraft also attacked Iraqi airfields, antiaircraft missile batteries, and air defense command centers. "This was not a gradual rolling back of the Iraqi air defense system," the Pentagon later noted. "The nearly simultaneous suppression of so many vital centers helped cripple Iraq's air defense system, and began seriously to disrupt the LOCs [lines of communication] between Saddam Hussein and his forces in the KTO."[77]

Before the first day of the war was over, Coalition forces had achieved "air superiority" over Iraq and Kuwait. Unimpeded by enemy aircraft or ground defenses, they then began to attack and destroy Iraqi military bases, communications facilities, supply depots, bridges, refineries, and other facilities vital to the Iraqi war effort. By the end of the first week of the air war, U.S. aircraft had conducted well over 10,000 sorties (individual combat missions) against targets in Iraq and Kuwait, with most such attacks directed against the military and industrial infrastructure of the Iraqi state.[78]

By January 23, when General Powell provided the first briefing on Phase I of Desert Storm, the destruction of known Iraqi WMD and missile production capabilities was already well advanced. As for Iraq's nuclear weapons program, he noted, "the two operating reactors they had are both gone, they're down, they're finished." Similarly, "we have done considerable damage to their ability to continue producing chemical weapons."[79] Thus, after only a few days of bombing, many of the key strategic goals of the war, it was claimed, had already been accomplished.[80]

To achieve Washington's remaining strategic objectives, particularly the destruction of the Republican Guards and other major ground formations, Coalition forces carried out five weeks of intensive bombing in Kuwait and southern Iraq. A total of 35,000 combat sorties were mounted by Coalition aircraft against Iraqi ground units in the KTO, including 5,600 against the Republican Guards alone. To destroy Iraqi fortifications and sap the morale of enemy defenders, thousands of tons of conventional bombs were dropped on Iraqi positions from B-52s and other U.S. aircraft.[81] It was this constant drubbing, more than anything else, that led to the ultimate collapse of Iraqi ground forces. "They were under constant bombardment 24 hours a day, five weeks in a row, without a let-up," an American general later reported. "No one has ever had to experience that in the history of warfare. It's no wonder the place was coming unglued at the seams."[82]

In attacking enemy forces, the Pentagon employed the complete panoply of non-nuclear weapons in their possession. At the time, much media emphasis was placed on the use of "smart" weapons, such as the Tomahawk cruise missile, various laser-guided bombs, and the Standoff Land Attack Missile (SLAM) for attacks on such pinpoint targets as radar stations and radio towers. Most of the munitions used in the KTO, however, were aimed at wide-area targets—troops, supply dumps, fortifications, and vehicle parks— rather than at small "point" structures. To obliterate these larger targets, the United States relied on the massive use of cluster bombs and other wide-area munitions. The MLRS, for instance, fired 9,660 rockets at Iraqi troop positions during the course of the fighting, sufficient to blanket 25,000 acres with a deluge of lethal metal fragments.[83] These weapons, and others like them, probably accounted for the largest number of battle deaths among Iraqi soldiers.[84]

To insure that Iraqi troops would not escape this intense bombardment at night, American forces also used a wide range of infrared and night-vision systems to locate, track, and engage enemy units after dark. This night-fighting capability was a distinguishing feature of the AH-64 Apache attack helicopter, which was widely employed in nocturnal operations against Iraqi ground forces. "I just didn't envision" that it was possible to go up there "and shoot the hell out of everything in the dark and have them not know what the hell hit them," said one Apache pilot after such an assault. "They had no idea where we were or what was hitting them."[85]

By "G-Day," the start of the allied ground campaign in Kuwait, U.S. aircraft had flown over 60,000 combat sorties against ground forces in Iraq and Kuwait, while U.S. ships had launched 288 Tomahawk missiles. In addition to inflicting enormous damage on Iraq's communications, logistics, and air defense capabilities, these strikes resulted in the destruction of thousands of tanks and artillery pieces.[86] According to U.S. intelligence, Iraqi front-line units in Kuwait had by this point been reduced in effectiveness by fifty percent or more through desertion, lack of equipment, or casualties inflicted by air strikes.[87]

Once the ground war began, it became a race against time. U.S. commanders struggled to liquidate Iraq's remaining war machine before Saddam Hussein caved in to U.S.–U.N. conditions for a cease-fire.[88] By the fourth and final day of the allied offensive, Iraqi forces were in total retreat, and American warplanes engaged in what was described by one U.S. pilot as a "turkey shoot" against exposed and defenseless troops.[89] General Schwarzkopf later indicated that he would have liked to continue the fighting in order to destroy more Iraqi units, but President Bush suspended the slaughter after one hundred hours of land combat.[90]

Even though the U.S. offensive was halted before all enemy units in Kuwait had been annihilated, Desert Storm inflicted enormous damage on the Iraqi war machine. According to the Department of Defense, Coalition forces captured or destroyed 3,847 Iraqi tanks during the course of Desert Storm, along with 1,450 personnel carriers and 2,917 artillery pieces.[91] In addition, 184 Iraqi combat planes were shot down or destroyed on the ground, and another 109 were flown to Iran and later confiscated by the Iranian government.[92] Also destroyed were Iraqi military bases, air defense systems, and many of the factories used to produce arms and ammunition.[93]

In announcing the end of hostilities against Iraq, President Bush asserted that the strategic goals of the war had been fully accomplished. "Tonight in Iraq, Saddam walks amidst ruin," he told a joint session of Congress on March 6. "His war machine is crushed. His ability to threaten mass destruction is itself destroyed."[94] Bush also asserted that Hussein "has been stripped of his capacity to project offensive military power."[95] Subsequent on-site research by U.N. investigators revealed that some of Baghdad's hidden nuclear facilities had escaped destruction during the war, but, this aside, there is no doubt that Iraq's capacity to invade, let alone conquer, other nations in the region had been largely destroyed.

THE "ROGUE DOCTRINE" CONFIRMED

From the perspective of the U.S. military establishment, Operation Desert Storm represented a remarkable success. It constituted a decisive victory over a significant regional power, achieved with few losses and in a matter of weeks. For the first time in decades, American forces had worked together under a unified command and executed a combat plan that maximized their already massive advantages over the enemy. Pentagon officials may have greatly exaggerated the capabilities of the Iraqi military and employed an army far larger than needed, but there is no doubt that their forces exercised total mastery over the battlefield.

In fact, the real American achievement was the attainment of competitive supremacy in so many combat areas that the Iraq-Kuwait theater of operations was transformed into something of an experimental battlefield, an enormous testing ground for the Pentagon's new weaponry and combat techniques. With the Iraqi military suffering from so many vulnerabilities and deficiencies, not to mention the strategic incompetence of Saddam Hussein, the conflict was, in the end, little more than a systematic slaughter.

As an overwhelming battlefield success, it had the effect of leveling adversaries at home, as well as in the Gulf. When the victorious

Generals Schwarzkopf and Powell faced Congress and the American public in the immediate aftermath of the war, they could declare the new U.S. military posture totally validated. Who, now, could deny the correctness of the operational concepts so recently adopted by Powell and his staff, or the global military doctrine cobbled together in the aftermath of the Berlin Wall's fall—a doctrine that, only six months earlier, had lacked an actual adversary?

For the Department of Defense, success was now at hand—not only on the battlefields of the Persian Gulf, but on the funding battlefields in Congress, the publicity battlefields in the mass media, the research and development battlefields of industrial America, and on that most important of all battlefields, the public mind. "Competitive strategies" seemed to be working in the United States itself; for, wherever one looked, adversaries of all sorts—their vulnerabilities exposed—were falling back in disarray. Not since the early years of the Cold War had the Department of Defense seemed to wield such a potent and winning strategic message—and Pentagon officials wasted no time in using it to promote the various dimensions of the Rogue Doctrine.

Scarcely was the Gulf conflict over before military officials began speaking of the need to prepare for armed combat with the "Iraqs of the future." On March 19, 1991, only two and a half weeks after the fighting ended, Secretary Cheney told Congress that "the Gulf war presaged very much the type of conflict we are most likely to confront again in this new era—major regional contingencies against foes well-armed with advanced conventional and unconventional munitions." However large its military, Iraq was not the only rising Third World power with potent arsenals. "There are other regional powers with modern armed forces, sophisticated attack aircraft, and integrated air defenses."[96]

On this basis, Cheney called for the accelerated transformation of America's Cold War defense establishment into a Third World–oriented force. "We must configure our policies and our forces to effectively deter, or quickly defeat, such regional threats," he told the House Foreign Affairs Committee.[97] For the foreseeable future, most senior policymakers would second Cheney's basic premise: America's future military posture should be governed by the need to prepare for an endless series of Desert Storm–like engagements with rising Third World powers.

Chapter Three

THE TRUE PATH TO VICTORY

Lessons of Desert Storm

WITH THE SUCCESSFUL conclusion of Operation Desert Storm, U.S. military leaders had achieved their most important post–Cold War strategic objective: convincing Congress and the American people of the need to prepare for a succession of regional encounters with Iraq-like powers in vital areas of the Third World. Whatever doubts had existed on this point before August 1990 were swept away by the Iraqi invasion of Kuwait and the subsequent conflict in the Gulf. Now, senior military officials embarked on a new campaign to convince Congress and the public that the Pentagon's preferred manner of fighting such wars—that employed in the Gulf conflict—should be embedded permanently in American military doctrine. To this end, the Department of Defense sought to define the "lessons" of Desert Storm—and, thereby, to determine how U.S. forces would be trained and equipped for the wars of the future.

By the close of 1991, dozens of studies were under way to trace the course of the Persian Gulf conflict and draw conclusions about the relative effectiveness of the strategies, forces, and weapons em-

ployed by America's armed services. From the military's point of
view, the most significant of these were two reports on *The Conduct
of the Persian Gulf War* submitted to Congress by Secretary of Defense
Dick Cheney. (The *Interim Report* was published in July 1991, the
Final Report in April 1992.) Similar reports were issued by the individual military services, the House Armed Services Committee, and
think-tanks and research institutes associated with the Department
of Defense.[1] Also important were studies conducted by the Center
for Strategic and International Studies, the International Institute of
Strategic Studies, and various academic analysts.[2]

In conducting these reviews, military analysts were keenly aware
that the Persian Gulf conflict represented a pivotal event: the first
large-scale conflict of the post–Cold War era, and the first war ever
to employ a full array of space-age weaponry. They were also aware
that these studies had potentially enormous political and budgetary
significance, in that the strategies, force structures, and weaponry
collectively deemed having been most successful in the Gulf naturally
stood the greatest chance of eliciting continuing White House and
Congressional support. For the Department of Defense and each of
the military services, shaping the lessons of the war therefore became
almost as important as winning the war itself had been.

The struggle to define the lessons of Desert Storm took place on
two fronts: the actual battlefields in Iraq and Kuwait, where particular weapons and forces had been used against Iraqi military units;
and the hypothetical battlefields of future Desert Storm–like engagements. "As we reshape America's defenses," Secretary Cheney
explained in 1992, "we need to look at Operations Desert Shield
and Desert Storm for indications of what military capabilities we may
need not just in the next few years, but ten, twenty, or thirty years
hence. We need to consider why we were successful, what worked
and what did not, and what is important to protect and preserve in
our military capability."[3]

Because the United States had committed so many weapons and
forces to the Gulf conflict, such analysis extended to many levels. At

a purely tactical level, the war had tested the effectiveness of an unusually broad range of new weapons systems, including the Patriot antiaircraft/antimissile missile, the ship-launched Tomahawk land-attack missile, the M-1A1 main battle tank, the F-117 Stealth fighter-bomber, and the JSTARS airborne reconnaissance system. On a strategic level, the war had tested the validity of various post-Vietnam modifications in U.S. military doctrine, including the concepts of decisive force, rapid deployment, and strategic mobility. Indeed, few aspects of military strategy (save those regarding the use of nuclear weapons) were left untested by the Persian Gulf conflict.

Not surprisingly, the Department of Defense went to great lengths to insure that its interpretation of Operation Desert Storm was decisive. In speech after speech, senior military officials sought to persuade Congress and the public of the accuracy of their assessments of the war, and to cast doubt on all other possible interpretations. Aided by a largely appreciative media, these efforts generally proved successful, and most policymakers continued to view Desert Storm as a triumphant application of American military power that should strongly influence future U.S. combat behavior.

The vigor of the Pentagon's postwar propaganda blitz should not, however, obscure the existence of other interpretations of the war's lessons, even within the military, and the need for caution in relying on Operation Desert Storm as *the* model for future wars. Alternate interpretations generally conclude that conditions in the Gulf were politically and militarily unique, unlikely to be repeated. "Desert Storm was the perfect war with the perfect enemy," a senior commander observed after the war. "We had the perfect coalition, the perfect infrastructure, and the perfect battlefield. [Hence], we should be careful about the lessons we draw from the war."[4]

Critics of the Pentagon assessment have also argued that some of the technical successes of the Gulf campaign were more publicity coups than combat triumphs. They claim that the war actually exposed a number of significant flaws in U.S. military planning, ranging from weaker-than-advertised performances by particular weapons systems (including the much-vaunted Patriot and Tomahawk) to questions regarding the validity of such strategic concepts as long-range power projection.[5]

LESSONS DRAWN

Pentagon analysts were quick to draw critical "lessons" from the U.S. military's Gulf War performance. These ranged from the technical and specific—for example, calculations of the effectiveness and "lethality" of particular weapons systems under various conditions of battle—to the strategic and conceptual. Most of these findings fell under four broad categories: (1) *high-technology works*; (2) *air power rules the battlefield*; (3) *all four military services are needed*; and (4) *enhanced strategic mobility is essential.*

Technology Works

The most important lesson drawn by the military was that high-technology works. The United States employed a wide array of high-tech weapons and support systems in the Gulf, including many never before used in full-scale combat. These included airborne surveillance systems that could locate enemy forces twenty-four hours a day, radar-evading aircraft that penetrated enemy air defenses with ease, and precision-guided munitions that struck enemy facilities with what was claimed was near-perfect accuracy. "Technology greatly increased our battlefield effectiveness," Secretary Cheney affirmed in 1992. "Our forces often found, targeted, and destroyed the enemy's before the enemy could return fire effectively."[6]

In discussing the role of technology, Pentagon officials placed particular stress on munitions and support systems employed for the first time in Operation Desert Storm.[7] Notable among these were the F-117A Stealth aircraft, the Tomahawk land-attack cruise missile, the Patriot air defense missile, the M-1A1 Abrams tank, the Multiple-

Launch Rocket System (MLRS), and the AH-64 Apache attack helicopter. Also making their debut were a number of advanced communications, surveillance, and targeting systems, including JSTARS, the NAVSTAR Global Positioning System (GPS), and the Pioneer unmanned spy plane.[8]

These systems all combined a variety of advanced technologies to outclass and overpower comparable systems in the Iraqi inventory. The F-117 employed radar-deflecting materials and a chisel-shaped profile to evade enemy radars and attack high-value targets in downtown Baghdad with relative impunity. The Tomahawk missile used built-in radar and a computerized memory bank to steer itself from "standoff" locations at sea to critical inland targets. The Patriot missile used a sophisticated radar and guidance system to intercept incoming Scud missiles while in flight. The Apache helicopter used infrared radar scopes and advanced night-vision devices (electronic devices that amplify natural light in order to produce a visible image of the nocturnal landscape) to locate enemy troop concentrations in the dark and destroy them with onboard missiles and rockets. All of these weapons benefited from the precise targeting and locational data provided by reconnaissance satellites, JSTARS, and Pioneer.

For Secretary Cheney and others in the Pentagon, the introduction of these high-tech systems represented a military breakthrough whose effects would be felt for decades to come. "This war demonstrated dramatically the new possibilities of what has been called the 'military-technological revolution in warfare,' " Cheney declared in 1992. "This technological revolution encompasses many areas, including stand-off precision weaponry, sophisticated sensors, stealth for surprise and survivability, night vision capabilities, and tactical ballistic missile defenses." The exploitation of these new technologies, he argued, will "change the nature of warfare significantly, as did the earlier advent of tanks, airplanes, and aircraft carriers."[9]

The technological changes touted by Cheney all derived from a common root: the ability to miniaturize complex electronic devices, and so endow munitions with the capacity to locate particular enemy

targets—even mobile targets—and strike them with a high degree
of accuracy. In previous conflicts, U.S. forces had difficulty locating
many key targets, and were forced to expend a vast supply of ord-
nance (bullets, bombs, and shells) in order to hit and destroy them;
as a result, wars often dragged on and produced a great deal of civilian
(in military parlance, "collateral") damage. In the Gulf War, according to Pentagon assessments, forces in the field were able to
pinpoint the location of critical targets and often succeeded in destroying them on the first or second shot—thereby reducing the
duration of the war and lessening collateral damage.[10]

The guided missiles used in attacks on heavily guarded Iraqi facilities certainly were the most visible examples of these new capabilities. The United States employed a wide variety of these
weapons to strike particular types of enemy assets: the Tomahawk
to destroy government offices and communications centers in downtown Baghdad; the Patriot to intercept incoming enemy missiles; the
Army Tactical Missile System to attack enemy bases and artillery
behind the front line of battle; and the Hellfire to destroy enemy
tanks and vehicles. Together, these weapons offered an impressive
capacity for destroying enemy weapons and installations. Shown on
television, moreover, they helped generate popular support for the
war by demonstrating America's ability to inflict significant damage
on the Iraqis while suffering little pain in return.

Pentagon analysts also emphasized the important role played by
advanced reconnaissance, surveillance, and communications technologies in the Gulf. By combining the data from space satellites,
the Airborne Warning and Control System (AWACS), JSTARS, and
television-equipped pilotless aircraft like Pioneer, intelligence officials were able to pinpoint the location of Iraqi military units and
transmit this information to allied combat units in "real time," almost
instantaneously. Equipped with such information, battle commanders were able to launch devastating air and missile attacks against
enemy units while they were moving or were otherwise vulnerable.
Because these systems operated around the clock, and because U.S.
aircraft, tanks, and helicopters were equipped with infrared and

night-vision devices, such attacks could be mounted at any hour of the day or night, depriving the enemy of any respite from constant bombardment.[11]

In one of the most dramatic incidents of the war, American forces used these capabilities to turn a nighttime retreat by Iraqi ground forces into a "turkey shoot," in which hundreds, if not thousands, of enemy soldiers perished. The massive Iraqi withdrawal from Kuwait began on the night of February 25–26, when it was already apparent that heavy fortifications would not stop the Coalition advance. As Iraqi troops began driving up the main highway from Kuwait City to Basra in southern Iraq, a JSTARS aircraft detected them on its moving target indicator radar and radioed the information to allied air commanders. Within minutes, the air above this "highway of death" was filled with U.S. combat aircraft. By the next morning, the fifty-mile stretch of road was a "mangled scene of destruction and death," with hundreds of burning vehicles and bloodsoaked bodies strewn across the desert.[12]

Such incidents, however troubling to some observers, were viewed by Pentagon analysts as evidence of the enormous advantages enjoyed by the United States owing to its superior technology. While American forces could fire at Iraq forces from safe distances, the Iraqis were unable to obtain shelter in their earthen trenches, even at night. The Iraqis may have compounded their predicament through poor strategic planning and a failure to challenge the Coalition's command of the air, but, in any case, they were at the mercy of superior weaponry, surveillance gear, and targeting systems. "Iraq seemed determined to fight in the style of the First World War, while the West fought in the style of the next century," observed Colonel Jeffrey McCausland of the Army War College."[13]

In the postwar battle of the budget, Pentagon officials were particularly determined to preserve America's lead in advanced technology. "The [Gulf] war showed that we must work to maintain the tremendous advantages that accrue from being a generation ahead in weapons technology," Secretary Cheney told Congress in 1992. Because other countries were likely to seek advanced weaponry of their own, he argued, the United States was obliged to continue spending vast sums on the design and procurement of high-tech munitions "to maintain our [technological] advantage."[14]

In support of this position, the various military services and their associated contractors conducted an elaborate media campaign on the need for continued procurement of high-tech systems of the sort used in the Gulf. As part of its contribution to the national celebration of Desert Storm, the Department of Defense staged a massive display of advanced weaponry on the Mall in Washington, D.C., on June 8, 1991. Billed as the largest (and costliest) military celebration in the nation's capital since General Dwight D. Eisenhower led a victory parade there after World War II, the extravaganza featured exhibits of Patriot missiles, Apache helicopters, Harrier jump-jets, and other Desert Storm weapons.[15] On a more substantive level, the services bombarded Congress with testimonials regarding the proven effectiveness of their favored weapons in the Gulf. The Air Force touted the F-117 and AWACS; the Army, the Patriot and Apache; the Navy, the Tomahawk and the Standoff Land Attack Missile. Such testimonials were considered essential to continued funding in the post–Cold War era. As one military official observed, "If you didn't get your chance to demonstrate your sexiness during Desert Storm, you are at risk" in seeking funds for future arms procurement.[16]

But, while such efforts certainly contributed to the impression that sophisticated weaponry had played the crucial role in the U.S. success, the high-tech systems had not performed flawlessly. Some that were highly touted by the Pentagon and the media have seen their accuracy ratings downgraded significantly as experts have looked more closely into their battle performance. The success rate of the Tomahawk missile in striking its designated target has been reassessed to less than sixty percent of all launches, rather than the eighty percent originally estimated, while the F-117A Stealth fighter is now reported to have struck its intended targets on only about sixty percent of its missions, not the ninety percent reported right after the war.[17] Furthermore, even these revised figures may overstate the effectiveness of many high-tech weapons used in the Gulf.

By far the greatest publicity setback befell the Patriot missile. On January 18, 1991, television watchers saw an elated General Schwarzkopf announce from Riyadh that the first Scud missile fired at U.S. forces in Saudi Arabia had been "destroyed by a United States Army Patriot Missile."[18] This statement, with accompanying video footage of the alleged Scud intercept, did much to boost the Patriot's popularity, and the popularity of high-tech weapons in general. However, it is now known that no Scud was fired at U.S. forces on that date, and that the Patriot shown on American television had exploded in midair as a result of computer error.[19] Subsequent research has also revealed that many other Patriots missed their targets entirely, or failed to destroy incoming warheads—which then crashed to earth and exploded.[20] According to Representative John Conyers, Jr., who conducted a ten-month investigation of the Patriot system, "there was little evidence to prove that the Patriot hit more than a few Scud missiles launched by Iraq during the war—and there is doubt about even those engagements."[21]

Even when high-tech systems did perform flawlessly, moreover, their success did not automatically translate into enhanced combat effectiveness. A case in point involved the distribution of intelligence data: while many air- and space-based surveillance systems were used to collect detailed information on the location and orientation of Iraqi forces, this information did not always reach the ground commanders who needed it most with sufficient speed to make a difference on the battlefield.[22] U.S. forces "could have been more effective had there been a greater ability to process and disseminate target and other information," the House Armed Services Committee noted in its 1992 study of the war.[23] Each service's predilection for its own communications gear also impeded the timely communication of intelligence data to combat units. For example, the Air Force's AWACS radar surveillance plane could relay information over secure channels to other Air Force aircraft, but not to Navy fighters, which impeded coordinated strikes against Iraqi aircraft.[24]

In addition, the Iraqis discovered ways to foil satellite and surveillance systems by employing camouflage or by moving key systems rapidly from place to place. These techniques proved particularly effective in thwarting efforts to target and destroy Iraq's mobile Scud launchers. Although the Air Force devoted some twenty to thirty percent of all air strikes to anti-Scud operations, it was unable to locate many of the mobile launchers, and Iraq continued to fire Scuds throughout the course of the war. These attacks did not have a significant impact on the war's outcome, but they did illustrate the difficulties that even advanced high-tech systems may face against a determined opponent.[25]

Indeed, there were many occasions on which the military itself chose to rely on older, low-technology systems. While precision-guided "smart" bombs were featured in televised military briefings, more than ninety percent of the bombs used in Desert Storm—perhaps 228,000 out of 250,000—were old-fashioned "dumb" bombs of the sort used in Korea and Vietnam. Indeed, many analysts credited incessant bombing by thirty-year-old B-52s using unguided iron bombs with breaking the morale of Iraqi forces and ensuring a rapid allied victory in the ground campaign.[26]

Moreover, even such clear-cut high-tech successes as Tomahawk and JSTARS must be understood in the context of this particular theater of war. The forces against which they were deployed were of such technological inferiority that the United States was able to proceed with very little interference. In many respects, the Gulf conflict was more akin to a large-scale proving ground for new tactics and weaponry than an actual battlefield. Indeed, one Air Force general observed that Desert Storm "could be the greatest laboratory experiment for force structure mix that we've ever had."[27] The Iraqis never seriously challenged U.S. control of the air, nor did they employ electronic systems to disrupt or disable American planes or surveillance systems. Had the Iraqis proved more adept at anti-air and electronic warfare, American forces would have had a much more difficult time exploiting the advantages of their high-tech weaponry.[28]

Although the Iraqis did not—could not—take effective action against these high-tech systems, it cannot be assumed that this would be the case in future encounters of this type. Military leaders in every country have now studied the Desert Storm campaign, and are undoubtedly minimizing their vulnerability to the sort of beating Iraq experienced. Of course, few of these countries will ever approach the technological proficiency of the United States, but any increase in future opponents' anti-air and electronic warfare capabilities would greatly diminish America's advantage in future wars.[29]

Air Power Rules

The second major lesson taken from the Gulf War by Pentagon strategists was that air power rules the battlefield. This is not to say that air power did it all—a conclusion that Pentagon officials do not want drawn from Desert Storm. They prefer to highlight the ways in which the U.S. advantage in air power was crucial in destroying the Iraqi military infrastructure and eroding the enemy's capacity to resist attack by allied ground forces. "The decisive character of our victory in the Gulf War is attributable in large measure to the extraordinary effectiveness of air power," Secretary Cheney affirmed after the war. "Drawing in large part on new capabilities, air power destroyed or suppressed much of the Iraqi air defense network, neutralized the Iraqi air force, crippled much of Iraq's command and control system, knocked out bridges and storage sites, and, as the war developed, methodically destroyed many Iraqi tanks and much of the artillery in forward areas."[30]

In the Pentagon's view, early success in gaining control of the airspace over Kuwait and Iraq was the critical triumph from which all else followed. It enabled allied forces to attack Iraqi ground forces at will and allowed them to employ high-tech munitions in coordinated attacks on key elements of the Iraqi war machine. This, in turn, permitted the application of "decisive force" and "competitive strategies" in erasing the enemy's capacity to resist. Echoing this view, the House Armed Services Committee asserted in 1992 that "the mass and precision of the [air] attack induced systematic shock and paralysis from which the political and military leadership [of Iraq] never recovered."[31]

For the Air Force, this was a moment to be savored. Ever since the days of General William ("Billy") Mitchell, the first American proponent of air power, Air Force leaders had dreamed of assuming the dominant role in warfare. In World War II, Korea, and Vietnam, the Air Force had offered assurance that its planes could deliver a knockout punch against enemy forces, only to be frustrated by imperfect equipment and enemy resistance. In Iraq, however, Air Force pilots encountered perfect conditions in which to demonstrate their prowess: not only did the Iraqis fail to challenge U.S. control of the air, but Saddam Hussein presided over a highly centralized political-military infrastructure that was exceptionally vulnerable to air and missile attack.[32]

To exploit these vulnerabilities, Coalition air forces had first attacked Iraq's air defense system, and then, when the Iraqis could no longer defend themselves, launched a systematic air campaign against enemy communications, intelligence, and logistical capabilities. To further hamper enemy operations, U.S. aircraft had attacked and destroyed key elements of the Iraqi electrical power grid.[33] Finally, to choke off the supply of oil and lubricants to enemy fighting forces, American planes had repeatedly bombed Iraqi oil refineries and storage facilities.[34]

Even more important, the relentless air campaign against Iraqi ground units in Kuwait and southern Iraq had produced huge numbers of casualties, and eroded the enemy's morale. According to the Department of Defense, U.S. and allied aircraft flew some 70,000 combat sorties during the five weeks of Desert Storm, most of them aimed at Iraqi troop positions.[35] These attacks "drastically wore down the ability and the will of the Iraqi Army to fight," the House Committee concluded. "Iraqi ground forces were so devastated and demoralized by the time the ground war started that they lacked the conviction to fight for their own soil, much less [for] Kuwait."[36]

Indeed, so potent did allied air capabilities seem that, at various stages in the crisis, a number of analysts suggested the United States eschew a ground campaign altogether, and rely entirely on air power to achieve its strategic objectives. This view did not sit well with General Powell and other senior commanders, who wanted to make sure that every service would have a conspicuous role in Operation Desert Storm. In the end, therefore, the Air Force (and carrier-based Navy aircraft) had to share some of the glory of Desert Storm with the Army and the Marine Corps.[37]

Despite such accommodations, the importance of air power had been firmly established. According to Colonel McCausland of the Army War College, Iraq's crushing defeat in the 1991 Gulf conflict confirmed that "chronic inferiority in air power is a strategic liability for which it is almost impossible to compensate in normal conventional warfare."[38] Nevertheless, Desert Storm revealed a number of important limitations on the application of air power in conflicts of this sort. Even under the particularly advantageous circumstances of the Gulf conflict—a war in which the enemy lacked not only sophisticated air defenses but air cover of almost any sort—U.S. air strikes had failed to achieve a number of key objectives.

One of the principal goals of Operation Desert Storm had been the destruction of the Iraqi nuclear and chemical capabilities, and at the war's end, senior U.S. officials announced that this objective had been fully achieved. Hussein's "war machine is crushed," President Bush told a joint session of Congress on March 6, 1991. "His ability to threaten mass destruction is itself destroyed."[39] Several months later, however, when U.N. investigators began their on-site inspection of Iraqi WMD installations, they discovered that while most chemical facilities had been destroyed, many key nuclear installations—including the gas centrifuge plant at Al Furat and the nuclear bomb assembly plant at Al Atheer—had been largely untouched.[40] This resulted not from poor aim, but from U.S. intelligence analysts' failure to appreciate the complexity and magnitude of the Iraqi nuclear weapons program. Many nuclear facilities had never been identified, let alone placed on the target list for Operation Desert Storm. While this represented a failure of intelligence rather than of air power, it also suggested that air power, when used in a strategic role, was only as effective as the target intelligence it drew upon. If that intelligence was faulty or incomplete, air power alone could not perform a strategic mission successfully.[41]

The U.S. effort to crush the central political authority of the Hussein regime was similarly unsuccessful. Although the Bush administration never admitted to planning the outright assassination of Saddam Hussein and his inner circle, Pentagon officials did admit to a desire to liquidate Iraq's senior military leadership—in Pentagon parlance, to effect the "decapitation" of the Iraqi war machine—through air and missile strikes on their underground command facilities.[42] But, while U.S. aircraft often targeted these facilities with pinpoint accuracy, U.S. intelligence had never been able to determine who was occupying any given bunker at any given time. Efforts to liquidate Hussein and his senior lieutenants failed, while an attack on the Amariya bomb shelter in Baghdad, thought to house senior military personnel, instead resulted in the death of more than three hundred Iraqi civilians.[43]

The intelligence failure at Amariya points to another major problem associated with the use of air power: it can be very difficult to determine, from a plane traveling at hundreds of miles an hour, who on the ground is a friend and who is a foe. At various times during the war, U.S. aircraft shot at American vehicles in the mistaken belief that they were Iraqi tanks. This accounted for many of the 107 U.S. casualties attributed to "friendly fire." Such self-inflicted losses represented seventeen percent of all casualties suffered by U.S. forces during the war, a very high ratio by historical standards.[44] (In World War II and Korea, friendly fire accounted for only two percent of U.S. casualties.) Because such mistakes are certain to recur in any future conflict of this sort, the Department of Defense has launched a high-priority effort to develop new IFF ("identification friend or foe") systems that will enable U.S. aircraft to better identify allied vehicles.[45] Even with such systems, however, the risk of friendly fire will undoubtedly accompany any effort to increase reliance on air power as an instrument of war.[46]

Despite exceptionally favorable circumstances, the United States was not able to validate Mitchell's belief in the ability of air power to achieve momentous strategic effects. "The air war against Iraq proper disappoints the central claim that has been made on behalf of strategic bombardment since the 1920s," wrote Pentagon critic Jeffrey Record in 1993. Although highly effective in pulverizing enemy ground units, the air war failed "to destroy or even paralyze the institutional foundations of Saddam Hussein's political domination of Iraq and Iraqi military forces."[47]

Balanced Forces

Notwithstanding the critical importance attached to air power, General Powell and other senior officials were very careful to stress the need for a balanced force composed of all four military services (Army, Navy, Marine Corps, and Air Force) in achieving a conclusive victory. Anything else would have defeated the military's principal political objective in the Gulf: demonstrating the need for a large, Cold War–like military establishment in the post-Soviet era. As a result, lesson number two, that air power was decisive, had to be accompanied by a third lesson: all four services are needed to defeat major regional adversaries like Iraq.

The maintenance of four separate military services, each with its own command structure, installations, academy, and arms supplies, has been an article of faith in American military thinking since the end of World War II, when the Air Force was effectively detached from the Department of the Army. With the end of the Cold War, however, some analysts questioned the need (not to mention the affordability) of such an elephantine structure. But any attempt to streamline the U.S. military establishment, no matter how appealing on paper, would have provoked intense conflict and competition among the services, and undermined Powell's efforts to win Congressional support for a scaled-back version of the existing military structure. By the same token, any blueprint for fighting Desert Storm–like encounters by using the Air Force (or any other service) alone automatically would have called into question the logic of a four-service establishment, and so would have been considered heretical by Powell and his associates.

A prime example of the conflict between these competing agendas was the political firestorm ignited by Air Force Chief of Staff General Michael J. Dugan, who, in a September 1990 interview in the *Washington Post*, proposed that the Air Force take sole responsibility for defeating Iraq. "Air power is the only answer that's available to our country" if we seek to avoid a bloody ground war in the Gulf, he had argued. Drawing on the strategic precepts of Billy Mitchell and Italian air power theorist Giulio Douhet, Dugan had advocated a concentrated bombing campaign against government facilities in downtown Baghdad, including Saddam Hussein's palace and head-quarters. "If I want to hurt you," he had been quoted as saying, "it would be at home, not out in the woods someplace."[48]

These remarks had been too provocative for Colin Powell and the leaders of the other military services, who had prevailed on Secretary of Defense Cheney to have Dugan fired.[49] Nevertheless, Dugan's views had been picked up by other strategists. "The United States must not let itself be drawn into a ground war under any circum-stances," Edward N. Luttwak of the conservative Center for Inter-national and Strategic Studies wrote in November 1990. If combat is required, "America should, insofar as possible, limit its response to the air bombardment of Iraq's military infrastructure."[50]

Such views obviously were attractive to those in Congress who opposed a ground campaign against Iraq, fearing that it might pro-duce many American casualties and turn into a protracted "quag-mire" of the sort experienced in Vietnam. For this reason, members of the Senate Armed Services Committee invited Luttwak and others of his persuasion to address their much-publicized prewar hearings on the crisis in the Gulf. But General Powell railed against such an approach, arguing that it would undermine efforts to drive the Iraqis from Kuwait. "Many experts, amateurs, and others in this town believe that this can be accomplished by such things as surgical air strikes or perhaps a sustained air strike," he told the same Senate committee; but such attacks are not decisive. "I have no question about the competence and ability of our United States Air Force to inflict terrible punishment [on Iraq]," he said. "But one can hunker down. One can dig in. One can disperse to try to ride out such a single dimensioned attack."[51]

Powell went on to argue the case for a multiservice attack, asserting that nothing else would achieve America's principal objectives in the Gulf. If the Iraqis were to be physically driven from Kuwait, the Coalition must be prepared to conduct a sustained ground campaign designed to do just that. "Based on our analysis of the mission," Powell noted, the Joint Chiefs of Staff had proposed a strategy "which seizes the initiative and which forces the Iraqis to consider the consequences of a combined, overwhelming, air/land/sea campaign against a powerful Coalition force."[52]

Powell and his subordinates had developed a campaign blueprint that offered each service a prominent role. The Air Force, aided by carrier-based Navy aircraft, was to destroy Iraq's military-industrial infrastructure, preparing the way for the ground offensive. The Army had been given the primary responsibility for driving Iraqi forces out of Kuwait, but the Marine Corps had also been assigned a major role in the ground campaign. The Navy and Marine Corps had also been given a conspicuous role in an elaborate deception organized by General Schwarzkopf and his staff to keep the Iraqis off-balance: the deployment of a large amphibious assault force off the Kuwaiti coast that had never been committed to battle, but had been used instead to lure Iraqi forces away from the Coalition's actual line of advance in the south and west.[53]

Although the Army and Air Force had made up the bulk of the forces committed to Operation Desert Storm, military officials had gone to great lengths to credit all four services for the victory in the Gulf. As noted by Cheney, "the collective weight of air, maritime, amphibious, and ground attacks was necessary to achieve the exceptional combat superiority" enjoyed by Coalition forces.[54] Moreover, we can assume that any plans developed by Pentagon strategists for future encounters of this sort will employ a similar, multiservice format. "The nature of modern warfare demands that we fight as a team," a postwar Pentagon manual on "joint warfare" states. "The ability to apply overwhelming force from different dimensions and directions is essential to victory."[55]

While this format may continue to find favor among senior Pentagon officials, it is by no means certain that the President will always choose to proceed in this fashion when U.S. forces are employed in combat abroad. Any commitment of American ground troops, whether drawn from the Army or the Marine Corps, automatically raises greater anxiety among members of Congress and the public than does the commitment of air and sea power, as air and sea forces generally are less vulnerable to enemy fire than land forces, and much easier to withdraw from combat if the situation gets out of hand. As the defense budget continues its decline, moreover, the armed forces are likely to revert again to intense interservice rivalry over their respective "roles and missions."[56]

Enhanced Strategic Mobility

As their final major lesson of Desert Storm, Pentagon strategists identified the urgent need for enhanced "strategic mobility," or the ability to transport large military forces from the United States to distant battlefields. Although the Department of Defense had been largely successful in moving its forces and equipment to the Gulf area in 1990–91, U.S. strategists argued that the war had exposed a number of weaknesses in logistical capabilities that had to be corrected if the Pentagon's two-war strategy were to be fully implemented.

The importance of adequate logistics to a campaign on the scale of Desert Storm cannot be overstated. "Moving a combat force halfway around the world, linking supply lines that spanned the entire globe, and maintaining unprecedented [combat] readiness rates" were the prerequisites for a U.S. victory, the Defense Department noted in its history of the war.[57] Such capabilities will become even more vital as the Pentagon shifts its strategic focus from Europe to the Third World. Because the Department of Defense cannot afford to maintain large combat forces in every region, it must be able to

transport large numbers of troops—along with their weapons, supplies, and ammunition—from bases in the United States to likely
combat zones abroad. As General Powell noted in 1992, "It is essential to our new [strategic] focus to possess the ability to move
quickly anywhere in the world with sufficient combat forces and
accompanying support elements."[58]

Fortunately for Powell and his colleagues, the United States retained a robust logistical capability from the Cold War era. In accordance with prior military doctrine, the Department of Defense
had maintained substantial air and maritime transport fleets in order
to permit the rapid reinforcement of NATO forces with U.S.–based
contingents, and to facilitate military intervention in other areas.
These assets included hundreds of long-range transport planes, including 97 C-5 Galaxies and 249 C-141 Starlifters, along with numerous tanker planes (to refuel U.S. aircraft in flight) and supply
ships. These ships and planes, along with others chartered from private firms, had enabled Washington to move an army of 540,000
from the United States and Europe to Saudi Arabia in record time.

Given the scale of the U.S. effort, Pentagon officials were understandably proud of their logistical feats in the Persian Gulf. "There
can be no doubt that this was one of the largest and most successful
deployment operations in our nation's history," Powell told the Senate Armed Services Committee. "No other country could have attempted or even contemplated doing what we have accomplished."[59]
In the first six weeks of the crisis, U.S. aircraft ferried more supplies
to Saudi Arabia than were carried in the sixty-five-week Berlin Airlift; by four months into the crisis, they had completed the equivalent
of two-and-a-half Berlin Airlifts.[60] All told, U.S. planes and ships
had delivered an estimated 3.6 million tons of supplies and equipment to the Gulf area between August 1990 and February 1991.[61]

But while the Department of Defense performed great logistical
wonders, it must be remembered that American forces enjoyed exceptional advantages in the Persian Gulf crisis. First, the Iraqis never
challenged or interfered with logistical operations, even though U.S.
forward bases had been within range of Iraqi military aircraft. Sec-

ond, the United States had been able to use elaborate air and naval facilities built up under American supervision in Saudi Arabia in the 1970s and 1980s. Without these facilities, it would have been nearly impossible to deploy such a large force in such a short period. Third, the Saudis had provided all of the petroleum products used by American forces, obviating the need to transport oil to the Gulf. Without this, the task of supplying allied troops with sufficient fuel would have severely taxed the Pentagon's logistical capabilities.[62]

While the United States learned a great deal about long-range supply operations in preparation for Desert Storm, it did not, in the words of one senior U.S. official, "learn how to engage in a combat scenario . . . where you did not have a large indigenous infrastructure to depend upon for support."[63] This understated remark is more damning than might first appear, because the strategic mobility concept articulated by General Powell called for sending large forces to *any* distant combat zone, whether or not equipped with extensive in-theater logistical facilities, and irrespective of any harassing operations undertaken by the belligerent or belligerents involved. For all the hoopla, Operation Desert Storm exposed significant deficiencies in America's capacity to conduct long-range logistical operations in areas lacking the facilities available in Saudi Arabia.[64]

Rather than reassessing their emphasis on strategic mobility in light of these deficiencies, military officials instead called for increased investment in airlift and sealift forces, and in the "pre-positioning" of arms and equipment in likely areas of conflict. "Now, more than ever, as regional scenarios become the focus of planning, mobility is essential to the U.S. defense strategy," the Defense Department noted in 1992.[65] In particular, the Pentagon called for the accelerated procurement of cargo planes (especially the new C-17 airlifter), logistics ships, and maritime pre-positioning ships (cargo vessels filled with military supplies and stationed in overseas waters).[66]

It remains to be seen whether Congress will go along with these plans. For many in Congress, the procurement of unglamorous cargo planes and supply ships takes second place to the acquisition of new weapons—especially when the Department of Defense is emphasizing the need for costly (and alluring) high-tech munitions. It is doubtful, therefore, that the Department of Defense will ever be able to assemble a strategic mobility capability of the sort needed to implement General Powell's two-war strategy.

LESSONS AVOIDED

For every major lesson that U.S. military leaders have drawn from Operation Desert Storm, they chose to avoid another important insight. These hidden lessons are concerned less with particular military deficiencies than with the utility of armed forces in the post–Cold War era, and with the basic assumptions of the new military strategy itself. For obvious reasons, the Defense Department has been reluctant to acknowledge or publicize any insights from Desert Storm that might undermine the logic behind its favored military posture. Three, in particular, deserve attention: (1) *military victory does not always produce political solutions;* (2) *the United States is highly dependent on foreign allies to carry out its military plans abroad;* and (3) *the circumstances of Operation Desert Storm were so unique as to make it a dubious model for future conflicts.*

The Limits of Military Action

When President Bush first authorized planning for an offensive military campaign against Iraq, his aims appeared relatively finite: to drive Iraqi forces out of Kuwait, to restore the Kuwaiti royal family to power, and to diminish Iraq's capacity to engage in further acts of aggression in the region.[67] However, as the crisis intensified, Bush and his associates articulated other objectives. As the onset of hostilities drew closer, the expectations riding on Desert Storm grew increasingly elaborate, reflecting inflated estimates of the military's ability to achieve complex political objectives.

Most prominent among these additional objectives was the overthrow of the Hussein regime in Baghdad, and its replacement by a government more respectful of American interests in the Gulf. President Bush never actually stated that U.S. policy was to topple the Hussein regime; rather, he suggested that the United States would look favorably on any action by Iraqi elites (presumably in the military) to depose Hussein and replace him with a more cooperative figure. "I hope that these actions [taken by the United States] will lead to an Iraq that is prepared to live peacefully in a community of nations," he said on August 11. But if Hussein proved unwilling to behave in this fashion, "I hope the Iraqi people do something about it so that their leader will live by the norms of international behavior that will be acceptable to other nations."[68]

As the crisis unfolded, Bush announced another major political objective: the establishment of a "new world order" of peace, justice, and stability. In an address to a joint session of Congress, the President suggested that the Persian Gulf crisis "offers a rare opportunity to move toward a historic period of cooperation." By resisting Iraqi aggression, he said, we can establish "a world where the rule of law supplants the rule of the jungle; a world in which nations recognize the shared responsibility for freedom and justice; a world where the strong respect the rights of the weak."[69] Although Bush never spelled out the implications of his grand scheme for the Persian Gulf region, he hinted that it would entail a greater degree of political democracy, increased respect for human rights (particularly with respect to minorities in the region, including the Iraqi Kurds and Shiites), and improved economic conditions for the Gulf's less affluent inhabitants.

The President received much criticism—and not a little ridicule—for proposing such lofty goals for intervention in the Gulf. Many policymakers argued that such objectives were exceedingly difficult to achieve and that U.S. strategy should be guided by more modest and attainable goals. But there is no doubt that such noble aims helped to legitimize American actions in the Gulf and to gain domestic and international backing for a military drive against Iraq.

As it turned out, many of these objectives were not achieved. Kuwait was liberated from foreign occupation and Iraq lost a good deal of its offensive military strength, but Hussein remained in power, and the regime lost none of its authoritarian character. Nor were Bush's other regional goals accomplished. Certainly, there was no significant progress toward genuine democracy in Kuwait or Saudi Arabia, and resident foreign workers there (especially Palestinians and Yemenis, some of whom had expressed support for Saddam Hussein) were subjected to increased repression and abuse. Whatever "new order" Bush might have been envisioning did not arise in the wake of Desert Storm.

To even imagine accomplishing more, Bush would have had to instruct the armed services to take on additional military missions and to remain far longer in the Gulf than originally planned. To topple Hussein, for instance, U.S. forces would have had to attack and occupy Baghdad; and this, in all probability, would have provoked far more determined and prolonged resistance than anything encountered by American forces in the liberation of Kuwait. A drive on Baghdad would have produced many American casualties and significantly delayed the return home of U.S. soldiers—a price that the Pentagon, fearing a sharp drop in domestic support, was unprepared to pay.

A prolonged military presence in the region would also have been necessary to protect the Iraqi Kurds and Shiites. In March 1991, evidently believing that the United States would come to their rescue—a belief nurtured by Bush's earlier statements regarding the desirability of an Iraqi *putsch* against Hussein—the Shiites in the south, and then the Kurds in the north, took up arms against the Iraqi army. But Washington had no desire to become embroiled in a bitter civil war or to preside over the dissolution of Iraq, and so U.S. forces did nothing when Hussein's forces counterattacked and slaughtered thousands of Kurds and Shiites. The United Nations, with U.S. backing, later declared a "safe haven" for surviving Kurds in the extreme north, and established a "no-fly zone" (from which Iraqi military aircraft were barred) over Kurdish and Shiite areas, but none of these moves involved the deployment of U.S. ground troops, and their effects have been limited.[70]

The campaign against Iraq was to have heralded a new era in the

Middle East, with greater regional peace, democracy, human rights, and economic equity. For the most part, however, conditions after the war remained largely as they had been before August 1990: Hussein still ruled in Baghdad, the Sabah family retained control of Kuwait, Israel and its Arab neighbors continued to build up their military stockpiles, and the region's vast oil wealth remained the exclusive property of wealthy elites. The defeat of Iraq did contribute to the decision of Jordan, Syria, and the PLO to negotiate a new *modus operandi* with Israel, but this move probably owed more to the collapse of the Soviet Union and internal political pressures than to American military action in the Gulf. Except for the liberation of Kuwait and the contraction of Iraqi military capabilities, U.S. intervention appears to have achieved relatively little in the way of long-term political change.

Operation Desert Storm represented the greatest commitment of U.S. military power since the end of World War II. The fact that it accomplished so little of a lasting political nature should caution against placing much confidence in the ability of military action to achieve U.S. objectives in a period of such turmoil and uncertainty. At certain times, and under certain conditions, military power—when applied with sufficient strength against adversaries with the glaring vulnerabilities of Saddam Hussein's Iraq—can achieve certain narrow, specific objectives. It cannot, however, bring into being a "new world order" or resolve deeply rooted ethnic, religious, and socioeconomic antagonisms—and its long-term effects are always unpredictable.

The Need for Allies

In many respects, the war against Iraq was an American campaign, fought by American soldiers equipped with American weapons and led by American officers. The United States provided most of the combat personnel for Desert Storm (540,000 out of 795,000), along with most of the warships (165 out of 230), and a vast majority of the aircraft (some 1,600 out of 2,430). American leaders determined the timing of military operations, the strategy employed, and the general distribution of military resources and responsibilities. For these reasons, most Americans viewed the victory in the Gulf as an American one, and as a testament to America's ability to triumph over any known or potential adversary.

Military officials were aware, of course, that other states played key roles in the war against Iraq, but they chose to nurture the image of Desert Storm as an all-American event because it was essential to their arguments for the maintenance of sufficient military strength to conduct two Desert Storm–like regional conflicts *simultaneously* and *unilaterally*.[71] In fact, the Department of Defense elected to play down certain aspects of international participation in Operation Desert Storm that were critical to its success. Although acknowledged in most official histories of the war, the roles played by other Coalition members did not receive the degree of attention they deserved. Without a tally of these states' contributions, however, no serious assessment of the challenges Washington claims to face in a future replay of Desert Storm is possible.

First, and most critical, was the decision by King Fahd of Saudi Arabia to "invite" U.S. ground forces to come to his nation's defense. Without this invitation—which had to be exacted from him by a hastily assembled team of U.S. officials, including Secretary Cheney and General Schwarzkopf[72]—it would have been impossible to deploy sufficient military strength in the region to carry out an offensive military campaign. Not only was Saudi Arabia needed as a staging area, but Saudi oil and money (a total of $17 billion) helped to sustain the operation. Equally important, Saudi political support provided legitimacy in the Middle East for an essentially Western military campaign against an Arab nation that had been released from colonial rule less than four decades earlier.[73]

While Saudi Arabia made the greatest non–U.S. contribution to the allied success, other states also played an important role. Britain and France together committed 60,000 troops to Desert Storm, many of whom participated in the ground campaign against Iraq, and several other NATO countries provided specialized air and naval units.[74]

Of particular political importance was the participation of troops from Egypt and Syria (23,000 and 19,000, respectively), lending Desert Storm significant legitimacy in the Arab world, and further isolating Saddam Hussein.[75]

There was also the critical issue of money. The total incremental cost to the United States of Desert Storm, the amount spent over and above what would have been allocated to U.S. forces in any case, has been estimated at $61 billion.[76] Had the United States been forced to bear this cost alone, President Bush would have been compelled to impose a tax increase or add to already high levels of deficit spending—either of which would have eroded domestic support for the war. Fortunately for Bush, Washington was able to persuade its allies, especially Germany, Japan, Kuwait, and Saudi Arabia, to assume about ninety percent of this added cost, thereby averting a potential political backlash at home.

The real lesson of Desert Storm, then, may be that allies are essential. The United States still bore the brunt of the fighting, and assumed most of the logistical burden for the joint operation. But, without the support of other nations, American forces could not have conducted an offensive ground campaign of the sort mounted in Iraq. "The lesson is clear," researchers at the Center for Strategic and International Studies affirmed in July 1991: "The United States was dependent on allies before, during, and after this war, and there is little prospect of being less dependent in any major future war."[77]

The Uniqueness of Desert Storm

Virtually from the moment that the war against Iraq was concluded, military officials were touting Operation Desert Storm as the model for future U.S. encounters with rising Third World powers. "This was a victory that rested, in the final analysis, on the capability of the United States to project war-winning power from the continental United States and from Europe and to fight jointly on land, in the air, and at sea," General Vuono of the Army averred in 1991. "That capability, of course, is the essence of our new strategy."[78]

But this model reflected a unique set of circumstances unlikely to arise again in future Third World conflicts. The uniqueness of Desert Storm was the product of two sets of extraordinary circumstances: first, the exceptional advantages enjoyed by Coalition forces in the Gulf; and, second, the profound vulnerability of the Iraqi forces.

On the American side of the equation, the advantages enjoyed included:

• *Technological superiority.* Although Saddam Hussein had spent many billions of dollars to acquire high-tech weaponry from the Soviets and the West, Coalition forces enjoyed uncontested technological superiority in every category of military hardware, enabling them to overpower and outmaneuver the Iraqis at every turn.

• *Numerical superiority.* Despite much talk of Iraq's million-man army, the Iraqis probably had only some 250,000 to 300,000 troops in the Kuwait area when the ground war began, about half as many troops as the combined Coalition army.[79]

• *Established logistical facilities.* Without the existence of a prepared military infrastructure in Saudi Arabia—the only place in the world outside Europe and North America where such an infrastructure existed—the United States never would have been able to bring such powerful forces to bear in the Gulf in such a short amount of time.

• *Favorable terrain.* The war against Iraq was fought in the arid, unpopulated Arabian desert, a locale where U.S. advantages in air power, precision-guided weaponry, and high-speed armor could be brought to bear with unprecedented effectiveness.

On the Iraqi side of the equation, major vulnerabilities included:

• *Significant military deficiencies.* No matter how large the Iraqi military establishment, it simply was in no condition to take on a consortium of major Western powers armed with a full array of high-tech weapons.

• *Lack of allies.* Although Iraq enjoyed the support of the Palestinians and other disaffected groups in the Islamic world, not a single state came to its aid when Operation Desert Storm commenced.

• *Incompetent leadership.* While Saddam Hussein had achieved mastery of the political skills needed to retain control of Iraq, he possessed little grasp of the exigencies of modern, high-tech warfare, and, as a result, he (and his obedient commanders) made one strategic blunder after another.

• *Internal divisions.* Although Saddam Hussein was firmly in control of the levers of power in Baghdad, he did not command the loyalty of major segments of the Iraqi population, and thus, even at the height of the fighting in Kuwait, he could not commit all of his forces to combat with the Coalition.

Together, these respective advantages and vulnerabilities created a situation in which Baghdad had no hope of averting defeat on the battlefield or scoring major blows against its adversaries. But the very combination of factors that contributed so forcefully to the lopsided U.S. victory in the Gulf are unlikely to arise again. The terrain will be different; or the population distribution; or the availability of allied logistical facilities; or the strength and proficiency of opposition forces.

More than this, it is wholly unrealistic to assume that future adversaries will repeat Hussein's catastrophic mistakes. Surely, no major power will knowingly risk combat with the United States unless it has developed some antidote to American air and missile power and is equipped to foil U.S. advantages in surveillance technology, electronic warfare, and long-range artillery. "The whole world . . . [has] seen the results of a high technology war conducted against a low technology country," the Center for Strategic and International Studies observed in 1991. "Nations that pose threats to U.S. interests, before they confront U.S. armed forces in conflict, will choose some means of counteracting revolutionary U.S. technology."[80]

If future adversaries are unable to counter U.S. forces in the technological realm, they may take the opposite tack and employ such "unconventional" operations as guerrilla warfare, terrorism, and low-intensity combat. "Given the likely overwhelming U.S. superiority in the traditional, or conventional, measures of military power," suggested former Pentagon official Andrew F. Krepinevich, "America's adversaries will have great incentives to adopt a very unconventional approach [in future military engagements]." Indeed, this is exactly what U.S. forces encountered in Somalia, and would have faced in Bosnia had they intervened there in 1994.[81]

BEYOND DESERT STORM: THE "POST-INDUSTRIAL BATTLEFIELD"

Even while Pentagon officials were publicizing their chosen lessons of Desert Storm, other military strategists were beginning to look beyond the present and to develop plans for the U.S. war machine of the twenty-first century. Numerous study groups were set up by the armed services to facilitate these endeavors, and many think-tanks and research organizations launched similar efforts. These all sought to draw on the Gulf War experience to construct plausible images of the future battlefield.

These projects covered a wide range of subjects, from specific military-technical problems to major doctrinal issues, but all shared the desire to capitalize on the achievements of Desert Storm and maximize U.S. advantages in technology, air power, weaponry, and mobility—what Cheney dubbed the "military–technological revolution" in warfare.[82] Indeed, there appeared to be a semi-conscious effort to ignore the various deficiencies exposed in the Gulf, and to enter a new realm of machine-driven battle in which air power, guided missiles, and technology would reign supreme.

A major focus for such efforts was the modernization of the Army's AirLand Battle Doctrine (ABD), the reigning combat doctrine of the 1980s and early 1990s. Originally designed for warfare against Warsaw Pact forces in Europe, ABD called for U.S. forces to conduct rapid counterattacks against the enemy's flanks and weak spots, along with "deep strikes" by aircraft and missiles against the enemy's rear-area installations.[83] Although it had never been employed in Europe, the ABD concept was incorporated into plans for the ground offensive in Kuwait.[84]

With the Cold War rapidly fading from memory, U.S. strategists have attempted to revise the AirLand doctrine in light of the Persian Gulf experience. *AirLand Operations: A Concept for the Evolution of AirLand Battle for the Strategic Army of the 1990s and Beyond*, released by the U.S. Army's Training and Doctrine Command (TRADOC) on August 1, 1991, called for a more flexible version of ABD aimed at regional conflicts in the Third World. The key to success in such engagements, TRADOC affirmed, was to avoid traditional set-piece battles along a defined, continuous front line. Instead, battle commanders needed to acquire proficiency in "nonlinear operations"—combat operations conducted simultaneously at several disconnected locations at both front and rear.[85] As with Desert Storm, such operations were said to involve rapid flanking maneuvers, airmobile assaults on rear-area objectives, and air and missile attacks against the enemy's key "centers of gravity"—command centers, communications nodes, air defense radars, and so on.[86]

These principles were further developed in the 1993 version of the Army's Field Manual 100-5, *Operations*, described as the first full-scale revision of Army combat policy since the end of the Cold War. "The 1993 doctrine reflects Army thinking in a new, strategic era," the manual's introduction affirmed. "It is truly doctrine for the full dimensions of the battlefield in a force-projection environment."[87]

Here, too, the emphasis was on fast-paced, hard-hitting offensive operations that would engage enemy forces on all sectors of the battlefield—front, flanks, and rear. Drawing heavily on the lessons of Desert Storm, the manual instructed American commanders to employ surprise flanking maneuvers, sudden shifts of direction, nighttime operations, and rear-area assaults in order to keep enemy forces off balance and prevent them from mounting any counterattacks. "Several dynamic characteristics apply to offensive operations," the manual notes, "initiative on the part of subordinate commanders, rapid shifts in the main effort to take advantage of opportunities, momentum and tempo, and the deepest, most rapid and simultaneous destruction of enemy defenses possible."[88]

While these two documents did not constitute a fully developed, coherent theory of war, it was apparent that American military thinkers were beginning to construct a new concept or style of warfare, one that bore as little relation to the attrition-oriented battles of World Wars I and II as those did to the infantry-and-cavalry battles of the preindustrial era. They were seeking to meld the global reach of modern air and space systems, the high-precision destructiveness of advanced conventional weapons, and the speed of modern communications into a powerful, lightning-fast war machine capable of quickly defeating any military forces not so blessed with modern technology.

To characterize this new combat environment, U.S. strategists have coined the phrase "post-industrial battlefield." This term, says Lieutenant Colonel David F. Melcher of the Army staff, can be used "to describe the characteristics of warfare [found in] the modern environment in which we will fight—increased precision and firepower across expanded dimensions of the battlefield, increased speed and tempo, the ability to see the enemy anytime, anywhere, and to take the battle to him."[89] On such a battlefield, there will be no "front lines" as in earlier wars; rather, the fighting will take place in disconnected encounters all across the battle zone and in the airspace above it, and in the "cyberspace" of electronic warfare, high-tech surveillance, and instantaneous communications.[90]

On such a battlefield, information technology, whether provided by space-based surveillance systems, airborne reconnaissance planes, electronic listening devices, or computerized command centers, will prove more decisive in battle than purely "industrial" assets such as tanks, mortars, and artillery pieces. By tracking enemy forces at all times of the day and night and guiding bombs and missiles to the enemy's most sensitive and vulnerable facilities, information systems will determine the tempo, location, and outcome of warfare. As suggested by Colonel James McDonough of the Army, "Information is the lifeblood of modern war, just as fuel was the lifeblood of war of movement and just as munitions and gunpowder were the lifeblood of the Boer War or World War I."[91]

Such images have obvious attractions for the military in that they highlight American advantages in firepower and technology, while limiting the risk to soldiers on the battlefield. In a sense, the "postindustrial battlefield" represents a distillation of all the lessons the Pentagon would like to extract from Desert Storm, while excluding all those it would prefer to avoid. There are no politics on the postindustrial battlefield, no requirement for troops to remain on the ground for more than a few days at a time, no impassioned ethnic warriors who must be fought face-to-face and house-to-house; instead, there are only symbolic representations of enemy units on a screen, to be "zapped" by self-aiming, standoff weapons fired by distant operatives who never witness the bloody aftereffects of their actions.

Will such battlefields ever materialize? Nothing that has occurred since the Persian Gulf conflict would lead anyone to assume so. This has not, however, stopped the Defense Department from pursuing a strategic posture based on the assumption that American forces will be required to fight an endless series of Desert Storm–like encounters. By proceeding in this fashion, Pentagon leaders justify the maintenance of a large, multifaceted military establishment and continued—or even elevated—funding for a wide variety of high-tech weapons on the order of those employed in the Gulf. Their paramount task, and their greatest success, has been to persuade Congress and the American people of the validity of this assumption.

Chapter Four

FIGHTING "DEMONS

AND DANGERS"

Military Policy

in the Clinton Era

Equipped with a congenial set of "lessons of Desert Storm," Pentagon officials returned to the Congressional battlefront in mid-1991, armed for a new round in the budgetary struggle that had been suspended after the Iraqi invasion of Kuwait. Although most senior policymakers by now had accepted the basic tenets of the Rogue Doctrine, there was still much debate in Congress and the media over the range of likely threats and the forces and equipment needed to counter them. Flushed with victory from the Persian Gulf campaign, senior military leaders now geared up for a major struggle over the size, shape, and cost of the post–Cold War military establishment.

In some sense, this battle picked up where it had left off a year earlier: a tug-of-war between those who favored a substantial reduction in military strength that would produce a sizeable "peace dividend" for domestic use, and those who sought to preserve as much of the Cold War military establishment as possible. The terms of debate, however, had shifted considerably. No one of any influence in Congress was talking of a fifty percent cut in military spending (as proposed by former Secretary of Defense Robert S. McNamara in December 1989), or anything even remotely close to it; rather, the debate had narrowed to a dispute over exactly how many soldiers, tanks, and the like would be needed to implement a two-war, anti-rogue military posture.

But though the terms of the debate had narrowed, there was no reduction in the intensity of verbal battle. Instead, policymakers began to argue over the size and cost of the military with the same fervor with which they had earlier debated the size of the proposed peace dividend. In addition to the fate of specific military units, billions of dollars in federal procurement funds were at stake—funds that could be spent on new weapons and support systems, on retaining now-redundant military bases in the United States, or on sustaining such high-tech research projects as the Star Wars program. As the national celebration over the Desert Storm victory wound down, the debate over these allocations erupted with fresh vigor and urgency.

The renewed debate over defense policy simmered during the summer and fall of 1991, and approached boiling point early in the winter of 1991–92. Prominent figures in this debate included General Colin Powell, Secretary of Defense Dick Cheney, and President George Bush on one side; and such Pentagon critics as Representatives Les Aspin (Dem.-Wisc.), Patricia Schroeder (Dem.-Colo.), and Ron Dellums (Dem.-Calif.) on the other. Serving as something of a referee between the two groups was Senator Sam Nunn of Georgia, the influential chairman of the Senate Armed Services Committee. As the 1992 legislative session got under way, these forces began to gird for a major clash over the future composition of the military establishment.

THE "GUIDANCE DOCUMENT" FUROR

In early February 1992, just as Congress began to take up the defense budget debate, Washington was rocked by a political uproar over a secret Pentagon strategy document, the "Defense Planning Guidance Scenario Set," that had been leaked to the *New York Times*. Intended as a guide for military officials in planning force levels for future conflicts, the so-called scenarios document was an appendix to the Defense Planning Guidance issued each year to senior officers by the Secretary of Defense. Although the particular scenarios included in the 1992 version of the scenarios document were described as "illustrative" rather than "predictive," they were seen by many in Congress as reliable indicators of Pentagon thinking regarding U.S. involvement in future conflicts.[1]

Seven hypothetical encounters were described in the document: a repeat invasion of Kuwait by Iraq; an invasion of South Korea by North Korea; simultaneous invasions of Kuwait and South Korea by Iraq and North Korea; a coup d'état in Panama; a coup d'état in the Philippines; a Russian invasion of Lithuania; and the emergence of a new, Soviet-like superpower. The first three scenarios, which represented variations on the Rogue Doctrine, aroused only minor comment, although some observers wondered why states like Iran and Libya were not incorporated into the scenarios. Similarly, little concern was aroused by the next two scenarios, which were typical examples of the sort of "low-intensity conflict" that long had figured in U.S. military planning. Many lawmakers, however, were upset by the inclusion of a NATO-Russian conflict over Lithuania and a reborn, Soviet-type superpower—scenarios that clashed dramatically with the then current reality of a disintegrating Soviet Union.[2]

In the days that followed the publication of excerpts from this document in the *New York Times*, both Democrats and Republicans rose in Congress to ridicule the hypothetical scenarios and to challenge the Pentagon's spending plans. "Some of these scenarios are incredibly unlikely," observed Senator Carl Levin (Dem.-Mich.), a member of the Armed Services Committee. "If they are used for budget rationale, they could undermine the strength of the Pentagon's budget request."[3] Several lawmakers, including Senator John W. Warner of Virginia, the ranking Republican on the Armed Services Committee, noted that Russia was not likely to constitute a serious threat for a long time to come and that, in any case, the United States was unlikely to go to war over Lithuania. Others objected to the portrayal of Russia as a hypothetical enemy at a time when Washington was seeking to forge a new partnership with Boris Yeltsin and other Russian leaders.[4]

In response to these charges, Pentagon officials insisted that the scenarios were not meant to be taken literally, but were intended solely to provide military officials with a range of hypothetical contingencies to use in developing future troop requirements. "These do not represent war plans," Defense Department spokesperson Bob Hall declared. "They are not predictive of what's going to happen. . . . It's something which we use basically to crunch numbers."[5] Nevertheless, the document clearly indicated that senior Pentagon officials had not been thinking in terms of a significantly downsized military establishment, but rather of a large, capital-intensive force capable of engaging and defeating an array of regional powers, or even a future superpower.

Whatever doubts may have remained in Washington concerning the Pentagon's strategic intentions were dispelled on March 8, 1992, when the *New York Times* published extracts from another leaked document, the top-secret "Defense Planning Guidance for Fiscal Years 1994–1999," to which the scenarios document had been an appendix. This "guidance document," prepared annually by senior officials in the office of the Secretary of Defense, is intended to lay out basic assumptions regarding likely future threats to U.S. security, and to identify the forces, weapons, and strategies needed to counter those threats. Historically, it had focused almost entirely on the Soviet threat; only in 1992 did it begin to address the new strategic environment.[6]

The guidance document, as excerpted in the *New York Times*, envisioned a strategic role for U.S. forces far exceeding that staked out in the anti-rogue posture conceived by General Powell and his staff in early 1990. Perhaps emboldened by the euphoric domestic reaction to victory in the Persian Gulf, the authors of this report, deputies to Paul D. Wolfowitz, the Undersecretary of Defense for Policy, called for a military capacity virtually identical to that maintained during the Cold War era:

> Our first objective is to prevent the reemergence of a new rival, either on the territory of the former Soviet Union or elsewhere, that poses a threat on the order of that posed by the former Soviet Union. This is a dominant consideration underlying the new regional defense strategy and requires that we endeavor to prevent any hostile power from dominating a region whose resources would, under consolidated control, be sufficient to generate global power. These regions include Western Europe, East Asia, the territory of the former Soviet Union, and Southwest Asia.[7]

In accordance with this requirement, the document called for the maintenance of sufficient military strength to overpower any future adversary or combination of adversaries that might arise in any corner of the globe. Furthermore, it suggested that the United States must be prepared to defeat such threats unilaterally. "We will retain the pre-eminent responsibility for addressing selectively those wrongs which threaten not only our interests, but those of our allies or friends, or which could seriously unsettle international relations."[8]

The appearance of excerpts from this report in the *New York Times* touched off a new firestorm of criticism in Congress. The document was "myopic, shallow, and disappointing," Senator Robert C. Byrd of West Virginia, a strong proponent of reduced military spending, declared angrily. "The basic thrust of the document seems to be this: We love being the sole remaining superpower in the world, and we want so much to remain that way that we are willing to put at risk the basic health of the economy and well-being of our people to do so."[9]

Many critics were particularly disturbed by the document's apparent emphasis on a unilateral American response to future threats, as distinct from the coalition effort mounted in the Persian Gulf. This is a plan for "a 'Pax Americana,' " charged Senator Joseph R. Biden, Jr., of Delaware, a ranking member of the Foreign Relations Committee, "a global security system where threats to stability are suppressed or destroyed by U.S. military power."[10] Arch-conservative Patrick J. Buchanan, a contender for the Republican presidential nomination, also denounced the document. "This is a formula for endless American intervention in quarrels and war where no vital interest of the United States is remotely engaged," he told reporters on March 9.[11]

Critics also objected to its suggestion that future rivals might emerge in Europe or East Asia—thinly veiled allusions to possible future clashes with Germany or Japan. "In a spirit bordering on paranoia," wrote Peter Tarnoff of the Council on Foreign Relations, the document calls on Washington to contest the hegemonic aspirations "not only of Iraq, Libya, North Korea, and other known troublemakers," but also of friendly states in Western Europe and Asia.[12] Similarly, in an editorial dated March 10, the *New York Times* observed that "it's downright perverse to affront allies who dare to 'aspire to a greater role.' "[13]

Pentagon press officers, again thrown on the defensive, claimed unconvincingly that the text excerpted in the *New York Times* was a "low-level draft" that had not been seen or approved by senior officials.[14] They insisted, moreover, that the emphasis on unilateral action was a distortion of actual U.S. policy.[15] However, in an effort to muffle criticism, the guidance document was revised under Cheney's supervision, and a new, thoroughly sanitized version was "leaked" to the *New York Times* on May 24, 1992. In contrast to the earlier draft, it placed great emphasis on cooperation with other powers, and avoided all reference to potential adversaries in the industrialized world. Instead, the document focused on the more familiar, and now accepted, threat supposedly posed by rogue powers. American forces, it stated, must be able to "preclude any hostile power from dominating a region critical to our interests."[16]

Just as the Iraqi invasion of Kuwait had essentially silenced those policymakers who favored dramatic reductions in the military (and military spending), the 1992 furor over the guidance document silenced those in the Pentagon who envisioned a military posture aimed at Soviet-like industrialized powers. This left the Rogue Doctrine as the dominant strategic concept, viewed by all key actors as the template for a military posture in the post-Cold War era. All that remained was to determine the size and nature of the forces that would be retained to implement this strategy in the years ahead.

THE "WAR OF THE SCENARIOS"

Because Congress tends to fight over specific budgetary items, rather than strategic concepts, the ensuing debate over military posture evolved into a wrangle over how many Army and Marine Corps divisions, Air Force tactical fighter wings (TFWs), and Navy aircraft carrier battle groups (CBGs)—all basic military units—should be retained in the post–Cold War military establishment. (An Army division normally comprises about 17,500 soldiers, while a Marine division can number 20,000 or more; a typical TFW comprises 72 combat planes; a CBG normally comprises one aircraft carrier, a half-dozen escort vessels, and a number of supply ships.) The more of these units the Pentagon had in its lineup, the larger the military as a whole would be, and the greater its capacity to face several opponents simultaneously or to overpower a single enemy with crushing superiority; the fewer, the more limited its capacity to engage in multiple contingencies.

The Department of Defense's entry in this contest was the plan originally developed in the spring of 1990 by General Powell for a "Base Force" of twelve active Army divisions, three active Marine Corps divisions, fifteen active Air Force fighter wings, and twelve aircraft carrier battle groups (with an additional carrier used for training). (See Table 4.1.) According to Powell, this force would be strong enough to fight two major regional conflicts simultaneously while, at the same time, engaging in a number of smaller actions. Critics of this plan, led by Representative Les Aspin, chairman of the House Armed Services Committee, argued that a somewhat smaller establishment would be sufficient for U.S. needs in the post–Desert Storm security environment.

To provide Congress with a range of alternatives to the Pentagon plan, Representative Aspin in February 1992 published a set of four possible options for structuring the U.S. military establishment. In doing so, he made clear his firm allegiance to the Rogue Doctrine: "The most militarily demanding threats" for which America will need military forces "are those posed by regional aggressors," he said. Furthermore, his scenarios were all calibrated in terms of "Desert Storm Equivalents" (DSEs)—the force needed to defeat a state approximately as powerful as Iraq had been in 1990. Aspin also envisioned a "Panama Equivalent," a force as large as that used to depose Manuel Noriega of Panama in December 1989, and a "Provide Comfort Equivalent," representing the level of effort required to mount the operation to provide humanitarian aid and military protection to the Kurds in northern Iraq after the Iraqi crackdown of April–May 1991.[17]

Drawing on these three "building blocks," Aspin sketched out his four hypothetical planning models:[18]

- "Option A," the smallest of the four, would include one Desert Storm Equivalent plus one Provide Comfort Equivalent.
- "Option B" would include everything in Option A plus the air combat component of a second DSE, allowing for limited U.S. involvement in a second regional conflict.
- "Option C" would include everything in Option B plus additional forces for the first DSE and sufficient extra strength to conduct one Panama Equivalent.
- "Option D," which came closest to the Pentagon's Base Force proposal, would include everything in Option C plus additional forces for the second DSE and sufficient extra strength to conduct a second Provide Comfort Equivalent.

Of these, the option that attracted the greatest interest among Democrats in Congress was Option C, a force that would permit full-scale intervention in one major regional conflict and partial intervention in another, while also permitting a Panama-type invasion and participation in a major humanitarian aid operation. To carry out all of these activities, Option C called for a total military force of 1.4 million active-duty personnel (compared to the Base Force's 1.6 million), 9 active Army divisions (instead of 12), 2 active Marine divisions (instead of 3), 10 active fighter wings (instead of 15), and 11 carrier battle groups (instead of 12).[19] (See Table 4.1.)

Conceptually speaking, there was not much difference between Powell's Base Force and Aspin's Option C: both assumed that the country should possess sufficient strength to engage in two major regional conflicts simultaneously while also participating in several smaller contingency actions; both also assumed that the United States would take full responsibility for achieving victory in the first of the two major conflicts. Where they differed was in the level of U.S. participation in the second major conflict, with Powell calling for a capacity for full-scale, unilateral intervention, and Aspin calling for a more limited commitment, made up largely of air and naval forces, as part of a coalition effort.[20]

In the months that followed, Congress debated the two plans in what the *Washington Post* termed the "war of scenarios."[21] In general, Republicans and conservative Democrats favored the Base Force proposal, while liberal Democrats favored Aspin's Option C. Backers of the Base Force claimed that Option C did not provide sufficient strength to deal with a combined assault by two rogue powers, while backers of Option C claimed that the Base Force was simply a device for preserving the existing Cold War military establishment.[22] In the end, however, nothing was really decided, as Congress chose to go along with the Bush administration's proposed fiscal year 1993 budget despite its unaltered Cold War character.[23] With the 1992 presidential campaign just getting under way, most lawmakers evidently preferred to leave the major policy issues to the presidential candidates.

TABLE 4.1
POWELL'S "BASE FORCE" AND ASPIN'S "OPTION C"

	ACTUAL 1991 FORCE	POWELL'S BASE FORCE	ASPIN'S OPTION C
Army Forces:			
Active divisions	16	12	9
Reserve divisions	10	6	6
"Cadre" divisions*	0	2	0
Navy Forces:			
Combat ships	528	450	340
Carriers	15**	13**	12**
Submarines	87	80	40
Assault ships	65	50	#
Marine Corps:			
Active MEFs	3	3	2
Reserve MEFs	1	1	1
Air Force:			
Active TFWs	22	15	10
Reserve TFWs	12	11	8

* Divisions with leadership cadre only.
** Includes one used for training only.
\# = Not indicated
TFW = Tactical fighter wing
MEF = Marine Expeditionary Force (1 division + 1 air wing)

Sources: U.S. Department of Defense, *National Military Strategy of the United States* (1992); Representative Les Aspin, *An Approach to Sizing American Conventional Forces* (1992).

THE CLINTON PROGRAM

Defense policy was not Bill Clinton's strong suit during a presidential campaign that focused largely on domestic economic concerns. Clinton could not totally avoid addressing military issues during the campaign, however. As an opponent of U.S. involvement in the

Vietnam War and, at best, a lukewarm supporter of Operation Desert Storm, Clinton felt obliged to endorse a strong, if somewhat downsized, military establishment. While calling for cutbacks in some Pentagon programs—the Reagan administration's costly Star Wars program, for instance—he surprised both critics and supporters by proposing a significant buildup of U.S. power-projection capabilities.

Clinton's military views were first spelled out in a speech at Georgetown University in December 1991. Using language virtually indistinguishable from that employed in Bush's August 2, 1990, speech announcing the Pentagon's new regional strategy, Clinton averred that "we need a force capable of projecting power quickly when and where it is needed." This meant that "the Army must develop a more mobile mix of mechanized and armored forces; the Air Force should emphasize tactical air power and airlift, and the Navy and Marine Corps must maintain sufficient carrier and amphibious forces."[24] Clinton also called for maintaining America's lead in military technology, a stance closely linked to his emphasis on the promotion of high-tech industrial development as a means of revitalizing the U.S. economy.[25]

In retrospect, it is obvious that these positions reflected not so much Clinton's views—prior to the 1992 campaign, he had evidenced little interest in military issues—as those of his closest campaign advisers. In particular, they reflected the thinking of Representative Les Aspin of the House Armed Services Committee, a self-taught expert on military affairs; Anthony Lake, a Mount Holyoke professor and former State Department official; and Samuel Berger, a noted Washington attorney and former colleague of Lake's at State.

Along with other national security experts in the Clinton camp, these three advisers were not harsh critics of Pentagon spending, but rather favored a modest, graduated reduction in military strength. Like many Democrats in Congress, moreover, they were particularly concerned about nuclear proliferation, and advocated stepped-up efforts to curb the military ambitions of rising Third World powers. In a proposed policy blueprint for the new administration, Berger and an associate wrote that "the continuing proliferation of weapons of mass destruction throughout the world may pose the greatest peril in the coming years to American and international security." In response, they argued, Washington should increase its emphasis on weapons nonproliferation and enhance the country's capabilities "to project American power where it is needed to counter aggression that threatens our interests."[26]

A close reading of this text and other policy statements issued by the Clinton campaign apparatus reveals the degree to which the Rogue Doctrine had come to dominate the thinking of what would be the next administration's national security team. While seeking to distance themselves from the Bush administration, Clinton and his associates nevertheless adopted a virtually identical policy framework. Both camps emphasized the threat posed by rising Third World powers equipped with modern weapons; both called for stepped-up nonproliferation efforts; and both advocated the enhancement of U.S. power projection capabilities. Any difference between the two positions had to do with how much additional strength each thought would have to be reserved for the possible resurrection of Soviet/ Russian military power: Bush called for more; Clinton, for less.

Following his election, Clinton tapped Aspin, Berger, Lake, and others with similar points of view for key positions in the new administration. Aspin was made Secretary of Defense; Lake was named the President's Special Assistant for National Security Affairs; and Berger became Deputy National Security Adviser. Together with Vice President Al Gore and R. James Woolsey, a Washington lawyer and Clinton's choice for Director of the CIA, they constructed a security posture based on the Pentagon's now-familiar anti-rogue model.[27]

The administration's emerging outlook was first articulated by one-time Pentagon critic Les Aspin on March 30 and April 1, 1993, in identical statements to the House and Senate Armed Services Committees. "With the demise of the Soviet Union," he said, "threats to stability in key regions throughout the world have become America's principal military concern and major determinant of our defense budget priorities." The administration's goal, he stated, was to ensure that U.S. forces "can reach troublespots quickly and with over-whelming power to deter—and, if needed, defeat—aggression."[28]

To guide the development of a new strategic framework, Secretary Aspin ordered the Department of Defense to conduct what he promised would be a sweeping, "start-from-scratch" assessment of its programs and policies. Known as the "Bottom-Up Review," this assessment was intended to reshape defense policy for the "post–Cold War, post–Soviet Union World."[29] Work on the review began in early 1993 and continued throughout the spring and early summer.

TWO WARS OR ONE AND A HALF?

By initiating the Bottom-Up Review, Aspin invited military officials to engage in a wide-ranging debate over the size and shape of America's post–Cold War military posture. As we have seen, however, the terms of that debate had already been narrowed. All thoughts of a future superpower-type conflict had been put aside in favor of some version of the Rogue Doctrine. The principal remaining issue was how many major regional conflicts (MRCs) the United States should be prepared to fight simultaneously. Although this dispute lacked the drama of the guidance document furor of March 1992, significant interests were at stake: a force capable of fighting two or more MRCs simultaneously would have to be considerably larger, and more costly, than one designed to fight only one, or one and a half, such conflicts. As Aspin suggested, the outcome of this debate would be "the biggest issue that's going to determine the size and shape of the United States' defense budgets" in the late 1990s and beyond.[30]

Initially, senior military officers and the Joint Chiefs of Staff favored the Base Force, "two-war" capability, while Secretary Aspin and his associates favored the Option C, "one-and-a-half-war" capability. Proponents of the two-war model charged that adoption of a one-and-a-half-war posture could jeopardize American security; hostile states, they argued, might be tempted to conduct a combined assault on U.S. allies abroad on the assumption that Washington could not organize an effective response to a two-pronged attack. Aspin countered with a modified version of his Option C plan; known as "win-hold-win," this called for U.S. air and ground forces to quickly defeat one opponent while relying on air power alone to contain ("hold") a second opponent for a period of weeks or months until such time as ground troops from the first campaign were available for use in the second.[31]

Although the Aspin plan was supported by some elements of the military—the Air Force was especially keen on win-hold-win, because air power would play the dominant role during the "hold" phase of a two-war campaign—criticism of the plan by the other three services intensified. Suggesting that the "holding" forces in such a scenario could be defeated before sufficient reinforcements were brought in from other locales, one four-star Army general went so far as to term the Aspin plan a recipe for "win-lose-lose." Another Pentagon critic termed it the "win-hold-oops strategy."[32]

"Win-hold-win" eventually fell victim to mounting Pentagon pressures and the quickening pace of international events. In the spring of 1993, as the United States expanded its support for the U.N. peacekeeping mission in Somalia and began preparing for possible intervention in Bosnia, advocates of a two-war strategy directed increasingly vociferous criticism at the Aspin plan. Although neither the Somalia nor the proposed Bosnia operations were comparable to a major regional conflict, they entailed a significant investment of air and naval power, and were characterized by Base Force proponents as adding to America's total military burden. Navy officials were particularly outspoken on this point, claiming that any reduction in carrier strength below the thirteen ships envisioned in the Base Force would jeopardize the Pentagon's capacity to conduct several combat missions simultaneously. "A smaller carrier force might be less expensive to operate and maintain in the short run," a 1993 Navy position paper declared, "but it would be at the long-term expense of being incapable of protecting United States interests."[33]

As the Bottom-Up Review approached completion, Secretary Aspin backed away from his fallback win-hold-win concept, and endorsed the two-war ("win-win") posture advocated by senior military officers. He had been unable to persuade the Joint Chiefs of Staff to soften their opposition to his plan, and was unwilling to get into a brawl with them while the Clinton administration—already on the defensive following election campaign charges that Clinton had used deceit in avoiding the draft during the Vietnam War—was enmeshed in an emotional debate over the status of gays in the military. In a speech at Andrews Air Force Base on June 24, Aspin capitulated, declaring that "after much discussion and analysis, we've come to the conclusion that our forces must be able to fight and win two major regional conflicts, and nearly simultaneously." Why a capacity for two such conflicts? Because, he said, "if we're engaged in one major regional conflict, we don't want a potential aggressor in a second region to believe that we're vulnerable or cannot respond in full force"—essentially parroting the views of senior military officers.[34] Aspin also let it be known that he would press for a twelve-carrier Navy, rather than the ten-carrier fleet envisioned by the win-hold-win plan.[35]

THE REVIEW IS REVEALED

With all major points of dispute within the military worked out, finalization of the Bottom-Up Review proceeded rapidly. President Clinton approved the plan in midsummer, and it was released to the public on September 1, 1993, at a much-publicized Pentagon press conference. Noting that Cold War considerations could no longer determine the size and orientation of the military establishment, Secretary Aspin reported that the review had resulted in the design of a "mobile, high-tech force, ready to protect Americans in this new time." While this force would be slightly smaller than that envisioned by Powell's Base Force, he explained, it contained a number of "force enhancements"—additional airlift and sealift capabilities, improved weapons systems, upgraded intelligence systems—designed to insure the success of a win-win strategy while permitting a small reduction in the military budget.[36]

In laying out the parameters of the Bottom-Up Review, Aspin left no doubt that the entire construct had been shaped by the exigencies of the Rogue Doctrine, by a need to contain "rogue leaders set on regional domination through military aggression while simultaneously pursuing nuclear, biological, and chemical weapons capabilities." In meeting these threats, he asserted, the Pentagon's principal objective would be "to project power into regions important to our interests and to defeat potentially hostile regional powers, such as North Korea and Iraq."[37]

General Powell, who begrudgingly endorsed the Bottom-Up Review, and who joined Aspin at the September 1 press conference, described this policy in more graphic terms: "The Soviet empire has now been replaced by something quite different—an Iraq, a Korea, [and] other demons and dangers that come along of a regional nature." Although these demons and dangers may not be linked, "they are, nevertheless, the source of potential conflict, places where the United States armed forces might have to go and fight and win."[38]

In outlining the new posture, Aspin and Powell indicated that the Defense Department had conducted numerous war games and simulations of likely conflict scenarios. These all began with the premise that a remilitarized Iraq would launch a full-scale attack on Kuwait and Saudi Arabia at the same time that North Korea would begin an invasion of South Korea. Aspin explained that these scenarios, although entirely hypothetical, provided Pentagon planners with a valid test of U.S. ability to confront and defeat two regional rogues simultaneously. "Both scenarios assumed a similar enemy operation," he noted: "an armor-heavy, combined-arms offensive against the outnumbered forces of a neighboring state. U.S. forces, most of which were not present in the region when hostilities commenced, had to deploy to the region quickly, supplement indigenous forces, halt the invasion, and defeat the aggressor."[39]

To defeat both Iraq and North Korea in "near simultaneous" campaigns, the Bottom-Up Review called for a force of 10 active Army divisions (with 5 or more in reserve), a 346-ship Navy with 11 active aircraft carriers (plus one other in use as a training ship, but available for combat if needed), 13 active Air Force fighter wings (with 7 in reserve), 3 active Marine Corps divisions (with one in reserve), and an active-duty troop strength of about 1.4 million soldiers.[40] (See Table 4.2.)

The Bottom-Up Review also provided a rough blueprint for intervention in a major regional conflict (MRC) based on scenarios for

TABLE 4.2
THE BASE FORCE, "OPTION C,"
AND THE BOTTOM-UP REVIEW

	ACTUAL 1991 FORCE	POWELL'S BASE FORCE	ASPIN'S OPTION C	BOTTOM-UP REVIEW
Army Forces:				
Active divisions	16	12	9	10
Reserve divisions	10	6	6	5+
"Cadre" divisions	0	2	0	0
Navy Forces:				
Combat ships	528	450	340	346
Carriers	15	13	12	12*
Submarines	87	80	40	45–55
Marine Corps:				
Active MEFs	3	3	2	3
Reserve MEFs	1	1	1	1
Air Force:				
Active FWEs	22	15	10	13
Reserve FWEs	12	11	8	7

* 11 active plus 1 for training/reserve
FWE = Fighter wing equivalent
MEF = Marine Expeditionary Force (1 division + 1 air wing)

Sources: U.S. Department of Defense, *National Military Strategy of the United States* (1992); Les Aspin, *An Approach to Sizing American Conventional Forces* (1992); Les Aspin, *Bottom-Up Review* (1993).

a contest very much like the Gulf War. These envisioned the United States pitted against an Iraq-like enemy equipped with large numbers of tanks, artillery pieces, planes, and missiles. Indeed, the three-phased campaign described in the review is almost a play-by-play repeat of Operation Desert Storm:[41]

In *Phase I*, U.S. ground forces would aid local forces in attempting to slow down and if possible halt an enemy advance while aircraft attacked enemy ground forces and attempted to destroy their logistical support network. At the same time, other planes would seek to destroy enemy aircraft and air-defense systems, thereby establishing air superiority.

In *Phase II*, U.S. forces would mount round-the-clock air and missile attacks against enemy troops and supply networks, in order to steadily degrade the enemy's ability to mount large-scale combat operations. In addition, a large ground combat force would assemble behind a defensive screen established by the earliest-arriving American ground troops.

In *Phase III*, U.S. forces would launch a counteroffensive against the main bloc of enemy forces, using a preponderance of firepower to crush their defenses. The emphasis would be on breaking the enemy's will to resist by conducting nonstop, high-speed flanking and enveloping attacks and by inundating enemy positions with bombs, shells, and missiles.

To conduct such a campaign, the Bottom-Up Review called for the commitment of a combined force not unlike that assembled for Desert Storm: 4–5 Army divisions, 4–5 Marine expeditionary brigades (approximately one and a half divisions), 10 Air Force fighter wings, 100 Air Force heavy bombers (B-1s, B-2s, and B-52s), 4–5 carrier battle groups, assorted Special Operations units, and a host of supporting elements. This "MRC Building Block," as Aspin termed it, was said to be strong enough to prevail in any conceivable regional conflict. Because the review assumed that the United States must be capable of fighting *two* such campaigns simultaneously, the Pentagon's ultimate requirement would be for a force approximately twice the size of this single-MRC capability.[42]

Furthermore, to insure that these campaigns would proceed smoothly and result in a decisive victory (while minimizing American losses), the Bottom-Up Review called for the maximum exploitation of the country's technological prowess. In particular, the report stressed the need for improved battlefield surveillance systems and enhanced communications between airborne intelligence units and the "shooters" on the ground. So that U.S. forces would be equipped with such capabilities, the review favored accelerated procurement of the Joint Surveillance and Attack Radar System (JSTARS) aircraft, the MILSTAR satellite communications system, and an upgraded version of the E-3 Airborne Warning and Control System (AWACS).[43]

Equally crucial, the review argued, was the acquisition of advanced self-guiding munitions—particularly munitions that could be employed in strikes against enemy tanks and armored vehicles while on the move. Many such weapons had been used to great advantage during Desert Storm, and new versions, currently under development, would further enhance the "kill effectiveness" of American combat systems. These weapons included the Longbow missile system (a helicopter-mounted antitank weapon based on the Hellfire missile), the CBU-97B Sensor Fuzed Weapon (a wide-area guided munition that can destroy many vehicles at once), the Brilliant Anti-Tank (BAT) submunition (a self-aiming projectile that can be delivered by a variety of missile systems), and the SADARM (Search and Destroy Armor) self-guided artillery warhead.[44] Such systems, Aspin noted, "hold promise of dramatically improving the capabilities of U.S. air, ground, and maritime forces to destroy enemy armored vehicles and halt invading ground forces."[45]

Because most of these new munitions were to be delivered by aircraft, the Bottom-Up Review called for the continued enhancement of U.S. air capabilities. Existing aircraft, including the F-117 fighter and the B-2 Stealth bomber, were to be provided with improved navigation and targeting systems in order to permit high-precision attacks with advanced conventional weapons. In addition, the review endorsed the procurement of the Air Force's new air-superiority fighter, the F-22, and the advanced, "E/F" model of the Navy's F/A-18 carrier-based multirole aircraft. Two other aircraft— the Navy's proposed A/FX attack/fighter plane and the Air Force's proposed multirole fighter—were cancelled by Aspin; the review did, however, propose the development of a Joint Advanced Strike Technology (JAST) aircraft for deployment early in the twenty-first century.[46]

Finally, to deal with the fact that future adversaries might possess nuclear weapons or other weapons of mass destruction, the Bottom-Up review called on U.S. forces to be better prepared to destroy such weapons before they could be used and to defend against them, should those efforts fail. Such "counterproliferation" efforts, as Aspin termed them, would include improved intelligence on enemy WMD, the procurement of enhanced antimissile missiles, the development of protective clothing and equipment, and "improvements in the ability of both our general purpose and special operations forces to seize, disable, or destroy arsenals of nuclear, biological, and chemical weapons and their delivery systems."[47]

THE BOTTOM-UP REVIEW AFTER ASPIN

Three and a half months after the release of the Bottom-Up Review, Les Aspin announced his resignation as Secretary of Defense. No single reason was given for his decision; rather, he was said by reporters to have alienated too many key players in Washington with his "hesitant," indecisive manner and his bookish, unmilitary bearing. Aspin also took some of the heat for President Clinton's backtracking on issues such as intervention in Somalia and gays in the military.[48] While few Pentagon officials expressed sadness over Aspin's departure, most were quick to praise his role in supervising the Bottom-Up Review, which, according to President Clinton, would "guide our nation's military for many years to come."[49]

Aspin's successor at the Pentagon, William J. Perry, was known more for his managerial proficiency than for his mastery of strategic issues. A mathematician and an electronics expert, he had served as Director of Defense Research and Engineering in the Carter administration, and as Deputy Secretary of Defense under Aspin. After being selected to replace Aspin, he paid due homage to his predecessor's strategic contributions, in the process signaling that he was not about to tamper with the inherited blueprint for America's post–Cold War military posture. "Secretary Aspin left us with an excellent legacy in his Bottom-Up Review," he told the Senate Armed Services Committee in February 1994. "We will build on that excellent base."[50]

As Perry settled into his new position at the Department of Defense, questions began to emerge in Congress and the military community about the viability of the Aspin plan. These questions took two forms: doubts about America's ability (and willingness) to pay for a two-war capability at a time of economic uncertainty, when reducing the federal deficit was an issue of growing significance; and skepticism about the Pentagon's strategic assumptions regarding future military threats.

Doubts about the affordability of the proposed Bottom-Up Review Force Structure (BURFS) of ten active Army divisions, twenty active and reserve fighter wings, and twelve carriers surfaced almost immediately. By December 1993, three months after release of the Bottom-Up report, the White House Office of Management and Budget reported that because of higher inflation estimates and a recent military pay increase, the armed services would have approximately $40–50 billion less to spend than had originally been assumed over the next five years. An even larger shortfall, of $110–$150 billion, was later predicted by the General Accounting Office. President Clinton promised to restore some $25 billion to the defense budget in December 1994, but it remained unlikely that the Department of Defense would receive sufficient funding to acquire all the new high-tech weapons it sought while sustaining a force on the scale of the proposed BURFS.[51]

Leaders of the various services were already beginning to make plans for a smaller force than that envisioned in the Bottom-Up

Review. Air Force Chief of Staff General Merrill A. McPeak, for instance, announced that the heavy bomber fleet (composed of B-1s, B-2s, and B-52s) might decline to one hundred deployable aircraft by the end of the decade—the number cited by Aspin as required for a *single* major regional conflict. To compensate for this shortfall, McPeak proposed to arm existing bombers and fighters with advanced bombs and missiles, but even this would not compensate for the decline in deployable aircraft.[52] The Army also warned that it might be forced to reduce active divisions from ten to seven or eight if additional funds were not provided. And John Deutch, the Deputy Secretary of Defense, said in August 1994 that it might be necessary to scrap the F-22 fighter and V-22 tilt-rotor troop transport in order to save the basic BURFS plan.[53]

It is possible, of course, that the Republican-dominated Congress elected in November 1994 may seek to restore some of the funds removed from the defense budget in 1993–94. Such a move would certainly be consistent with the rhetoric employed by House Speaker Newt Gingrich and other Republican leaders. But the Republicans also seek to reduce taxes while balancing the federal budget, and this will argue against any significant increase in military spending.

Questions about the Bottom-Up Review's strategic assumptions were slower to emerge, but no less pointed. In general, they addressed the nature of America's future adversaries and doubts about the particular scenarios built into the BURFS blueprint. As noted, the Bottom-Up Review assumed that America's adversaries in future regional wars would resemble the Iraq of August 1990. Specifically, the review posited an aggressor state fielding 400,000–750,000 active-duty soldiers, 2,000–4,000 tanks, 500–1,000 combat planes, 100–200 naval vessels (with up to 50 submarines), and 100–1,000 Scud-class ballistic missiles.[54] But a survey of potential Third World adversaries revealed only one state—North Korea—that came close to this model; all other likely enemies fell short of it. In light of this, critics of the Bottom-Up Review once again suggested that the force structure proposed by the Department of Defense was far larger than needed to deal with the most likely regional threats.[55]

Critics of the BURFS also charged that future enemies were likely to learn from Iraq's mistakes in the 1991 Gulf conflict, so that U.S. forces would face a very different sort of scenario than that envisioned in the Bottom-Up Review. "Given Iraq's spectacular failure against the U.S.–led coalition, it is difficult to accept that future potential aggressors would attempt to repeat Baghdad's folly," observed Andrew F. Krepinevich of the Defense Budget Project. "It would seem far more likely that they would attempt to be highly innovative, both in the types of forces they field and the kind of military doctrine they employ." By focusing solely on Iraq-like threats, such critics claimed, the Bottom-Up Review might lead the United States to procure the wrong types of forces and pursue the wrong strategies for responding to future threats.[56]

Along with other critics, Krepinevich, a former Army officer, suggested that future enemies might look less like the Iraqi forces in Kuwait and more like General Aidid's forces in Somalia or the Serbian militias in Bosnia—forces that would seek to avoid direct confrontations with American power, but might use terrorism, ambushes, and other unconventional tactics not easily defeated by a force organized along Desert Storm lines.[57] Although there is no evidence that the Department of Defense is prepared to abandon the Desert Storm model or modify the BURFS in any fundamental way, budgetary constraints and unanticipated overseas challenges are likely to eat away at the feasibility of a two-MRC strategy, forcing military leaders to adapt.[58]

THE QUESTION OF NUCLEAR WEAPONS

One key topic not addressed by the Bottom-Up Review was the thorny issue of nuclear weapons. The military apparatus that the Clinton administration inherited in 1993 included vast nuclear stockpiles and a massive array of aircraft and missile delivery systems. Historically, these weapons had served a single function: threatening the Soviets with catastrophic retaliation if they invaded Western

Europe or otherwise jeopardized American security interests. With the Soviet Union out of the picture, the U.S. nuclear arsenal had lost its *raison d'être*. Pentagon strategists were forced to consider what, if any, function such weapons might perform in the post–Cold War era.

For forty-five years, from the onset of the Cold War to its conclusion, nuclear weapons had been at the heart of U.S. military strategy. Although the USSR might have attained superiority in some aspects of conventional power, American leaders had always sought to retain superiority in the nuclear realm, to assure that Washington would be able to threaten the USSR with annihilation in the event of a superpower showdown. To this end, the United States had built up a mammoth arsenal of nuclear weapons, along with an immense and costly complex of military reactors, nuclear weapons fabrication plants, and nuclear test facilities. Equally significant, American strategists had constructed an elaborate theory of "deterrence" to justify the acquisition and deployment of ever more sophisticated and potent nuclear weapons systems. With the end of the Cold War, the futures of both the physical and theoretical components of this vast enterprise were suddenly thrown into question.

In 1990, the U.S. nuclear arsenal consisted of approximately 21,000 nuclear warheads, along with 1,000 intercontinental ballistic missiles (ICBMs), 608 submarine-launched ballistic missiles (SLBMs), 324 long-range bombers (B-1s and B-52s), and thousands of shorter-range, tactical weapons.[59] These numbers began to drop in 1991, with the signing of the Strategic Arms Reduction Treaty (START-I) and a unilateral U.S. decision to retire many tactical nuclear weapons. By the time President Clinton assumed office, the warhead total had declined to approximately 18,500, while the number of ICBMs stood at 550, that of SLBMs at 440.[60] Further reductions in warhead numbers were expected in accordance with START-I, but the missile force was not expected to drop much below 1,000.[61]

Just exactly what function these remaining weapons will serve has yet to be determined. President Bush did not address this issue during his term in office, choosing to focus instead on problems of U.S.–Soviet (and later U.S.–Russian) arms control. President Clinton did not address this question prior to taking office; once in the White House, he delegated it to Secretary of Defense Les Aspin. Aspin did not take this up in the Bottom-Up Review, but instead initiated a separate study, the Nuclear Posture Review, for that purpose.[62]

In defining a new policy for nuclear weapons, Pentagon analysts were free to consider fundamental changes in U.S. strategy. With the Cold War over, and many of the nuclear weapons of the former Soviet Union in storage or in the process of being dismantled, it certainly would have been possible to conceive of a much smaller arsenal. Indeed, some strategists, including former Secretary of Defense Robert S. McNamara, suggested that the United States could safely reduce its nuclear stockpile to a very small number (assuming that the former Soviet states agreed to do likewise), and ban all future production of nuclear weapons materials.[63] Other analysts, citing the continued existence of potent nuclear arsenals in Russia, Ukraine, and China, along with the spread of nuclear weapons to other states, argued for the preservation of a slightly downsized version of existing nuclear forces. Still other experts argued for the acquisition of new types of "low-yield" nuclear weapons (weapons with a smaller explosive yield than those dropped on Hiroshima and Nagasaki in 1945); these would supposedly be better suited to a world of rising Third World powers armed with chemical and/or nuclear weapons.

The first post–Cold War assessment of possible approaches to nuclear strategy was conducted in late 1991 by a committee of senior military officials headed by former Air Force Secretary Thomas C. Reed. The committee, known as the Joint Strategic Target Planning Advisory Group, called for retention of a sizeable nuclear arsenal and the targeting of "every reasonable adversary" of the United States with nuclear weapons. The joint committee argued that, while most of these weapons should be aimed at the former Soviet Union, a portion should be committed to a "nuclear expeditionary force" aimed at China and other potentially hostile Third World powers.

This force would be used to deter these states from acquiring weapons of mass destruction and for retaliation, should some country choose to use WMD against the United States or its allies.[64]

In a companion paper, Reed and an associate spelled out their rationale for targeting Third World powers with nuclear weapons. Although the nuclear threat posed by Russia and other ex-Soviet states was likely to decline, they argued, "more nuclear-weapon states are likely to emerge, especially in the more unstable regions of the Third World." No matter how strong the international norm against proliferation, moreover, some ambitious Third World leaders were likely to pursue nuclear weapons in the belief that "with such weapons, they can seek to deter the United States and others from interfering with their regional aggressions." Therefore, the United States should retain a capacity to threaten—and, if obliged, engage in—nuclear retaliation, in response to blatant acts of aggression. Foreign leaders, they said, should not "be allowed to believe that they can embark on major aggression against the United States, its deployed forces, or its allies and friends, while enjoying personal sanctuary from American weapons, including nuclear weapons."[65]

Not surprisingly, these documents provoked considerable criticism from strategists who believed that the United States could, and should, reduce its reliance on nuclear weapons. Suggesting that Washington was highly unlikely to use nuclear weapons in response to regional aggression when it could inflict immense damage with conventional weapons, McNamara characterized the Air Force report as "weakly argued and weakly constructed."[66] John Steinbruner of the Brookings Institution commented that "the whole tenor of the report is to preserve the [nuclear arms] business as best one can, while recognizing that a lot has changed."[67]

In the months that followed, policymakers grappled with the issues raised by the Reed Committee's report without reaching any firm conclusions. While few military strategists were prepared to eschew all nuclear options aimed at Third World powers, many questioned the credibility (if not the morality) of threatening such attacks with the powerful "city-busters" now in the U.S. nuclear arsenal. "For a nuclear deterrent to be credible," Pentagon arms expert Thomas F. Ramos argued in 1991, "an adversary must believe that the use of the weapons is plausible." Because the United States might hesitate to use city-busters against a small or medium-sized power, he noted, any retaliatory threats based on the use of such weapons would carry little plausibility, and so would possess little deterrent effect. For this reason, he argued, the Defense Department should develop new, "low-yield" nuclear weapons that would be more suited to a "multipolar world of lesser regional powers."[68]

In a similar vein, two analysts at the Los Alamos National Laboratory, Thomas W. Dowler and Joseph S. Howard II, proposed the establishment of a nuclear arsenal made up of small, very-low-yield weapons. Such weapons, they suggested, would fall into a middle ground between the Hiroshima bomb, which unleashed the destructive force of 15,000 tons (15 kilotons) of TNT, and standard conventional bombs, which typically carry 500–1,000 pounds of high explosive. Specifically, Dowler and Howard called for the development of a family of "micronukes" with a yield of 10 tons of TNT, "mininukes" with a yield of 100 tons, and "tinynukes" with a yield of 1,000 tons. Such weapons could be used to destroy enemy airfields and bunkers, intercept enemy missiles, and blunt enemy offensives. Seeking to confer legitimacy on the use of small nuclear weapons— a proposition long championed by U.S. nuclear strategists and rejected by most arms control advocates—they claimed that such explosives would be "true battlefield weapons, not weapons of indiscriminate mass destruction."[69]

Although Dowler's and Howard's proposals have not received official endorsement from senior officials, they continue to be the subject of study by analysts at Los Alamos and other nuclear weapons laboratories.[70] For now, such proposals are likely to remain in the conceptual stage; the Clinton administration has pledged to suspend nuclear testing (so long as all other nuclear powers do likewise), and all existing nuclear weapons plants have been shut down for budgetary and safety reasons. Should this situation change, proposals for small nuclear weapons probably will receive a sympathetic response from many in the military establishment.

While the United States is unlikely to resume the production of nuclear weapons—whether "mini" or not—in the immediate future, many of the strategic assumptions articulated by Reed and his associates, and by Dowler and Howard, seem to have been incorporated into Pentagon thinking. According to a 1994 editorial comment in the *New York Times*, the Department of Defense plans to use nuclear weapons to deter and retaliate against the use of *any* weapons of mass destruction—including chemical and biological weapons—by rogue regimes in the Third World.[71] Despite Secretary of Defense William Perry's official denial, knowledgeable observers have cited additional evidence of such a posture.[72]

Although many details of the Nuclear Posture Review have not been released, its principal conclusions have been made public. Rejecting the argument that, with the Cold War over, the United States can dispense with nuclear weapons (or, at the very least, radically reduce their number), administration officials insist that a robust nuclear capability is needed to cope with unspecified future threats. "We will retain strategic nuclear forces sufficient to deter any future hostile leadership with access to strategic nuclear forces from acting against our vital interests," President Clinton declared in July 1994. "Therefore we will continue to maintain nuclear forces of sufficient size and capability to hold at risk a broad range of assets valued by such political and military leaders."[73]

According to published accounts, the Nuclear Posture Review called for the retention of a significant nuclear arsenal and for preserving the option of employing nuclear weapons against WMD-armed Third World powers. Although the U.S. stockpile will be reduced to about 3,500 warheads in accordance with the START-II agreement, no further cuts are contemplated. This will result in a future force of 450 land-based Minuteman-III ICBMs, 14 Trident missile-carrying submarines with 24 missiles each, and 66 nuclear-armed B-52 bombers. In addition, the United States will retain an unspecified number of "non-strategic nuclear forces" for use in attacks on states other than the former Soviet republics.[74]

TURNING UP THE PRESSURE: NONPROLIFERATION POLICY IN THE CLINTON ERA

In line with developments in U.S. military policy, President Clinton's foreign policy placed great stress on nonproliferation activities and on pressuring unfriendly Third World countries into complying with U.S.–backed technology controls. Senior officials, from the President on down, repeatedly identified proliferation as a significant factor in U.S. relations with arms-seeking and arms-supplying powers. "I have made nonproliferation one of our nation's highest priorities," Clinton told the U.N. General Assembly in September 1993. "We intend to weave it more deeply into the fabric of all of our relationships with the world's nations and institutions."[75]

President Clinton's plans in this regard were spelled out in his first post-election press conference. Asked about his foreign policy objectives, he declared that he intended to appoint a Secretary of State who could be relied on to "restrain the proliferation of weapons of mass destruction."[76] From their earliest moments in office, Clinton's top foreign policy officials placed considerable emphasis on the strengthening of global nonproliferation efforts. In seeking confirmation as Secretary of State, for instance, Warren Christopher told the Senate Foreign Relations Committee that "we must work assiduously with other nations to discourage proliferation though improved intelligence, export controls, incentives, sanctions, and even force when necessary."[77] Similar views were expressed by other prospective officials, including Les Aspin and James Woolsey.

Once in office, these officials continued to stress the importance of vigorous nonproliferation efforts. At first, they followed more or less in the path carved out by the Bush administration, seeking to strengthen existing nonproliferation agreements like the Nuclear

Non-Proliferation Treaty and the Missile Technology Control Regime and encouraging nonparticipating states to comply with these measures. As time went on, however, it become possible to detect a more distinctive Clinton administration approach to proliferation. This involved more overt forms of pressure on noncooperating states, and a greater readiness to impose sanctions and threaten military action when such states failed to heed Washington's instructions.

The new position was first articulated by the President during a visit to Asia in July 1993. In a series of speeches in Tokyo and Seoul, he warned that proliferation posed a new and increasingly serious threat to regional security. "No specter hangs over this peninsula and this region more darkly than the danger of nuclear proliferation," he told South Korea's National Assembly.[78] In response, he noted the United States would step up its efforts in the nonproliferation field, and would ask its allies to do likewise. Clinton further indicated that his preferred approach was the use of diplomacy and economic incentives to persuade the proliferators in the region, especially China and North Korea, to discontinue their objectionable behavior.[79] He let it be known, however, that Washington was prepared to use force—even extreme force—to punish unacceptable proliferation behavior by "outlaw regimes." In a visit to the Demilitarized Zone between North and South Korea, he took an even more aggressive stance. It would be "pointless" for the North Koreans to build nuclear weapons in the face of certain U.S. retaliation in the event of their use: "It will be the end of their country," he said.[80]

The administration's tougher stance on proliferation was also evident in subsequent comments by Anthony Lake, the President's Special Assistant for National Security Affairs. In a 1993 address at Johns Hopkins University, Lake described a new framework for American foreign policy: in place of "containment" of the Soviet Union, as practiced during the Cold War era, the United States would now pursue a policy of "enlargement," seeking to expand the community of nations committed to democracy and capitalism. At the same time, Lake warned against the "backlash" states—his term for rogues and outlaws—that stood in the way of global progress. Such states, he suggested, "are more likely to sponsor terrorism and traffic in weapons of mass destruction and ballistic missile technology." It would be necessary, he said, for the United States to seek to isolate such states and cut off their access to sensitive military technology; if this failed to prevent aggressive action on their part, "we clearly must be prepared to strike back decisively and unilaterally."[81]

Nor was the administration's response to "outlaw states" and "rogue regimes"—terms that appeared with growing frequency in official statements—limited to an escalation in rhetoric. Beginning in the summer of 1993, the White House ordered a number of punitive actions against states accused of trafficking in WMD-related materials or in violating key provisions of the Non-Proliferation Treaty.

In August 1993, U.S. warships attempted to prevent the *Yin He*, a Chinese ship said to be carrying materials used in the manufacture of chemical weapons, from unloading its cargo in Iran. In defending this move, U.S. officials claimed they had obtained convincing intelligence that the ship had sailed from a Chinese port with large quantities of thiodiglycol (a chemical used in making mustard gas) and thionyl chloride (used in making nerve gas). Chinese authorities strongly denied these charges, but allowed the ship to be searched by Saudi and U.S. inspectors at the Saudi Arabian port of Dammam. Much to the embarrassment of Washington, no supplies of the suspect chemicals were found aboard the ship, which was allowed to go on its way. Nevertheless, this incident set a possibly important precedent for future naval action in blocking WMD shipments.[82]

The Clinton administration also beefed up its military capabilities in South Korea, and threatened to impose tough economic sanctions on North Korea if it failed to discontinue its efforts to manufacture nuclear weapons. "Our diplomacy has reached a critical point," Secretary Christopher declared in March 1994. "We have made it clear to North Korea that it must become a responsible member of the international community or that community will have no choice but to pursue progressively stronger measures."[83] When North Korea instead thwarted efforts by the International Atomic Energy Agency to inspect a key nuclear facility in May 1994, the White House

announced that it would seek international support for the imposition of economic sanctions against the North—a step that prompted
North Korean threats of war and stepped-up activities by both sides
to prepare for a full-scale military encounter.[84]

It was during the North Korean nuclear crisis of May–June 1994
that the language of the Rogue Doctrine truly came into its own.
Major newspapers, including the *New York Times* and the *Wall Street
Journal*, regularly described the North Korean government as "a
rogue regime" with nuclear ambitions, and such terms figured prominently in Congressional debate on the crisis. In addition, many pundits and policymakers began to speak openly of the need for military
action against the North. Former National Security Council official
Richard N. Haass wrote in June that if Pyongyang failed to halt its
nuclear program, America should "launch a preemptive military
strike against North Korea's nuclear facilities."[85] Other strategists
called for the immediate imposition of sanctions, even at the risk of
prompting an all-out war.[86] The crisis finally abated in late June,
following a peacemaking mission to North Korea by former President
Jimmy Carter—but not before many in Washington became con-
vinced that a "Second Korean War" was imminent.[87]

The Korea crisis also crystallized another aspect of the Rogue Doctrine: the equation of "enemy-ness" with the pursuit of weapons of
mass destruction in violation of (and hidden from) international
nonproliferation institutions. North Korea's "crime" was not that it
had attacked South Korea, or deployed nuclear weapons in a threatening manner—the United States had yet to determine beyond reasonable doubt that Pyongyang actually possessed functioning nuclear
munitions, let alone that it could deliver them—but that it had frustrated efforts by the International Atomic Energy Agency to calculate
its supply of bomb-grade plutonium. On this basis alone, the Clinton
administration was prepared to impose sanctions on North Korea
and risk a full-scale war.

Where all of this will lead is anyone's guess. It is possible that
crises will break out from time to time on one proliferation front or
another, then subside for a while as the focus of attention turns

elsewhere. But there is no doubt that repeated threats, imposition of sanctions, and the ratcheting up of pressure is likely to strain U.S. relations with such "problem" states as China, Iran, Iraq, Libya, Pakistan, Syria, and North Korea. While such moves may not in themselves cause a war, ensuing reprisals and countermoves might easily escalate into one. Indeed, such a "snowball effect" constitutes one of the scenarios most likely to lead to large-scale U.S. military action, now that proliferation has replaced communism as the greatest perceived threat to U.S. national security.

Chapter Five

ROGUES, OUTLAWS, AND

HEGEMONS

A Pentagon Roster of the

"Iraqs of the Future"

THE BOTTOM-UP Review Force Structure, like the Base Force before it, rested on one fundamental premise: that the United States must be prepared to conduct a succession of Desert Storm-like engagements with rising Third World powers. From the Pentagon's point of view, such states ideally should possess a large military establishment, a substantial supply of modern weapons, and a desire for weapons of mass destruction. Furthermore, to fully satisfy the review's basic assumptions, they should exhibit hegemonic inclinations regarding states in their region, or harbor ambitions that would otherwise threaten U.S. interests. To describe such states, military officials are wont to speak of "other Iraqs" whose aggressive behavior could eventually provoke a military clash with the United States.

The concept of "other Iraqs" was first articulated by Secretary of Defense Dick Cheney in the immediate aftermath of the Persian Gulf War. "Iraq's forces were considerable, but not entirely unique," Cheney told the House Armed Services Committee on March 19, 1991. "There are other regional powers with modern armed forces, sophisticated attack aircraft, and integrated air defenses. . . . By the year 2000, it is estimated that at least 15 developing nations will have the ability to build ballistic missiles—eight of which either have or are near to acquiring nuclear capabilities."[1]

This prognosis soon became a standard feature of the Pentagon's long-range strategic outlook. "Iraq is not the only heavily-armed developing country with designs on its neighbors," Army Chief of Staff General Carl E. Vuono wrote in 1991. Because such violence-prone states will eventually be driven to challenge vital U.S. interests, "this nation cannot and must not sacrifice its ability to deal with the Iraqs of the future."[2]

By the time the Clinton administration took office, the development of a capacity to fight the "Iraqs of the future" had become the principal goal of the Department of Defense. So unquestioned was this proposition that the only real issue of debate in 1993 was *how many* of these countries the United States should be prepared to fight at any one time. As we have seen, the senior military leaders pushed for a "two-war" capability, while Secretary of Defense Aspin initially supported a "one-and-a-half-war" capability, before capitulating to the Joint Chiefs of Staff.

But just exactly which countries, in particular, should the United States be prepared to fight? On this vital point, the Department of Defense was notably vague: it rarely identified likely enemies, other than Iraq and North Korea, by name, preferring to speak vaguely of "hostile powers"—or, to use Secretary Aspin's term from the Bottom-Up Review, "a new class of regional dangers." Included in this class, Aspin stated, were states with "rogue leaders set on regional domination through military aggression while simultaneously pursuing nuclear, biological, and chemical weapons capabilities."[3]

A further insight into administration thinking was provided by Anthony Lake, Clinton's Special Assistant for National Security Affairs, who wrote menacingly in *Foreign Affairs* magazine of "backlash" states that threatened to undermine global progress toward democracy and market reform. "Our policy must face the reality of recalcitrant and outlaw states that not only choose to remain outside the family of nations but to assault its basic values." Such states—he specifically mentioned Iran, Iraq, Libya, and North Korea—were often "aggressive and defiant," and sought to enhance their military might through the acquisition of weapons of mass destruction. To counter this threat, he argued, the United States must "deploy military capabilities sufficient to deter or respond to any aggressive act" by these states.[4]

From these and other such statements, it is possible to construct a plausible list of the Pentagon's leading candidates for "future Iraqs." At the top of this list is North Korea, followed by four other countries often described as "rogues" and "outlaws" by U.S. leaders: Iran, Iraq, Libya, and Syria. All four of these states have been characterized as hostile to the United States and its allies, as sponsoring or condoning terrorism, and as having pursued the acquisition of chemical and/or nuclear weapons. All four, moreover, are said to be ruled by authoritarian leaders who espouse militant anti-Western beliefs, and are prepared to threaten fundamental U.S. interests in their regions.[5]

Given the history of U.S. relations with these five states and the frequency with which they have been named as rogues and renegades by the media, it has not been difficult for the Department of Defense to persuade U.S. policymakers of the need to be prepared to defend America's "vital interests" against their aggressive intentions. Many members of Congress were quick to call for a buildup of American forces in South Korea during the June 1994 crisis over nuclear inspections in the North, and calls for military action against the other four frequently have followed allegations of their involvement in international terrorism or illicit proliferation activity. In fact, the likelihood of periodic clashes with these five states has become an article of faith among U.S. policymakers.

But while the Department of Defense can take pleasure in the popularity of its anti-rogue stance, this position faces a fundamental problem: the above-named five rogues simply do not constitute a large enough group of rising Third World powers to justify maintenance of the massive military apparatus envisioned by U.S. military officials. Although the new posture assumes a U.S. capability to fight two Iraq-like adversaries simultaneously, of the five so-called rogues, only one—North Korea—can claim a military establishment as large and as potent as that fielded by Saddam Hussein in August 1990. The others are too weak or possess too few tanks, planes, and artillery pieces to constitute an Iraq-like menace.

Recognizing this, the Department of Defense has not limited its planning scenarios to conflicts with the five existing rogues. Rather, it has assumed that the current crop of outlaws will eventually be joined by other Third World powers, drawn from what might be called "prospective" rogues. These candidate enemies—China, Egypt, India, Pakistan, South Korea, Taiwan, and Turkey—are not characterized as "rogues" per se, but are described as emerging regional powers with hegemonic aspirations and, in most cases, an interest in the acquisition of weapons of mass destruction (WMD). While most of these prospective rogues are allied with or friendly to the United States, military analysts suggest that their leaders may well shift loyalties in response to future events, or be overthrown by forces hostile to the West.

In supporting a military posture based on the hypothetical threat posed by these candidate rogues, Pentagon officials maintain that it is necessary to consider not only the political stance of a given state, but its military capabilities as well. Because a country's accumulation of large quantities of arms could be the harbinger of hegemonic or aggressive behavior, it is necessary to monitor such buildups carefully.[6] "Instability may arise in areas where nations are acquiring increasingly sophisticated and expensive military equipment," the Joint Chiefs of Staff observed in 1992. "This tendency undermines regional stability and the balance of power, [thus] expanding the opportunities for violent conflict."[7]

The seven states named above all consistently score high on the Pentagon's charts of troop strength, military spending, arms holdings, and pursuit of WMD. Pentagon analysts view prospective rogues as the countries most capable of joining the five nominal rogues on a list of twelve possible "future Iraqs." Other states may, in fact, be more likely to provoke a serious clash with the United States, but only these twelve possess sufficient military strength to serve as major regional adversaries in the combat scenarios incorporated into the Bottom-Up Review. (See Table 5.1.)

One additional Third World state satisfies the Pentagon's criteria for an emerging regional power: Israel, which has a large and well-equipped military establishment, devotes a sizeable portion of its GNP

TABLE 5.1
EMERGING REGIONAL POWERS

COUNTRY	NUCLEAR WEAPONS	CHEMICAL WEAPONS	BALLISTIC MISSILES	ARMED FORCES	HEAVY TANKS	COMBAT AIRCRAFT
"Rogues"						
Iran	u.d.	yes	yes	473,000	700+	293+/−
Iraq (1993)	no*	no*	no*	382,000	2,200+/−	?
Libya	no	yes	yes	70,000	2,300+	409
No. Korea	u.d.	yes	yes	1,100,000	3,700	730
Syria	no	yes	yes	408,000	4,500	639
"Prospective rogues"						
China	yes	prob.	yes	3,000,000	7,500+	4,970
Egypt	no	prob.	u.d.	430,000	3,167	546
India	yes	prob.	yes	1,300,000	3,400	707
Pakistan	yes	prob.	u.d.	577,000	1,890+	393
So. Korea	no	prob.	yes	633,000	1,800	445
Taiwan	no	prob.	yes	442,000	309	484
Turkey	no	no	no	480,000	4,835	539
Others						
Argentina	no#	no	no#	70,800	266	180
Brazil	no#	no	u.d.	296,700	0**	326
Cuba	no	no	no	173,500	1,575	140
Indonesia	no	poss.	no	270,900	0**	80
Israel	yes	prob.	yes	176,000	3,960	662

* Earlier efforts terminated by Desert Storm.
** Inventory includes some light tanks.
\# Earlier efforts suspended voluntarily.
prob. = probable
poss. = possible
u.d. = under development

Sources: International Institute of Strategic Studies, *The Military Balance 1993–1994*; other reports cited in text.

to defense, and has built up a substantial stockpile of nuclear and chemical munitions. Israel's military posture is so closely aligned with that of the United States, however, and the probability of Israel ever severing its links to Washington is so low that U.S. military officials do not view it as a potential adversary.

The fact that the seven potential rogues named above have been included in the Pentagon's list of potential adversaries does not, of course, mean that the United States is destined to go to war with any of them; nor does it mean that the United States will forbear going to war with states not on that list. Rather, these seven states are seen as prime examples of the *type* of enemy against which the U.S. military apparatus supposedly is destined to fight. To justify retention of a two-war strategy, moreover, the Department of Defense must operate on the assumption that at least some of these countries will eventually join the five nominal rogues as possible "Iraqs of the future."

Given the centrality of this assessment to current U.S. military thinking, it is essential that we view these rogues and prospective rogues through the eyes of Pentagon strategists, highlighting those aspects of their behavior and capabilities that could prove most threatening to U.S. interests in the years ahead. In particular, this means focusing on these states' strategic outlook, their net military potential, and their involvement (if any) in illicit proliferation activities. In many cases, such an approach exaggerates the "roguishness" of these countries, while downplaying the more hopeful trends; only in this manner, however, can we appreciate the perspective of senior Pentagon officials.

What follows is a strategic assessment of the twelve states viewed by U.S. military planners as the most likely candidates for the "Iraqs of the future." The assessment begins with a profile of North Korea, and is followed by profiles of the four other states most often described as rogue powers: Iran, Iraq, Libya, and Syria. It concludes with profiles of the seven prospective rogues: China, Egypt, India, Pakistan, South Korea, Taiwan, and Turkey.[8] But it must be remembered that much can change in the years ahead. The death of North

Korean president Kim Il Sung on July 8, 1994, is a reminder that the leaders of several of the states in question are quite elderly, and while they may be replaced by other figures of a similar outlook, it is possible that their passing will lead to political upheaval and the rise of a new group of leaders with different views. In a number of states, moreover, a shift in the political orientation of the ruling party, or an electoral victory by opposition candidates, could significantly alter foreign and military policies. Economic crisis, natural disasters, and social unrest could also transform these countries' capabilities and outlooks.

NORTH KOREA

When U.S. strategists began looking for the "Iraqs of the future," most eyes in Washington turned to North Korea—the last remaining Stalinist regime in Asia and a longtime foe of the United States. Although North Korea did not receive much attention from American policymakers in the 1980s, largely because of greater U.S. concern over developments in other areas, its highly publicized resistance to nuclear inspections by the International Atomic Energy Agency (IAEA) made it a natural focus of U.S. interest in the 1990s. By May 1994, North Korea's nuclear weapons program had emerged as one of the Clinton administration's most pressing foreign policy concerns, and American officials had begun speaking of a possible war on the Korean peninsula.[9]

The United States and North Korea had traded threats and insults before, and tension along the Demilitarized Zone (DMZ) between North and South was nothing new. However, the developments of March–June 1994 had a qualitatively different feel. U.S. policymakers began to speak openly of the need for preemptive military strikes against suspected North Korean nuclear weapons installations, and North Korean officials threatened to turn Seoul into a "sea of fire."[10] Furthermore, both sides began to bolster their forces along the DMZ, and to stockpile fuel and ammunition in the battle zone.[11] General

John Shalikashvili, the chairman of the Joint Chiefs of Staff, reportedly described the situation in Korea as the "most dangerous crisis" facing the United States since the end of World War II.[12]

The Democratic People's Republic of North Korea (DPRK) was ruled from 1946 until his death in 1994 by Communist Party leader Kim Il Sung, who was succeeded by his son, Kim Jong Il. The elder Kim, the longest surviving communist dictator of the Stalinist era, harbored an unremitting hostility toward the United States, fueled by memories of U.S. intervention in the Korean War and continued U.S. support for the anticommunist leadership of South Korea. Once backed by China and the Soviet Union, North Korea in 1990 found itself largely isolated in a rapidly changing world; but, while other communist states sought to moderate their anti-Western policies and to forge economic ties with the outside world, Pyongyang adhered to its highly centralized economic and social system, shunning any accommodation with the West.[13]

As a consequence of the continuing mutual hostility between North and South, the Korean peninsula became one of the most highly militarized regions on earth. With 1.13 million men under arms, North Korea maintains the fifth-largest military establishment in the world (exceeded only by those of China, Russia, the United States, and India) and possesses large numbers of Soviet and Chinese weapons systems, including some 3,700 tanks, 2,500 armored personnel carriers (APCs), and 9,000 major artillery pieces. South Korea's military, numbering some 630,000, has fewer tanks and planes than the North's, but its equipment is considered of better quality. Moreover, the South Koreans are backed up by 35,500 U.S. troops (26,000 Army, 9,500 Air Force) stationed in their country.[14]

Aside from its sheer numbers, the North Korean military has been a source of concern to U.S. strategists for several reasons. An estimated seventy percent of North Korean ground forces are deployed within sixty miles of the DMZ, which at one point is only about twenty-five miles north of the South Korean capital of Seoul. The North Koreans have also deployed thousands of heavy artillery pieces, many of which can reach the outskirts of Seoul from their present positions, in the border zone. Adding to North Korea's war potential is a large inventory of Scud missiles and a substantial chemical warfare (CW) capability.[15]

Despite all this, U.S. military commanders have repeatedly expressed optimism about their ability to defeat the North Koreans in battle. "I am very, very confident," General Shalikashvili declared on December 14, 1993. "Even the more pessimistic studies [show] that the South Koreans, together with our reinforcements, will stop the North Korean attack far short of reaching their war objectives."[16] Most analysts agree, however, that any war between North and South Korea would be extremely violent and destructive, and would result in high numbers of military and civilian casualties. Because Seoul is so close to the DMZ, and because both sides are likely to concentrate their forces there, the fighting in and around the South Korean capital—home to some 14 million people—could prove especially intense and bloody.[17] "Those on the forward edge of the battle area are going to get chewed up very badly," observed Paul Godwin of the National War College in 1994. "The reinforcements will have to come in to take care of absolutely incredible casualties."[18]

For this reason, leaders of China, Japan, and other Asian countries have long sought to moderate tensions on the Korean peninsula, meeting with officials of both sides in a continuing effort to promote reconciliation between North and South. Their efforts appeared to have achieved a major breakthrough in December 1991, when representatives of the two Koreas signed an "Agreement on Reconciliation, Non-Aggression, and Exchanges and Cooperation." This important agreement, the first of its kind between North and South, was followed by the signing, on December 31, 1991, of a second major agreement banning the production and deployment of nuclear weapons in both North and South Korea.[19] Under immense pressure from Moscow, moreover, Pyongyang signed an all-important protocol with the International Atomic Energy Agency providing for IAEA inspection and monitoring of North Korea's nuclear facilities in order to ensure full compliance with the terms of the Nuclear Non-Proliferation Treaty (NPT).[20]

It was widely hoped that such on-site inspections would enable the IAEA to clear up important questions about North Korea's nuclear intentions. In 1986, the North Koreans had begun operation of a 25-megawatt gas-graphite reactor at Yongbyon, located some sixty miles north of Pyongyang. The Yongbyon reactor, said by the North Koreans to be for peaceful research purposes, was seen by many Western experts as a likely future source of plutonium for nuclear weapons. In 1989, the reactor was shut down for several months and some of its fuel rods were removed; at about the same time, North Korea began operating a nuclear reprocessing facility at Yongbyon that was thought by U.S. intelligence analysts to be intended for use in extracting plutonium from spent nuclear reactor fuel. By conducting various tests at the reprocessing site, IAEA inspectors sought to determine whether the North Koreans had, in fact, extracted sufficient plutonium from the fuel rods to produce one or more nuclear weapons devices.[21]

At first, the IAEA was granted access to North Korean nuclear facilities. Several inspections were conducted at Yongbyon in the summer and fall of 1992, and plans were laid for future visits in early 1993.[22] But then, suspecting that the North Koreans had hidden some of the plutonium believed to have been extracted from the fuel rods removed in 1989, the IAEA demanded access to certain facilities at Yongbyon that had not been listed by the North Koreans as being part of their nuclear program. North Korea refused the IAEA access to these facilities, charging that such action represented an infringement on its sovereignty. Thus set in motion an international crisis that continued well into 1994.[23]

Between March 1993 and June 1994, repeated efforts were made by the United States, Japan, China, and other states to overcome the impasse through negotiations. On March 12, 1993, North Korea announced its intention to withdraw from the Non-Proliferation Treaty. However, in response to promises of direct talks with senior U.S. officials about the normalization of U.S.–North Korean relations it later agreed to "suspend" its withdrawal and to allow regular IAEA inspections.[24] These talks appeared to be making slow but gradual progress when, in May 1994, North Korea shut down its 25-megawatt reactor for a second time and, with IAEA personnel barred from the site, removed all of its fuel rods, thereby precluding any future efforts to determine how much plutonium was extracted after the 1989 shutdown.[25]

The reactor shutdown and the threat of sanctions led to the most acute crisis in U.S.–North Korean relations since the end of the Korean War. The Clinton administration announced its intention to seek U.N. Security Council approval for the imposition of economic sanctions; Pyongyang responded by warning that such a move could precipitate North Korean military actions.[26] Both sides placed their forces on higher levels of alert, and began stockpiling fuel and supplies for a possible war.[27] With the tempo of military preparations increasing day by day, former President Jimmy Carter conducted a personal peacemaking mission to Pyongyang, and persuaded Kim Il Sung to freeze North Korea's nuclear efforts in return for a promise of fresh talks with the United States.[28] When North Korean officials confirmed this offer, President Clinton withdrew his call for sanctions and agreed to a new round of negotiations.[29]

Kim Il Sung died on July 8, 1994, shortly before the planned startup of the new round of U.S.–North Korean negotiations. After a period of mourning, however, Pyongyang agreed to proceed with the talks. Negotiators from the two countries met in Geneva on August 5; after a week of intensive negotiations, they agreed to a tentative accord. North Korea would suspend its nuclear program in return for a U.S. promise to help replace the North's existing gas-graphite reactors (which produce large quantities of weapons-grade plutonium) with modern light-water reactors (which do not). This accord was followed, on October 17, 1994, with the signing of an even more sweeping agreement, under which North Korea will terminate its nuclear weapons program entirely in return for massive infusions of U.S. economic and technical assistance. This agreement was welcomed by many in Washington, but criticized by some as overly generous to the North Koreans—a perception that could lead to problems in the years ahead.[30]

Nor is the nuclear issue the only aspect of North Korea's military behavior that is likely to produce friction in the U.S.–Korean relationship. American officials have expressed particular concern over Pyongyang's chemical weapons capability and its continuing production of ballistic missiles. The North Koreans are believed to possess a substantial CW capability, and to have developed CW warheads for their large inventory of ballistic missiles.[31]

North Korea currently manufactures an improved version of the Soviet Scud missile, the Scud-B (range: 190 miles), and a second variant, the Scud-C (range: 370 miles). These missiles are deployed with the North Korean military, and have been sold to Iran and Syria.[32] The North Koreans have also flight-tested a long-range Scud variant, the 600-mile NoDong-1 (also called RoDong-1), and are reported to be developing two long-range, multi-staged missiles, the Taepo Dong-1 and Taepo Dong-2.[33] The development of such missiles is particularly worrisome to Washington, because it could enable Pyongyang to attack American bases in Japan and Guam; U.S. officials also fear that North Korea might sell these missiles (or the technology to produce them) to other rogue powers, as it has the Scud-B and Scud-C. However, some experts question whether North Korea can successfully develop and manufacture multi-staged missiles.[34]

Ultimately, the fate of North Korea (and its relations with South Korea and the United States) hinges on the leadership succession from Kim Il Sung to his son, Kim Jong Il. The elder Kim was a tough and wily leader who successfully retained power for nearly fifty years; his son is thought to be less able to wield the reins of power. North Korea is also suffering from steep economic decline and widespread shortages of basic necessities, greatly adding to the pressures on the current regime.[35] Were Kim Jong Il to falter, a power struggle among competing military factions might break out, or mass riots and demonstrations might sweep through the country, as they did through East European countries in 1989–90.

THE ROGUES

Aside from North Korea, the countries most often described by U.S. officials as rogue states are Iran, Iraq, Libya, and Syria. All four are now ruled by authoritarian leaders—Ali Akbar Hashemi Rafsanjani in Iran, Saddam Hussein in Iraq, Muammar el-Qaddafi in Libya, and Hafez al-Assad in Syria—who have repeatedly voiced hostility toward the United States, its leaders, and its allies. All four have built up large military establishments that are viewed as threatening by neighboring states, and all have been accused of sponsoring terrorism or otherwise endangering international peace and stability.

Most significant, from a military point of view, is that all four have attempted to circumvent existing international restraints on the proliferation of weapons of mass destruction. Three of these states—Iran, Iraq, and Libya—have sought (or are thought to be seeking) the technology to produce nuclear weapons, and all four are believed to possess chemical weapons. All, moreover, possess or are developing ballistic missiles that could be used to deliver nuclear or chemical warheads to neighboring states.

Iran

"Iran is a revolutionary state whose leaders harbor a deep sense of grievance over the close ties between the United States and the [former] Shah," presidential adviser Anthony Lake charged in 1994. "Its revolutionary and militant messages are openly hostile to the United States and its core interests."[36] Ruled since 1979 by a clique of fundamentalist Islamic clerics, Iran has generally adhered to anti-Western, anti-American positions. Following the Persian Gulf conflict of 1991, in which Iran sided with, but did not join the anti-Iraq coalition, Iranian President Rafsanjani did attempt to restore Teheran's political and economic ties with the West. As the Clinton era commenced, however, U.S. intelligence officials were troubled by two key aspects of Iranian behavior: first, a drive by Teheran to increase its political and military influence throughout the Islamic world; second, the Iranians' costly and ambitious campaign to re-build their military capabilities (shattered during the 1980–88 con-flict with Iraq) and to acquire weapons of mass destruction.[37]

Iran has sought to increase its influence in a variety of ways, including extensive support for militant fundamentalist movements in Algeria, Egypt, Jordan, Lebanon, Tunisia, and the Occupied Ter-ritories under Israeli control; a *de facto* military alliance with the Moslem rulers of Sudan; extensive diplomatic and religious outreach to the Moslem states of the former Soviet Union; and a pattern of support for anti-Western terrorist groups.[38] Of particular concern to Washington are Iran's ties to the Party of God (or Hezbollah), the Lebanon-based group charged with a number of bombings of Jewish and Israeli organizations in the West.[39] Iran, Lake said, "is the fore-most sponsor of terrorism and assassination worldwide."[40]

At the same time, Iran has been engaged in a costly effort to modernize its armed forces and to replace aging American weap-onry—most of it supplied by Washington during the reign of the former Shah—with new Russian and Chinese equipment. The CIA estimated in 1992 that the Iranians were spending some $2 billion each year on imported weapons, although a subsequent downturn in oil prices may have lowered this amount.[41] Purchases from Russia have included two Kilo-class diesel submarines (with one more on order), thirty MiG-29 fighters, a squadron of Su-24 long-range strike aircraft, and several hundred T-72 tanks; in addition, the Iranians acquired SS-N-22 Sunburn anti-ship cruise missiles from Ukraine, F-7 fighters from China, and Scud missiles from North Korea.[42] These transactions significantly enhanced the combat capabilities of Iranian forces, making up for some of the losses incurred during its conflict with Iraq; nevertheless, Iran today remains far less powerful than Iraq in 1990 or, for that matter, Iran under the Shah.[43]

Especially troubling, from the American point of view, Iranian efforts to acquire nuclear, chemical, and ballistic missile technology. "Iran has embarked on an across-the-board effort to develop its military and defense industries, including programs in weapons of mass destruction," CIA Director Robert Gates told Congress in May

1992.[44] Gates did not provide any details at that time; five months later, however, the CIA reported that Teheran had launched a secret effort to develop nuclear weapons, using technology acquired from China and (by means of covert procurement channels) from commercial sources in the West.[45]

The Iranians have denied that they are working to produce nuclear weapons, but proliferation experts have reported a pattern of suspicious activities, including the construction of underground facilities at new nuclear research facilities at Isfahan, Qazvin, Moallem Kalayeh, and Karaj.[46] If these reports prove accurate, Iran might begin to manufacture a small number of nuclear weapons early in the twenty-first century.[47] More immediate, however, is the threat posed by Iran's growing chemical weapons stockpile. The Iranians first began producing CW munitions in the early 1980s, after being attacked with such weapons by Iraq, and are thought to have expanded their CW production capability in the intervening years.[48] Iran is also believed to be developing an array of ballistic missiles with assistance from China and North Korea.[49]

How far Teheran proceeds in modernizing its military and developing weapons of mass destruction will depend, to a considerable extent, on domestic political and economic developments. Although Iran's leaders clearly are eager to bolster its regional power status, they may be hampered by continued economic difficulties brought about by a steady decline in oil revenues and internal disputes over ideological and religious issues. Popular discontent over prevailing social and economic conditions may also undermine the leadership's regional aspirations.[50] If current policies remain in force, however, Iran may be headed toward a new round of clashes with the United States.

Iraq

Operation Desert Storm and subsequent disarmament measures imposed by the United Nations have largely destroyed Iraq's capacity to manufacture weapons of mass destruction, and have limited its ability to project military power into adjoining territories. Nevertheless, Iraq retains a sizeable military establishment, and U.S. intelligence officials believe it has hidden some of its chemical equipment and ballistic missiles from U.N. inspectors (although no evidence of this has yet been produced).[51] For these reason, Iraq is still viewed by U.S. military officials as a significant military threat.

At the conclusion of the Persian Gulf conflict, U.S. officials reported that a substantial proportion of Iraq's major combat equipment—some 3,800 tanks, 1,450 armored personnel carriers (APCs), 2,900 artillery pieces, and 184 combat planes—had been destroyed or captured by allied forces.[52] The war also destroyed many Iraqi combat units, reducing total armed strength by about half (to some 400,000 active-duty troops). Despite this, the Iraqi army still claims 30 combat divisions and large numbers of modern weapons, including some 2,300 tanks, 2,000 APCs, and 1,500 artillery pieces.[53] Much of this force is tied down within Iraq, fighting Kurdish and Shiite insurgents and protecting Saddam Hussein and his close associates from other potential foes, but it could be redeployed at some future date for military operations against neighboring states.

While Iraq is allowed to maintain conventionally armed military forces under the terms of the U.N.–imposed cease-fire of April 1991, it is not allowed to possess nuclear, chemical, or biological weapons, or any ballistic missiles of more than 150-kilometer range.[54] To enforce this ban, the Security Council established the U.N. Special Commission (UNSCOM), and empowered it to destroy all weapons of mass destruction that had survived the war. Despite periodic harassment by Iraqi officials, UNSCOM has succeeded in locating many Iraqi WMD production sites and destroying much of the weaponry remaining in Iraqi hands.[55] However, Iraq retains the scientific and technical manpower used in its weapons programs, along with any research and production technology that may have been hidden prior to the deployment of U.N. inspection teams. Thus, while Iraq poses no immediate proliferation threat, it will be subjected to close monitoring by U.S. intelligence analysts for years to come.[56]

Should such monitoring operations detect any sign of secret efforts by Iraq to rebuild their WMD capabilities, the United States almost certainly will engage in military strikes to halt these efforts. In a demonstration of what Baghdad might expect in this regard, then President Bush ordered a barrage of some 45 Tomahawk cruise missiles against the Zaafaniyah nuclear weapons plant in early 1993 when Iraqi officials attempted to impede UNSCOM's activities.[57] Any move by Iraq to again threaten Kuwait with invasion would also, of course, prompt a U.S. military response, as occurred in October 1994. "We will not allow Saddam Hussein to defy the will of the United States and the international community," President Clinton declared on October 10, 1994.[58]

Libya

Ruled since 1969 by Colonel Muammar el-Qaddafi, Libya has clashed frequently with the United States over a range of political issues, especially its support for terrorist groups and other anti-Western forces. In 1986, U.S. aircraft struck Qaddafi's living quarters in Tripoli, along with key government facilities, in retaliation for alleged Libyan involvement in terrorist attacks against U.S. citizens in Europe. Following the 1986 raid, Qaddafi seemed to adopt a more accommodating stance, backing away from his support of terrorist groups. However, U.S. officials have charged Libya with continuing involvement in terrorist activities, including the December 1988 bombing of Pan Am Flight 103 over Lockerbie, Scotland. Libya has been subjected to U.N.–imposed economic sanctions since April 1992 for its refusal to permit the extradition to Scotland of the two Libyan security agents named as defendants in the Lockerbie attack.[59]

The U.N. sanctions and growing economic difficulties within Libya have largely prevented Colonel Qaddafi from engaging in the foreign intrigues and adventurism. After years of meddling in Chad's politics (often through the dispatch of Libyan forces), Qaddafi agreed to submit Libya's claim to the "Aouzou strip" of northern Chad to international adjudication. (This territory was subsequently awarded to Chad by the World Court.) Qaddafi also mended his relations with other Arab leaders, including President Mubarak of Egypt. But the Libyan leader has always sought an elevated role on the world stage, and so future intrigues of one sort or another cannot be ruled out.[60]

Qaddafi is limited in what he can accomplish by the relatively small size of Libya's armed forces—some 70,000 active troops, with perhaps 40,000 in reserve. To compensate for his troops' inferiority in numbers, however, Qaddafi has provided them with vast quantities of modern weapons, mostly of Soviet or Russian manufacture. His army, with only 40,000 soldiers, possesses some 2,300 tanks (with another 1,200 in storage), an unusually large number for a force that size (the French army, with 260,000 troops, has half as many tanks). Similarly, Libya's small Air Force boasts 409 combat aircraft, including many late-model MiG fighters.[61] It is not known how effectively Libyan personnel can operate all this equipment— the Air Force, for instance, often relies on non-Libyan pilots—but the possession of so much modern weaponry endows the military with an offensive capacity far out of proportion to its actual size.

Of greater concern to U.S. strategists is Libya's pursuit of nuclear and chemical munitions. Arguing that the Arab powers needed a nuclear capability to counter that possessed by Israel, Qaddafi sought throughout the 1970s and 1980s to acquire sensitive nuclear technology from such states as Argentina, Belgium, Brazil, India, Pakistan, and the Soviet Union. Despite Libya's professed willingness to commit vast funds to these efforts, opposition by the United States and considerable wariness on the part of prospective suppliers resulted in few significant transfers of technology taking place.[62]

Having attained little in the nuclear area, Qaddafi apparently decided in the mid-1980s to seek a significant chemical warfare capability. In 1988, Libya was discovered to be constructing (with assistance from a West German chemical firm) a large CW plant at Rabta, some forty miles south of Tripoli. By 1992, production at Rabta had reached an estimated 100 tons of lethal CW agents (presumably mustard gas) per year. Production there was later suspended for reasons that are not altogether clear, but a second, underground CW plant reportedly is being built at Tarhunah.[63] The Libyans also possess a supply of Scud-B missiles, and are believed to be cooperating with Syria and North Korea in the development of more capable Scud variants.[64]

As in the case of North Korea, Libya's fate is very much tied up in the fortunes of its leader. Although Colonel Qaddafi undoubtedly enjoys the support of some Libyans, the depth of that support is unknown, and it may erode if Libya becomes more isolated in the international community. Qaddafi has been the target of several military revolts, most recently in 1993.[65] It is impossible to determine what impact a successful coup against Qaddafi would have on Libya's foreign policy; so long as he remains in power, however, Libya undoubtedly will continue to be seen as a rogue state by U.S. military officials.

Syria

The Syrian Arab Republic, ruled since 1970 by General Hafez al-Assad, continues to be viewed with distrust in Washington despite its active involvement in the anti-Iraq coalition and its subsequent participation in U.S.–sponsored Middle Eastern peace talks. This distrust stems from several factors: Syria's clashes with Israel in 1967, 1973, and 1982, and its continuing anti-Israeli military posture; Assad's support for radical Palestinian organizations and other groups linked by the U.S. government to terrorist activities; and Syrian efforts to acquire weapons of mass destruction. So long as some combination of these factors remains, Syria will be seen as a rogue state by U.S. military officials, no matter how cordial the formal relations between Washington and Damascus.[66]

Syria's military units have been battered repeatedly by the Israelis, most recently in 1982, but they were lavishly reequipped with modern Soviet weapons after each of these occasions, and still constitute one of the most powerful forces in the Middle East. As of 1994, the Syrian military numbered 408,000 regulars and 400,000 reserves. Its army possessed some 4,500 tanks, making it the sixth largest tank force in the world (after Russia, the United States, China, Turkey, and Ukraine, in that order), along with large numbers of APCs, multiple-rocket launchers, and artillery pieces. Syria's air force, decimated in the 1982 clash with Israel, has since been reequipped with late-model MiG and Sukhoi fighters.[67]

Although its efforts in the WMD area have not attracted as much attention as those of the other nominal rogues, Syria has long sought a strategic deterrent to Israel's nuclear and chemical capabilities. Lacking the infrastructure for a nuclear weapons program, Assad has concentrated on the development of chemical weapons and ballistic missile delivery systems. The Syrians are thought to have been able to produce chemical weapons in facilities evidently constructed with the assistance of West German companies since the mid-1980s, and reportedly have stockpiled large quantities of mustard gas and the nerve agents Sarin and Tabun.[68] Syria is also thought to have produced CW warheads for its large arsenal of Scud missiles (many of which were acquired from North Korea), thereby exposing all of Israel to the threat of chemical attack.[69]

Of all the "rogues," Syria appears the most likely to improve its relations with the United States. By agreeing to negotiate with Israel over the future status of the Golan Heights (Syrian territory captured by the Israelis during the 1967 war) and by curbing the operations of some of the terrorist groups based on its territory, Syria has earned U.S. officials' qualified approval.[70] Should Syria sign a peace accord with Israel and otherwise move to satisfy American security concerns, it may be dropped from the Pentagon's informal list of rogues; if, however, President Assad (or his successor) pursues a more hardline position toward Israel and accelerates Syria's proliferation activities, Washington will most likely adopt a more hostile stance toward Damascus and pursue tougher nonproliferation measures.

PROSPECTIVE ROGUES

Like the rogues, the seven prospective rogues—China, Egypt, India, Pakistan, South Korea, Taiwan, and Turkey—have all sought to become more self-sufficient in military terms, building large military establishments and/or acquiring the capacity to produce weapons of mass destruction. Five of these states—China, India, Pakistan, South Korea, and Taiwan—either possess or have attempted to manufacture nuclear weapons, and all but Turkey are believed to possess chemical weapons (or the capacity to produce them). All, moreover, have begun to produce advanced conventional weapons in their own factories.[71] What makes them especially worthy of attention, from the Pentagon's point of view, is that each has the potential to play a hegemonic role in its region; and each, should its leadership or political orientation change, might enter into an adversarial relationship with the United States.

Some of these potential rogues have been close allies of the United States for a long time, and continue to support U.S. positions on most international issues; others have a history of conflict with the United States, and only support American positions when it is to their immediate advantage. In the future, U.S. relations with these countries will be shaped by a variety of considerations, including the status of economic and trade relations; human rights issues, development policies; and their voting patterns at the United Nations and other international bodies. The profiles that follow will concentrate on the factors of greatest concern to the Department of Defense— the development of weapons of mass destruction and ballistic missile systems for their delivery, and the possibility that present governments will be taken over by more radical forces.

China

Of the seven prospective rogues, China is the most likely to slide one day into the military's rogue category. It has vigorously opposed the United States in the past, directly aiding America's adversaries in Korea (where one million Chinese "volunteers" participated in attacks on U.S. forces) and Vietnam. Although Sino-American relations have been relatively friendly since the Nixon era, China still poses a significant military threat to Taiwan, and Beijing often clashes with Washington on issues of trade, human rights, and proliferation. China, however, has also emerged as a major trading partner of the United States, accounting for a significant share of America's overseas commerce.[72]

Three aspects of Chinese are especially worrisome to U.S. officials: the continuing buildup of China's strategic nuclear capabilities; the expansion of China's power projection capabilities; and China's suspected role as a supplier of nuclear and missile technology to other states, including several of the rogues.

Although China's strategic nuclear capabilities—consisting of several dozen intercontinental and intermediate-range ballistic missiles and one missile-carrying submarine—are quite limited when compared to those of Russia, Britain, or France, they represent the only possible direct threat to continental North America that any potential rogue power may pose for the foreseeable future.[73] The Chinese are also developing several new ballistic missiles, and are building additional ballistic missile submarines; at the same time, they continue to conduct underground nuclear weapons tests at their Lop Nor test site, frustrating international efforts to impose a moratorium on nuclear testing.[74]

The buildup of China's power projection capabilities has been under way since 1985, when the Central Military Commission directed the People Liberation Army (PLA) to shift its primary strategic focus from preparation for an all-out war with the Soviet Union to readiness for limited conflicts on China's periphery.[75] In line with this shift, Beijing reduced the size of the PLA from four to three million soldiers, while bolstering its air, naval, and amphibious assault capabilities.[76] The PLA has also taken advantage of Russia's economic problems to purchase new planes, guns, and missiles at cut-rate prices.[77] Many of these new systems are believed to be aimed at China's neighbors to the South, several of which (including Malaysia, Taiwan, and Vietnam) have contested China's claim to ownership of the Paracel and Spratly island groups, large archipelagos in the South China Sea that are believed to sit astride potentially vast oil reserves.[78]

Of particular concern to U.S. military officials are China's sales of nuclear and chemical weapons technology to emerging powers in Asia and Africa. In an effort to gain hard currency for its military modernization programs, China has become a major supplier of research reactors and other nuclear systems to Algeria, Iran, Pakistan, and Syria.[79] Chinese officials insist that these sales are intended for civilian purposes only, but many have been shrouded in secrecy and associated with facilities suspected of possessing a military function (such as the Iranian nuclear research facility at Isfahan). The Chinese are also suspected of exporting chemical weapons precursors (chemical compounds used in the manufacture of chemical weapons) to Iran and Syria.[80]

In addition, China has become a major supplier of missiles and missile technology to the Middle East and Southwest Asia, providing the HY-2 "Silkworm" to Iraq and Iran (which used them in 1987 in attacks on Kuwait and on U.S.–flagged Kuwaiti ships in the Persian Gulf), the CSS-2 intermediate-range ballistic missile to Saudi Arabia, and parts for the M-11 mobile missile to Pakistan.[81] The Chinese are also believed to have provided Iran and Syria with production technology and components for the solid-propellent M-9 missile, a far more accurate and reliable weapon than the Scud-Bs and -Cs now in the arsenals of these countries.[82] These sales provoked considerable alarm in Washington, and, in August 1993, the Clinton administration imposed limited trade sanctions on Beijing for alleged violations of the Missile Technology Control Regime (MTCR).[83] China has since pledged to respect the MTCR, but doubts remain about its commitment to arms export restraint.[84]

As of this writing, China's relations with the United States appear to be at a turning point. By improving its human rights performance and curbing its sales of nuclear, chemical, and missile technology, Beijing could enjoy relatively "normal" relations with Washington. President Clinton's May 1994 decision to renew China's most-favored-nation trading status without conditions was a significant step in this direction. The Clinton administration also agreed to lift certain trade sanctions on China in return for a pledge by Beijing to suspend its sales of missile technology to other Third World countries.[85] On the other hand, if Chinese leaders adopt a more combative stance, they will strengthen the hand of those in the U.S. military who view China as a potential rogue superpower. How this plays itself out in the years ahead will depend, in part, on the outcome of the succession struggle expected to follow the death of Deng Xiaoping, the aging Communist Party official who has dominated Chinese politics for nearly twenty years.

Egypt

Egypt, like China, once was allied with the Soviet Union. Disappointed with the level of Soviet aid before and during the 1973 Arab-Israeli conflict, however, it revoked its Treaty of Friendship with Moscow and shifted its allegiance to the West. Since then, the United States has served as Egypt's principal supplier of arms and military assistance, providing some $16.4 billion worth of weaponry between 1975 and 1992.[86] Washington's ties with Cairo were further strengthened in August 1990, when Egypt agreed to provide 35,000 troops to the anti-Iraq Coalition army.

Despite its recent history of warm relations with the United States, Cairo has periodically clashed with Washington over sensitive security issues. In the mid-1980s, for instance, Egypt collaborated with Argentina and Iraq in the development of the Condor-II ballistic missile. The Condor program was canceled in 1990 under pressure from the United States, but not before Egypt had acquired considerable technology that could be applied to other missile programs.[87] In 1988, moreover, the United States charged two Egyptian military officers with conspiring to smuggle 432 pounds of carbon-carbon fiber (a material used in missile nosecones) to Egypt, presumably for use in the Condor or one of its successors.[88] While not considered serious enough to produce a breach in U.S.–Egyptian relations, these incidents have caused American intelligence officials to keep a close eye on proliferation activities in Egypt.

Proliferation aside, Washington's greatest worry is that Egypt's existing, pro–U.S. government will be toppled by Muslim fundamentalists with close ties to the clerical rulers of Iran and Sudan. Although President Hosni Mubarak remains in control of the army and the government, fundamentalist groups appear to be gaining strength in many parts of the country. With the Egyptian economy in tatters and the government accused of widespread corruption, militant Muslim forces are likely to pose an increasing threat to social and political stability.[89]

Were Egypt to be taken over by the fundamentalists or political factions loyal to their cause, it is likely to be reclassified as a rogue state by U.S. military analysts. In this capacity, Egypt might prove a formidable regional adversary. It is the most populous state of the Arab world (with a population of 55 million people) and a major center of Islamic culture. With 430,000 soldiers, its military is one of the largest in the region (dwarfed only by Iran's and Turkey's), and its army is one of the best equipped. Egypt is also thought to possess a large supply of chemical weapons, and, as noted above, has engaged in the development of ballistic missiles.[90]

India

Since its founding as an independent state in 1947, India has sought to acquire sufficient military strength to dominate the Indian Ocean area and to deter military intervention by the great powers. The Indian military, with 1.3 million active-duty troops, is the fourth largest in the world (after China, Russia, and the United States), and has developed both nuclear weapons and the missiles to deliver them.[91] Because of this, U.S. analysts worry about a possible future takeover of the government—whether through electoral or other means—by anti-Western forces or ultranationalistic military officers. U.S. officials also fear that a future clash with Pakistan or China might result in a regional nuclear war.

Relations between the United States and India have fluctuated from year to year. Washington chose to ally with Pakistan during the Cold War period (to secure sites for secret electronic listening posts and, after 1980, to support the anti-Soviet insurgency in Afghanistan), prompting India to align itself with the Soviet Union. India's close ties with Moscow—the two signed a Treaty of Friendship in 1971—gained New Delhi substantial infusions of military aid and technology from the Soviet Union, including the means to produce advanced tanks and planes. But India has never severed its ties with the West and, after the collapse of the Soviet Union, moved to improve its relations with the United States.[92]

Although Washington has welcomed India's new stance, U.S. officials remain concerned about its long-range nuclear intentions. India reportedly began work on nuclear weapons in the mid-1960s, building several "unsafeguarded" reactors (reactors that are not subjected to IAEA inspections) and developing the technology to separate plutonium from spent reactor fuel. In May 1974, Indian scientists conducted what they termed a "peaceful nuclear explosion," viewed by most Western analysts as a test of a functioning nuclear weapon. Since then, India has continued to expand its nuclear infrastructure and its stockpile of weapons-grade plutonium. By the early 1990s, it was believed to possess sufficient plutonium for 50–100 nuclear devices. American analysts do not know whether this plutonium has actually been incorporated into combat-ready weapons systems, but many suspect that India has acquired the know-how and materials to do so.[93] Moreover, India has developed two missiles believed capable of delivering nuclear warheads, the 150-mile-range *Prithvi* and the 1,500-mile-range *Agni*.[94]

The U.S. government periodically has condemned India's pursuit of nuclear weapons, but it has also allowed some transfers of high-tech equipment to India's nuclear and aerospace industries. Nonproliferation efforts were stepped up in 1990, when American intelligence analysts learned that both India and Pakistan might be prepared to employ nuclear weapons in their dispute over the divided territory of Kashmir.[95] New Delhi, however, continued to rebuff U.S. demands that it sign the Nuclear Non-proliferation Treaty or engage in nuclear arms control talks with Pakistan.[96] Washington also objected to India's ballistic missile development program, and in 1992 banned exports to the Indian Space Research Organization (which is believed to be diverting Russian space technology to India's ballistic missile program in violation of the Missile Technology Control Regime).[97]

Washington's concern over the rise of ultra-nationalist Hindu fundamentalism has been fueled by intensified sectarian violence and the growing popularity of the fundamentalist Bharatiya Janata Party (BJP). The BJP has made steady gains in the Indian parliament, winning 88 seats in the 1991 election (double its performance in the 1989 election) and acquiring the status of a major opposition party. In 1992, moreover, a Hindu assault on a sixteenth-century Muslim mosque at Ayodhya—believed by Hindus to have been built on the site of Rama's birthplace—produced a major government crisis, and subsequent Hindu-Muslim fighting has further eroded the authority of the ruling Congress (I) Party.[98] The BJP has opposed any compromise on the status of Kashmir and has called openly for the development of nuclear weapons,[99] so any future gains by the party would undoubtedly produce considerable alarm in Washington.

Pakistan

Until fairly recently, Pakistan maintained close military ties with the United States, and generally followed Washington's lead on key policy issues. It allowed the United States to set up anti-Soviet electronic listening posts on its territory and aided U.S. efforts to assist the Afghan rebels (*mujahideen*) in their struggle against Soviet occupation forces. Because of its strategic location and friendly stance, Pakistan has been a major beneficiary of U.S. military aid, receiving some $2.9 billion in grants and loans between 1950 and 1990.[100] In October 1990, however, the flow of aid to Pakistan was cut off. The reason for this move was Pakistan's continued development of nuclear weapons, in defiance of U.S. nonproliferation policy.

Pakistan began to develop a nuclear weapons capability following its crushing defeat in the 1971 Indo-Pakistani war and the establishment of Bangladesh (until then a part of Pakistan) as an independent state. Pakistani leaders, thwarted in their efforts to obtain a plutonium reprocessing facility from France, decided to pursue an alternative route to nuclear weapons—the use of high-speed centrifuges to produce highly enriched uranium. Using technology illicitly acquired from Western Europe, they established an enrichment facility at Kuhata and, in 1986, began to produce weapons-grade material.[101]

By all accounts, the Reagan administration possessed sufficient intelligence on the Pakistani nuclear effort to conclude that Islamabad had achieved its goal—the production of deliverable weapons—by 1986 or 1987. The White House, however, never passed this information on to Congress: in accordance with American nonproliferation statues, it would have triggered an automatic cutoff of U.S. aid to Pakistan—a move that Reagan was determined to prevent, as it would have jeopardized the secret U.S. effort to aid the Afghan *mujahideen*. Accordingly, the White House, under both Reagan and Bush, repeatedly "certified" to Congress that Islamabad did *not* possess a functioning nuclear device, thereby permitting the continuation of U.S. military assistance. Only in 1990, when the Pakistanis were believed to possess the materials and components for six to ten nuclear weapons, did President Bush decide to withhold such certification and thereby stop the flow of military aid.[102]

Since 1990, the United States and Pakistan have repeatedly clashed over nuclear proliferation. Although they deny that Pakistan possesses nuclear weapons, government officials, including Prime Minister Benazir Bhutto, have adamantly refused to suspend Pakistan's nuclear program.[103] A 1994 U.S. proposal that Pakistan freeze its nuclear arsenal at current levels in return for a resumption of U.S. aid was rejected by Islamabad because the proposal did not call for a similar cap on the Indian nuclear arsenal.[104] Meanwhile, Islamabad has strengthened its military ties with China, acquiring ballistic missile technology (including launchers and components for China's mobile M-11 missile) and know-how for the production of tanks and military aircraft.[105]

South Korea

Like Israel and Taiwan, South Korea has been a close ally of the United States for many years. Large numbers of U.S. troops have been stationed there ever since the 1950–53 Korean War, and the United States has also provided Seoul with considerable military assistance, amounting to some $7.8 billion in loans and grants by 1992.[106] As its economy has expanded, South Korea has become less dependent on U.S. aid, and has used its own funds to purchase advanced European and American arms. Today, South Korea boasts one of the largest and best-equipped military forces in Asia.[107]

Although U.S. analysts generally assume that South Korea will be a reliable American ally for many years to come, concerns remain that Seoul will resume its pursuit of nuclear weapons, and that South Korea will eventually absorb the North (with its military capabilities intact) and pursue a more independent regional role.

South Korea reportedly began work on nuclear weapons in the early 1970s, when the United States announced plans to diminish its military presence in Asia. Upon learning of the South Korean nuclear program, Washington pressured Seoul to abandon its weapons effort and to sign the Non-Proliferation Treaty (which it did in 1975). There is no evidence that Seoul has violated the NPT in any significant way, but some proliferation specialists believe that weapons-related research of some sort continued at least into the late 1970s, and perhaps much later.[108] South Korea has also developed a large civilian nuclear industry and has acquired much "dual use" technology that might be used in the manufacture of nuclear weapons.[109] For this reason, recent reports that South Korean leaders have begun to speak again of the need for an indigenous nuclear weapons capability—both to offset nuclear developments in North Korea and as a hedge against any future efforts by Japan to acquire such weapons—have generated concern among arms control experts.[110]

The future of U.S.–South Korean relations ultimately will hinge on the fate of North Korea and the prospects for North-South unification. A North Korean invasion of the South would undoubtedly result in American intervention on the side of the South and a U.S.–led drive to topple the North Korean regime, producing a merger through force. A merger might also occur were the succession process in North Korea to be followed by the rise of reform-minded military leaders who sought peaceful and voluntary unification with the South. In either case, the existing South Korean government might wind up in possession of a unified state with considerable military capabilities, producing much concern in Washington.

Taiwan

Taiwan—officially known as the Republic of China (RoC)—has long enjoyed friendly relations with the United States, and continues to receive much of its military equipment from American firms. In 1955, when it appeared that Communist China might use military force to crush the Nationalist (Kuomintang) government on Taiwan, the United States deployed its Seventh Fleet in the Formosa Strait, and threatened to attack China with nuclear weapons. When U.S. relations with mainland China improved following President Nixon's historic 1972 visit to Beijing, Washington downgraded its political and military ties with Taiwan. Although the United States no longer maintains formal diplomatic relations with Taiwan, Washington retains a quasi-embassy in the capital city of Taipei, and continues to supply the Taiwanese with advanced military hardware.

Although the threat of an invasion from the mainland has greatly diminished, Taiwan continues to maintain a large, well-equipped military establishment.[111] With abundant foreign exchange reserves, the Taiwanese have spent billions of dollars on the international weapons market for a wide variety of modern arms, including 150 F-16 fighters, 60 Mirage 2000-5 multirole aircraft, 6 French La-Fayette-class frigates, and 7 batteries of Patriot missiles.[112] The RoC has also embarked on a major drive to become self-sufficient in the production of basic combat systems, and now produces its own aircraft, ships, missiles, and tanks.[113]

Taiwan has also sought to develop an independent nuclear weapons capability. Its nuclear efforts were halted owing to U.S. pressure in the 1950s and again in the 1980s, but not before the Taiwanese had begun construction of a small-scale plutonium extraction unit.[114] At present, Taiwan is not known to be engaged in the full-scale development of nuclear weapons, but there are occasional reports from Taipei of secret research on nuclear projects with possible military applications.[115] The Taiwanese are also reported to have produced chemical weapons and long-range ballistic missiles.[116]

As South Korea's future is highly dependent on developments in North Korea, so Taiwan's is closely tied to developments in mainland China. Trade between Taiwan and China is growing rapidly, and it is possible that a new, post-Deng leadership in Beijing will seek an accommodation with Taipei. It is also possible that China will turn in a more hostile direction, spurring renewed Taiwanese involvement in illicit proliferation activities.

Turkey

Turkey is a member of NATO and a long-term ally of the United States. However, with the end of the Cold War and the subsequent dissolution of Yugoslavia and the Soviet Union, Turkey has sought to play a more independent role in its foreign relations, and at some times has clashed with Washington over key regional issues. Although Ankara is not known to possess (or to be seeking) weapons of mass destruction, it maintains a very large military establishment, and has developed an extensive military-industrial complex.

With a total active strength of 480,000 and a reserve strength of 1.1 million soldiers, the Turkish military is the largest in Europe (apart from Russia's) and the largest in the Middle East. Although its weaponry is not, for the most part, as modern as that possessed by Israel and the major European powers, Turkey does boast large numbers of tanks, aircraft, artillery, and missiles.[117] Moreover, with the aid of Germany and the United States, Turkey has been replacing many of its older weapons with more advanced and capable systems.[118] Even more significant, Turkey is building up its own arms manufacturing capabilities using technology imported from the United States and Western Europe, and is producing a wide variety of combat systems (including F-16 aircraft) under license.[119] If Ankara's current plans are realized, Turkey will be self-sufficient in the production of most basic combat systems by the early twenty-first century.[120]

During Operation Desert Storm, Turkey provided critical support to Coalition forces by allowing allied aircraft to attack Iraq from NATO bases on its territory. More recently, however, Turkish leaders have criticized the West's failure to stop Serbian aggression against the Muslim population of Bosnia, and have threatened to reduce U.S. access to Turkish military facilities.[121] Turkey has also generated some concern in Washington by siding with Azerbaijan in the conflict with Armenia over the former Soviet territory of Nagorno Karabakh, and by threatening to go to war with Greece over Athens' announced intention of extending the offshore territorial waters of its islands in the Aegean Sea.[122] Although closely aligned with the West, Turkey could be tempted in the years ahead to pursue a hegemonic role in the Middle East—a stance that could lead to clashes with the United States over a number of critical security interests.

OTHER CANDIDATES

At present, the five rogues and seven prospective rogues discussed above constitute the most likely candidates for "Iraqs of the future" in the eyes of U.S. military and intelligence officials. However, on the basis of past proliferation activities or unpredictable future developments, a number of other countries might become potential candidates. Included in this group are two countries that once pursued nuclear weapons and conceivably might do so again: Argentina and Brazil.

Both Argentina and Brazil launched nuclear arms development

programs in the 1970s, when each was under military rule and sought to assert its status as a major regional power.[123] These weapons programs were largely discontinued in the late 1980s, when Argentina and Brazil were restored to civilian rule, and the two countries have since agreed to open their nuclear facilities to bilateral inspection (following procedures established by the International Atomic Energy Agency).[124] At present, both countries face severe economic problems, and are not likely to divert scarce national resources to the expansion of their military capabilities. Should either or both of these countries again fall under military rule, however, it is possible that future leaders could seek to restart their nuclear weapons programs.

The list of future candidates for rogue state status must also include a number of other Third World countries with the potential to amass significant military power in the twenty-first century, including Mexico and Indonesia, both of which possess large populations and growing industrial bases. Mexico thus far has declined to convert its industrial strength into military power (in part, out of concern that this would provoke a strong negative response from Washington), and shows no signs of wanting to do so in the future. Indonesia, however, has embarked on an ambitious program of military industrialization, establishing factories for the production of helicopters, military aircraft, and warships, and appears poised to become a major regional power in the next century.[125]

Finally, the list of candidate rogues would have to include some of the remnants of the once-mighty communist bloc, including Cuba, Serbia, and the former republics of the Soviet Union. Indeed, Cuba and Serbia are often mentioned by military officials as "rogue" or "outlaw" states, and as possible future military foes. But neither of these countries possesses weapons of mass destruction, or is in any position to threaten fundamental U.S. interests in even the most localized sense.

As for the former republics of the USSR, most are too weak and internally divided to represent a military threat to any states not part of the former Soviet Union. Only Russia and Ukraine possess sufficient military potential to constitute such a threat, and Ukraine is likely to preserve what strength it has as a hedge against Russian attack. That leaves Russia as a potential adversary. While the rise of radical nationalist forces there has produced considerable alarm in Washington (as well as, undoubtedly, a certain yearning on the part of those who would welcome a return to a more familiar superpower rivalry with a known and identifiable enemy), most U.S. leaders hope to work with Moscow in promoting domestic reform and the downsizing of its military. Should these efforts fail, the United States and Russia could again become mortal enemies; but, were this to occur, Washington would find itself in an entirely new strategic environment, and the logic of the Bottom-Up Review would cease to have any relevance.

IN THE FINAL ANALYSIS

In accordance with the Pentagon's 1993 Bottom-Up Review, the U.S. military establishment is being configured to fight two major regional conflicts simultaneously, each of which is assumed to entail combat with one of the "rogues" or "prospective rogues" discussed above. But just how realistic is this scenario? Are there, in fact, two major regional powers that fit the Pentagon's planning model? The Department of Defense has never answered these questions adequately, despite their crucial importance to its entire post–Cold War strategic equation.

According to the Bottom-Up Review, "potential military aggressors" of the type that U.S. forces will be trained and equipped to fight should possess the following military capabilities:[126]

- 400,000–750,000 active military personnel
- 2,000–3,000 tanks
- 500–1,000 combat aircraft
- 100–200 naval vessels, and up to 50 submarines
- 100–1,000 Scud-type ballistic missiles

In addition, the Pentagon scenario assumes that these states possess (or seek to possess) weapons of mass destruction, and that the intended victims of their aggressive designs are relatively weak countries like Kuwait with close ties to the United States.

Using this model, a very specific set of conditions must be satisfied for the Pentagon's basic scenario to be credible. As evident from Table 5.2, however, only two of the five rogues—North Korea and Syria—come close to satisfying the model's criteria. Both of these countries possess large military forces plus ample stocks of tanks and aircraft, along with significant numbers of Scud missiles. But neither country satisfies the second major test, in that the likely targets of their aggression—South Korea and Israel—are not weak and defenseless states, but powerful, even potentially dominant actors on their own. Israel has repeatedly demonstrated its ability to defeat Syrian forces; South Korea is believed to enjoy technological superiority over the North. In any conflict involving North Korea and/or Syria, then, the bulk of the fighting would be performed by U.S. allies, not by the United States.[127]

The other rogues in this group—Iran, Iraq, and Libya—fail the Pentagon test on several grounds. Iran and Iraq do possess fairly large military forces, but their stockpiles of tanks, artillery, and aircraft have been severely depleted by warfare, and their weak economies put a distinct limit on whatever military buildups they might plan. Libya has a large number of tanks and aircraft, but a very small military force (its army numbers only 40,000 active-duty soldiers, less than one-seventh the number in Egypt's army). In addition, these countries face hostile or potentially hostile neighbors that possess equal or superior military capabilities (Iraq, Pakistan, and Turkey for Iran; Iran, Syria, and Turkey for Iraq; and Egypt for Libya), restricting further their opportunities for aggressive action.

TABLE 5.2
MILITARY CAPABILITIES OF POTENTIAL ADVERSARIES

POTENTIAL ADVERSARY	TOTAL TROOPS	TOTAL TANKS	COMBAT PLANES	MAJOR SURFACE VESSELS (SUBS)	SCUD MISSILE OR EQUIVALENT
"Rogues"					
Iran	473,000	700	293	8 (2)	Yes
Iraq	382,500	2,200	300?	1	No*
Libya	70,000	2,300**	409**	3 (5)	Yes
N. Korea	1,127,000	3,700	730	3 (25)	Yes
Syria	408,000	4,500	639	2 (3)	Yes
"Prospective rogues"					
China	3,030,000	7,500+	5,000	56 (45)	Yes
Egypt	430,000	3,167	546	5 (2)	Yes
India	1,265,000	3,400	707	24 (15)	Yes
Pakistan	577,000	1,890	393	14 (3)	u.d.
S. Korea	633,000	1,800	445	38 (4)	Yes
Taiwan	442,000	309	484	33 (4)	Yes
Turkey	480,000	4,835	539	19 (15)	No

u.d. = under development
* Iraqi missiles and weapons of mass destruction are being destroyed in accordance with U.N. Security Council Resolution 687.
** Many Libyan tanks and planes are in storage and believed to be of little utility

Source: International Institute for Strategic Studies, *The Military Balance 1993–1994* (for non-nuclear munitions); additional data from sources cited in Chapter 6.

It is hard to believe that any of these states would deliberately provoke American intervention by attacking a close ally of the United States. None could anticipate an easy victory over the intended targets of their aggressive designs, and none possesses sufficient strength to defeat the United States in armed combat. Moreover, no combination of these states could conceivably defeat the United States and its allies. While one or more of these powers might stumble into a confrontation with Washington through accident or misadventure, it is very hard to imagine that any of them, whether singly or in pairs, would *choose* to provoke such an encounter.

Turning now to the prospective rogues, we find six that satisfy the Pentagon's criteria in terms of their net military capabilities: China, Egypt, India, Pakistan, South Korea, and Turkey. Most of these states also border on weaker states that they might someday be tempted to invade: China faces Burma, Laos, Mongolia, and Vietnam; Egypt faces Libya and Sudan; India faces Bangladesh, Burma, Nepal, and Sri Lanka; Pakistan faces Afghanistan; and Turkey faces Armenia and Bulgaria. However, none of these potentially endangered nations is a close ally of the United States or harbors "vital interests" of the sort found in Kuwait. If any of them were to be invaded, it is highly unlikely that Washington would come to their defense. If, on the other hand, any of the prospective rogues were to invade neighbors allied to the United States—Taiwan in the case of China, Israel in the case of Egypt, Pakistan in the case of India, or Greece in the case of Turkey—they face rather formidable adversaries, not weak countries of the sort envisioned by the Pentagon model. Even if the current leaders of these states were to be replaced by others considered less friendly to Washington, there is no reason to assume that they would read the military equation significantly differently from those now in power.

In analyzing the military capabilities of rogues and prospective rogues, we must also ask how the acquisition of weapons of mass destruction, either now or in the future, might alter the strategic equation. Certainly, a potential adversary's possession of nuclear weapons would induce great caution on the part of U.S. leaders, were American troops to be involved in a military encounter with that state. However, none of the "rogues" now possesses nuclear weapons, and only North Korea is likely to acquire such weapons in the near future (and no more than a few of them). Even if they did employ chemical weapons (or, in the case of North Korea, nuclear weapons), they could neither defeat the United States in war nor prevent catastrophic retaliation. It is highly unlikely, therefore, that they would invite such devastation through the deliberate use of weapons of mass destruction. Of course, such weapons might be used in an act of desperation, but they would not alter the basic strategic equation in any encounter with the United States and its closest allies.

The situation is a bit different in the case of several of the prospective rogues, which possess significant arsenals of nuclear and/or chemical weapons. However, only one of these states, China, has the ability to reach North America with nuclear-armed intercontinental ballistic missiles (of which it possesses only a handful), and India is the only other country in this group that is likely to acquire such a capability in the next ten to twenty years.[128] It is almost impossible, then, to imagine a realistic scenario for a direct attack on the United States in the coming decades. And even if any of these countries were to use WMD in attacks on U.S. allies or any U.S. forces deployed in the region, they could not avert defeat by the United States no matter how much death and destruction they produced. American power is so vast and resilient that no imaginable attack by any of these countries could impair the United States' ability to inflict extreme punishment on the perpetrator of such extreme folly.

—

WHERE, THEN, DOES all of this leave us? While it is certainly true that the countries viewed as hypothetical enemies by the Department of Defense possess significant military capabilities, it is very difficult to find *any* state that conceivably might benefit from an armed encounter with the United States or its allies. No doubt, various regimes and revolutionary groups will cross swords with U.S. forces in the years ahead, if only in the course of peacekeeping or peace enforcement missions of the sort conducted in Bosnia and Somalia; but the prospect of two major regional powers provoking a war with the United States, as envisioned by the Bottom-Up Review, appears very dim indeed.[129]

If the actual threat environment of the post–Cold War era fails to conform to the alarmist imagery of the Rogue Doctrine, this is only to be expected from a posture that was created in response to domestic budgetary considerations rather than any calculus of external dangers. The "rogue state" model, while undeniably effective in mobilizing Congressional support for a two-war military capability, bears little resemblance to the various countries that U.S. forces supposedly are expected to fight.

What made the rogue state threat look far more plausible than it otherwise might was the spread of weapons of mass destruction to prospective adversaries in the Third World. Since 1990, the U.S. military has enthusiastically cited the dangers of nuclear, chemical, and missile proliferation to lend credibility to the otherwise limited threat posed by the available rogues. As with other aspects of the Rogue Doctrine, however, the proliferation picture is far more complex and ambiguous than it is often made out to be. It is essential, therefore, to examine this picture in its full complexity.

Chapter Six

THE AMBIVALENT CRUSADE

Washington's War Against

Proliferation

BY THE TIME the Clinton administration took office, the concept of rogue states had become intertwined in military thinking with the threat of proliferation. Just as the "Soviet threat" had once been described in terms of the plentitude of missiles, bombers, tanks, and the like in Soviet hands, so was the "rogue threat" framed increasingly in terms of the pursuit of nuclear, chemical, and biological weapons by potentially hostile Third World states. "The old nuclear danger we faced was thousands of warheads in the Soviet Union," Defense Secretary Les Aspin observed in 1993—"the new nuclear danger we face is perhaps a handful of nuclear devices in the hands of rogue states." Moreover, "the engine of this new danger is proliferation."[1]

Proliferation came to be seen as a significant danger for several reasons. First, there was the obvious risk that regional powers might use their weapons of mass destruction in attacks on their neighbors or, in the event of U.S. intervention, against American soldiers. This danger certainly existed during the Persian Gulf conflict of 1991, when some of Saddam Hussein's forces were armed with chemical weapons. Even if WMD-equipped states did not use their weapons, Washington considered the very fact that they might do so threatening because it gave the appearance of enhancing the hegemonic potential of rising powers, thereby diminishing the credibility of American promises to aid friends and allies if they were attacked by hostile states. Weapons of mass destruction "give rogue states disproportionate power, destabilize entire regions, and threaten human and environmental disasters," Secretary of State Warren Christopher warned in 1993. "They can turn local conflicts into serious threats to our security."[2]

Proliferation was also seen by policymakers as a dangerous repudiation of the interlocking system of controls that the United States and its allies had put in place over the past thirty years to prevent the spread of WMD capabilities to the Third World. These "regimes" were viewed as the cornerstones of the existing U.S.–dominated international system, and any attempt to circumvent or undermine them was seen as a threat to the world order.[3] As a result, protection of existing nonproliferation regimes against sabotage, cheating, and disregard became a major foreign policy objective. Just as an earlier generation of officials had sought to counter the threat of Soviet expansionism through a strategy of "containment," so a new crop of leaders came to believe that the threat of Third World proliferation should be "contained" through vigorous nonproliferation efforts.[4]

U.S. officials adopted a wide array of programs and policies to contain proliferation. Historically, the primary nonproliferation strategy had focused on *prevention*—efforts to dissuade potential proliferators from seeking weapons of mass destruction and/or to restrict their access to critical WMD materials and technologies. At the center of such efforts were various nonproliferation regimes, including the Nuclear Non-Proliferation Treaty, the Biological Weapons Convention, and the Missile Technology Control Regime.[5]

Increasingly, however, American leaders have emphasized options for *reversing* the process of proliferation once a state has crossed the WMD threshold. The primary option here is diplomacy; U.S. officials have beseeched WMD-producing nations to cease their activities and agree to destroy their stockpiles of nuclear, chemical, and biological weapons. The Department of Defense has also explored the possibility of using military force to destroy such stockpiles or deter their use.[6] Such attacks figured prominently in American planning for Operation Desert Storm, and no doubt are included in any U.S. plans for future military engagements with such states as Libya and North Korea.

In seeking support for these policies, U.S. officials have employed the sort of alarmist language once used to describe the threat posed by Soviet expansionism. "If we do not stem the proliferation of the world's deadliest weapons," President Clinton warned in 1993, "no democracy can feel secure."[7] The underlying message of such pronouncements is clear: "we"—the Western democracies—are on the side of nonproliferation; "they"—the Third World rogues and outlaws—are on the side of proliferation.

Images of containment and of a last-ditch global struggle against proliferation suggest a vigorous, uncompromising, and coherent strategy for combating the spread of WMD. Nothing, however, could be further from the truth. U.S. policy on proliferation has been ambivalent, indecisive, and inconsistent. While Washington on occasion has been forceful in opposing the proliferation activities of certain countries, it often has tolerated or ignored those of others. As a result, some weapons-seeking states have made great strides in pursuit of weapons of mass destruction; some have made moderate progress; and some have made very little progress at all. At least part of this discrepancy in the WMD accomplishments of weapons-seeking states has been the result of the dissimilar technical and industrial capabilities of emerging Third World powers; some states are simply better positioned to take on the complex tasks of producing weapons of mass destruction. More important, however, has been the reception that proliferation activities have received from the major powers, especially the United States. Nations such as Israel and India (and, until 1990, Iraq and Pakistan) that have experienced very little interference from the United States have made far more headway in their weapons efforts than Iran and Libya and others that have been the target of vigorous American nonproliferation efforts.

The U.S. government has never acknowledged its inconsistency in applying nonproliferation controls and sanctions, but it is not possible to explain the striking discrepancies in the relative accomplishments of WMD-seeking states otherwise. When determined to do so, the United States has been able to slow or stop the weapons programs of known proliferators. In a number of cases, however, Washington has turned "a blind eye to proliferation," electing to disregard irrefutable evidence of WMD activities and allowing such efforts to proceed virtually unimpeded.[8]

COLD WAR LEGACIES

Much of the ambivalence in the application of proliferation policy can be traced to continuing tension between two historic goals of American foreign policy in the post–World War II years: the containment of the Soviet Union, and the prevention of global nuclear and chemical weapons proliferation. In the Cold War era, both of these goals were considered essential to national security, and each resulted in significant initiatives on Washington's part. To promote containment, the United States spurred the formation of NATO and established a string of military bases around the Soviet Union; to promote nonproliferation, Washington sponsored the Nuclear Non-Proliferation Treaty and other measures for curbing the spread of WMD technology. But these two goals were never considered of equal importance, and whenever Washington perceived a potential conflict between the two, containment of the Soviet Union was always accorded higher priority.[9]

Such conflicts arose from time to time with particular urgency because of U.S. interest in building up the military power of friendly Third World countries. Once the U.S.–Soviet competition shifted from Europe to the developing countries in the mid-1950s, both superpowers sought to attract and retain allies by providing favored leaders with military and technical assistance. In return for such aid, recipient states were expected to support their patron in various ways—by allowing their patron to build bases on their territory, providing troops to joint military operations (as South Korea and Thailand supplied troops for the U.S. war effort in South Vietnam), and cooperating in various covert activities.[10] Yet, as Washington's dependence on such allies grew, America's Third World "surrogates" found that they had gained a certain degree of leverage over U.S. leaders, at least when it came to bargaining for ever more powerful weapons and even greater levels of military assistance. As some of these states began to develop weapons of mass destruction, moreover, Washington found it increasingly difficult to consider cutting off its flow of aid and weaponry—or even impeding these WMD efforts—for fear of alienating allies, driving them into the "Soviet camp," or losing their support for U.S. endeavors.[11]

A prime example of this clash in priorities can be found in the American response to Pakistan's nuclear weapons program. In April 1979, after acquiring clear evidence of the Pakistani nuclear effort, the Carter administration suspended military aid to Pakistan, as mandated by the 1976 Symington Amendment to the Foreign Assistance Act. However, when Soviet troops occupied Afghanistan in December 1979, Congress overruled the Symington Amendment and allowed a $3.2 billion sale of American arms to Pakistan. Between 1980 and 1990, the Pakistanis played a key role in American efforts to aid anti-Soviet Afghan rebels via covert channels. In return, Washington agreed to supply Pakistan with advanced weapons and to overlook its ongoing nuclear program. Only in 1990, after the Soviets had completed their pullout from Afghanistan and the Pakistanis had succeeded in producing operational nuclear devices, did President Bush acknowledge Pakistan's nuclear weapons status and impose a belated cutoff in military assistance.[12]

The same inclination to subordinate proliferation concerns to what were considered more compelling strategic considerations has been evident in Washington's response to Israel's nuclear weapons program. Although senior American officials were aware of the secret

Israeli nuclear reactor and weapons plant at Dimona in the Negev desert by the early 1960s, they consciously chose to ignore this effort, not even acknowledging its existence lest they be obliged to punish Israel—a move that might have jeopardized Washington's "strategic relationship" with Tel Aviv.[13]

The United States has also been remarkably tolerant of India's nuclear weapons program, visible since its 1974 test of a nuclear explosive device. Although Washington cut off supplies of nuclear materials to India following the 1974 test, and restricted other forms of U.S. aid, it has not otherwise penalized New Delhi for its failure to sign the NPT and its continuing pursuit of nuclear weapons. Again, Cold War considerations were largely responsible: although India signed a Treaty of Friendship with the Soviet Union in 1971, and obtained most of its conventional weaponry from the Soviets, U.S. policymakers were reluctant to drive a wedge in U.S.–Indian relations and thereby push India into a closer embrace with Moscow.[14]

Other cases of selective application of nonproliferation restraints abound. On several occasions, for instance, Washington has applied pressure to Taiwan and South Korea to discontinue work on nuclear weapons. On the other hand, the United States has taken no visible action to halt the efforts of either country to develop ballistic missiles, and has never made an issue of their suspected chemical weapons capabilities; nor has Washington taken action against suspected chemical weapons programs in Egypt and Israel. (All four of these states are described by U.S. military officials as "probably possessing" chemical warfare capabilities.[15])

After 1989, American officials attempting to implement a coherent, vigorous policy on proliferation were no longer caught in a squeeze between containment and nonproliferation. However, they still confronted the checkerboard pattern of arms diffusion that forty years of Cold War thinking had produced. If they had begun to apply sanctions against the states with the most developed WMD capabilities, they would have been forced to punish some of America's closest friends in the Third World. Washington chose to pursue a more selective policy, reserving its strongest actions for states such as Iran, Libya, and North Korea, whose WMD endeavors were generally less advanced.[16]

American efforts to combat the spread of WMD technologies have also been hampered by another major legacy of Cold War thinking: Washington's desire to deny to others, particularly rising Third World powers, military capabilities that it sought to retain for itself (and, in some cases, its closest European allies). At the height of the Cold War, U.S. leaders were reluctant to part with any weapon they thought might be needed for combat with the Soviet Union. The military therefore built up large stocks of chemical and biological munitions, as well as nuclear weapons. In 1969, the United States announced its intention to forgo biological weapons (it signed the Biological Weapons Convention in 1972), but the country retains a vast inventory of nuclear weapons and ballistic missiles, and only in 1992, with the signing of the Chemical Weapons Convention, did Washington agree to destroy its stockpile of chemical weapons.

Washington's reluctance to part with weapons considered necessary for combat with (or deterrence of) the Soviet Union led to an American preference for "discriminatory" nonproliferation regimes under which the major powers would be allowed to retain their supplies of certain weapons, while all other states would be barred from receiving or producing them. The Nuclear Non-Proliferation Treaty, for instance, allows the United States and four other declared "nuclear weapon states" (Britain, France, Russia, and China) to maintain their nuclear arsenals while denying this privilege to other states. Similarly, the Missile Technology Control Regime allows member states—mainly the advanced industrial powers of Europe and North America—to possess unlimited numbers of ballistic missiles, but obliges them to ban sales of missile technology to nonmembers.[17] In the chemical weapons field, the United States sought to exempt itself from any worldwide ban on such weapons until 1991, when President Bush finally agreed to sign a universal, nondiscriminatory CW ban.

At one time, American officials defended their support for discriminatory nonproliferation agreements on the grounds that the United

States could not forgo developing any vital military capability when locked in a struggle for survival with the Soviet Union. It was also claimed that the existing powers were more adept than emerging ones at negotiating arms control and conflict avoidance measures. (There was the added implication that Third World leaders could not be trusted as could those of the First World to have weapons of such power in their hands.) In the case of the NPT, the United States and the other four nuclear powers did agree, under Article VI, to conduct talks "in good faith" aimed at the eventual elimination of all nuclear weapons; not surprisingly, however, such talks have never been convened.[18]

American nonproliferation efforts have been viewed with understandable suspicion by many Third World leaders, and at times have been fiercely opposed by some who viewed these efforts as a form of imperialism. "Underlying the proposition that advanced industrial nations have a right to develop sophisticated weapons, while the developing nations do not, appears to be the old attitude of 'white man's burden,' " observed C. Raja Mohan and K. Subrahmanyam of the Institute for Defense Studies in New Delhi. While most Third World leaders have endorsed the general concept of nonproliferation, many have expressed opposition to discriminatory measures that allow the developed countries to preserve or add to their existing WMD stockpiles, and have called instead for the adoption of nondiscriminatory regimes under which *all* states are obliged to surrender or eschew particular weapons.[19]

Third World leaders' suspicions of U.S. nonproliferation policy have been especially evident in their criticism of the Missile Technology Control Regime. Unlike the NPT, the MTCR is not a formal treaty but a suppliers' cartel under which the leading industrialized powers—described as the "Partners" in MTCR protocols—agree not to share their missile and space technology with nonmembers. On several occasions, the United States has imposed economic sanctions against Third World states accused of building ballistic missiles in violation of the regime, provoking angry complaints from the leaders of the states involved.[20] "If the Americans continue this unfair degree of pressure on us then we will just go ahead and develop the technology ourselves," an official of the Indian Ministry of External Affairs avowed in 1992, following such an incident.[21]

By persisting in its commitment to discriminatory controls, Washington has lost much of its moral authority in the proliferation debate, and has helped to legitimize—at least in the eyes of their own populations—the WMD programs of some Third World states. American leaders may deplore this reaction to their policies, but they cannot entirely ignore the consequences of Washington's historic preference for discriminatory nonproliferation controls.

THE OTHER SIDE OF THE EQUATION

From the dawn of history, states or empires in possession of advanced weaponry have sought to prevent its spread to rising powers on their peripheries, fearing that this would diminish their capacity to stave off attacks from challengers. By the same token, up-and-coming states on the periphery have sought to gain access to advanced technologies in order to reduce their military inferiority vis-à-vis the dominant powers. Throughout history, then, there has been a struggle between those seeking to curb the diffusion of technology and those seeking to accelerate it—between nonproliferation and proliferation.[22]

This epic contest acquired particular intensity in the post–World War II era because of the potency of the weapons involved. The mere possession of these weapons, given their immense destructive force, was thought to confer power and prestige on their owners. Furthermore, by constructing their military strategies around nuclear weapons (and, later, long-range ballistic missiles) the United States and the Soviet Union signaled to all other countries that membership in the class of "major" powers was limited to states in possession of such weapons. This prompted first Britain and France, then China, Israel, India, Pakistan, Argentina, Brazil, South Africa, Iraq, and North Korea to seek weapons of these types for themselves.[23] Still other states, lacking the industrial resources required to manufacture nuclear weapons, have sought membership in the WMD club by producing chemical and biological munitions.[24]

These weapons-seeking states have been spurred by a number of motives. Aside from a desire to gain entry into the exclusive circle of major powers, many have felt threatened (or anticipated being threatened) by the superpowers, or by other states allied to one of the superpowers and already in possession of WMD. In this, there was often something of a "domino effect": China sought nuclear weapons in the 1950s because the United States—then its principal adversary—threatened Beijing with nuclear strikes during the Korean War and then the Formosa Straits crisis of 1955; India sought such weapons at least in part because China, an adversary in the 1960s, was building them; Pakistan felt compelled to acquire nuclear weapons to offset the nuclear advantage of its arch-enemy, India. Similarly, a number of the Arab powers, including Egypt, Iraq, and Syria, sought chemical weapons as a counterweight to the nuclear weapons they suspected were in Israel's arsenal. Each of these states hoped that the possession of WMD would deter an attack by some rival power or powers; or, if such attacks did occur, would provide them with powerful weapons with which to stave off defeat.[25]

Against this backdrop, American leaders must now confront the reality that a dozen or so states, including several close allies, do not accept Washington's views on the urgency of nonproliferation and are prepared to circumvent any regimes established for this purpose. As the United States increases its pressure on these states to terminate or suspend their proliferation activities, it is likely only to strengthen their determination to conceal their efforts ever more thoroughly from public view.

The tendency of weapons-seeking states to conceal their WMD activities or to deny their existence has produced another policy dilemma for American policymakers. To effectively counter such activities in the face of evasions and denials, the United States must produce evidence to back up its suspicions, and be prepared to risk an international crisis. It is a course fraught with danger, as the June

1994 crisis over North Korea's nuclear program demonstrated. As a result, it has often proved more convenient for Washington to accept such denials at face value—even when they are patently false—rather than to provoke a major confrontation. Needless to say, American leaders have been more prone to proceed in this fashion when dealing with friendly powers like Israel and India than with hostile ones like Iran and Libya.

American efforts to combat proliferation have also been compromised to some degree by the desire of private American and European companies to sell nuclear reactors, space technology, advanced computers, and other "dual-use" goods (goods that can be used for both civilian and military purposes) to suspected proliferators. Much of the equipment used by such states in the development and production of WMD and missiles has been of this character, and weapon-seeking states have been able to acquire significant supplies of such items from Western firms on the not-always-believable pretext that they are intended for non-military purposes. Because such sales can be quite lucrative for the firms involved, they have campaigned—often successfully—for a liberal interpretation by American and European officials of what constitutes a "civilian" product.[26]

Probably the most egregious example of such commercialized proliferation occurred in Iraq during the 1980s. Throughout this period, Western firms flocked to Baghdad in search of contracts for the supply of sophisticated dual-use equipment sought by the Iraqi government. Between 1985 and 1990, the U.S. Commerce Department licensed the sale of some $1.5 billion worth of high-technology products to Iraq.[27] Although Iraqi officials always insisted that such items were intended for legitimate civilian use in fields like metallurgy and oil refining, it was apparent to many proliferation experts that they were actually intended for military purposes. This suspicion was subsequently confirmed when, following the 1991 Gulf conflict, U.N. inspectors visited Iraqi weapons installations and discovered that many high-tech commercial systems supplied by the West had been used in the development of ballistic missiles and nuclear, chemical, and biological munitions.[28]

Although some efforts have since been made to tighten up international technology controls, it is still possible for weapons-seeking states to obtain militarily significant equipment through commercial sales channels. Indeed, to facilitate American sales of high-tech equipment to overseas customers, the Clinton administration has sought to speed up and "streamline" the process of reviewing applications for dual-use exports—an effort that has been criticized by some experts as increasing the risk of the very sort of illicit transactions that the administration has sworn to prevent.[29]

American efforts to tighten controls on the illicit trade in WMD-related products has also been hampered by the growing "leakage" of nuclear materials—including weapons-grade plutonium—from military and civilian facilities in the former Soviet Union. With the dissolution of the Soviet state into fifteen sovereign republics and the subsequent decline in living standards for many former Soviet citizens, including senior military and scientific personnel, security at many government installations has deteriorated. As a result, it has become increasingly easy for criminal organizations to procure sensitive nuclear materials from cooperative government employees. The seriousness of this problem was brought into sharp relief in August 1994, when German authorities arrested a smuggler who had flown from Moscow to Munich with some ten to twelve ounces of plutonium—perhaps one-tenth of the amount that would be needed to manufacture a crude nuclear device.[30] Although Russia has since promised to improve security at its nuclear installations, Western officials are fearful of further leaks of sensitive materials from the former Soviet Union.[31]

THE PROLIFERATION HIERARCHY

These factors of supply and demand, vigilance and negligence, opportunism and greed have produced an uneven pattern of WMD proliferation. Not every Third World country has pursued weapons of mass destruction: many are too poor to acquire WMD technology, or lack the technical capacity to make use of it if they did; others have simply chosen to do without such weapons. When the two key factors of desire and capability have been combined, however, significant proliferation has occurred. What we find, then, is a relatively short list of about fifteen states that over the past twenty or thirty years have succeeded in procuring weapons of mass destruction.

The list of WMD-possessing countries is as short as it is because even desire and significant technical and financial resources generally are insufficient to insure that a state's military aspirations will be satisfied. In most cases, it must also obtain specialized materials and technologies covered by one or another nonproliferation regime. This, in turn, requires the assistance of a country already in possession of such items or commercial firms willing to supply the needed equipment and materials, along with proficiency in circumventing existing nonproliferation controls. An ability to put together some combination of these ingredients has been the determining factor in the relative progress in acquiring weapons of mass destruction achieved by the fifteen or so active proliferators.

As suggested by Table 6.1, the major WMD-seeking states can be divided into three broad categories according to their success in the proliferation area:[32]

- *"Advanced proliferators"* possess a substantial nuclear arsenal, are capable of producing chemical warfare (CW) and biological warfare (BW) agents, and have acquired (or are developing) ballistic weapons with a range of more than 1,000 kilometers. Only three states—China, India, and Israel—currently fall into this category.
- *"Intermediate proliferators"* have made progress in some aspects of WMD production, but have lagged in others; or have suspended some or all of their WMD activities. Eight countries—Argentina, Brazil, Iraq, North Korea, Pakistan, South Africa, South Korea, and Taiwan—belong in this group.
- *"Struggling proliferators"* currently lack the technical and industrial resources to produce nuclear weapons on their own, though they may have attempted to purchase them from other countries or

are seeking the know-how to manufacture them in the future. They are also likely to possess chemical weapons and imported ballistic missiles. Four countries—Egypt, Iran, Libya, and Syria—fit into this group.

These categories are, of course, somewhat arbitrary, and there is a degree of overlap among the various groups. But the discrepancies in the relative rate of their WMD development is unmistakable. Given the inherent capabilities of WMD-seeking countries and the inconsistent policies of the major powers, these discrepancies are likely to persist for a long time.

TABLE 6.1
WEAPONS OF MASS DESTRUCTION CAPABILITIES
OF MAJOR THIRD WORLD PROLIFERATORS

Advanced proliferators

• *China:* the first Third World country to acquire nuclear weapons; is now believed to possess an arsenal of some 400 nuclear warheads. It is the only Third World country to have produced an intercontinental ballistic missile (the DF-5) capable of reaching North America, and has also produced a variety of other missiles. China is thought to possess CW and BW production facilities.

• *Israel:* after China, the Third World country with the largest nuclear arsenal, thought to comprise some 200–300 warheads. It also produces a 1,450-kilometer-range missile, the Jericho-II, and is believed to possess CW and BW production capabilities.

• *India:* first tested a nuclear device in 1974, and is now believed to possess sufficient nuclear material for 75–100 bombs (although it is not known how many functioning bombs have actually been assembled). It has developed and tested the *Agni*, a ballistic missile with an estimated range of 2,400 kilometers, and is thought capable of manufacturing CW agents (if it has not done so already).

Intermediate proliferators

• *Argentina:* conducted a secret nuclear weapons program in the 1970s and 1980s, but suspended this effort in the late 1980s before any functioning weapons had been produced. It also developed a 1,000-kilometer-range missile, the Condor-II, but this effort, too, was terminated prior to completion. It is not known to possess chemical weapons.

• *Brazil:* like Argentina, conducted a secret nuclear weapons program in the 1970s and 1980s that, like Argentina's, was suspended in the late 1980s before a functioning weapon had been produced. It has developed a 300-kilometer-range missile, the SS-300, but work has been suspended due to economic difficulties. It is not known to possess chemical weapons.

• *Iraq:* was in the process of developing nuclear weapons when Operation Desert Storm commenced in 1991. It had also established a large CW production capability and had begun producing longer-range versions of the Scud missile. All Iraqi WMD activities have been halted under United Nations supervision in accordance with U.N. Security Council Resolution 687.

• *North Korea:* is believed to possess sufficient bomb-grade plutonium for the production of one or two nuclear weapons, but may not have succeeded as yet in packaging this material in functioning nuclear weapons. It has developed and tested a long-range derivative of the Scud, the 1,000-kilometer NoDong-1, and is thought to be developing missiles with even longer ranges. It is also believed to possess CW and BW production capabilities.

• *Pakistan:* began producing nuclear weapons in the late 1980s, and is now thought to possess 15–20 warheads. It has also attempted to develop short-range missiles, but has not yet succeeded in efforts to produce a long-range weapon. It is thought to be capable of manufacturing CW agents.

• *South Africa:* conducted a secret nuclear weapons program in the 1970s and 1980s and, by its own admission, had produced six nuclear bombs by 1991, when it agreed to terminate its nuclear efforts. It has also developed and tested a variant of the Israeli Jericho-II missile, the 1,450-kilometer Arniston, and is thought to be capable of manufacturing chemical weapons.

• *South Korea:* commenced the development of nuclear weapons in the early 1970s, but was later persuaded by Washington to abandon this effort in 1975 (although some secret weapons research may have continued). It has developed a short-range ballistic missile, the 250-kilometer NHK-1, and is believed to possess chemical weapons.

• *Taiwan:* like South Korea, conducted nuclear weapons research in the early 1970s until persuaded to halt these efforts by the United States (although, as in the case of South Korea, weapons research may have continued in secret). It has developed a 900-kilometer ballistic missile, the *Tien Ma* (Sky Horse), and is thought to possess CW and BW production capabilities.

Struggling proliferators

• *Egypt:* has not attempted to produce nuclear weapons, but is known to possess a significant CW production capability. It has been unsuccessful in manufacturing ballistic missiles on its own, but possesses Scud missiles acquired from the Soviet Union and North Korea.

• *Iran:* has been charged by U.S. officials with conducting a secret nuclear weapons development program, but at this point is believed to be at least ten years away from producing functioning weapons. It is attempting to produce ballistic missiles with Chinese and North Korean assistance, and possesses Scud missiles acquired from North Korea. It is also believed to possess a CW and BW production capability.

• *Libya:* made several attempts in the 1970s and 1980s to purchase functioning nuclear weapons and nuclear weapons technology from other states, but without success. It has built a CW production facility with the assistance of German chemical firms, and possesses Scud missiles acquired from the Soviet Union.

• *Syria:* has not attempted to produce nuclear weapons, but is believed to have developed a CW and BW production capability with foreign assistance, and has acquired Scud-B and Scud-C missiles from North Korea.

Sources: OTA, *Proliferation of Weapons of Mass Destruction* (1993); L. Spector, *Nuclear Ambitions* (1990); Spector, "Nuclear Proliferation Status Report" (1992); "Missile and Space Launch Capabilities of Selected Countries," *Nonproliferation Review* (Winter 1994); other sources cited in text.

STRATEGIES OF PROLIFERATION

The production of weapons of mass destruction is not a simple or cost-free endeavor. Prospective proliferators must assemble a wide array of rare and costly materials, secure considerable scientific and technical know-how, and acquire proficiency in a variety of sophisticated industrial processes—all while circumventing international restraints established to impede these endeavors. In attempting to procure WMD in the face of these impediments, weapons-seeking states have sought to minimize their dependence on other nations and to rely as much as possible on indigenous sources of know-how and materials. Few Third World countries, however, are self-sufficient in all the commodities needed for the production of weapons of mass destruction, and so they must of necessity turn to foreign sources for at least some critical items. In certain cases, such as Iraq's and Libya's pursuit of chemical munitions, this may mean the purchase of finished weapons or weapons-making facilities; in others, it may mean the purchase of detailed blueprints, special machinery, exotic alloys, or scientific instruments. Because these products are generally available from only a handful of countries, and often are covered by a nonproliferation regime, a proliferator must find ways to circumvent such restraints and gain the cooperation of willing suppliers.

In seeking foreign technology, prospective proliferators have used a number of approaches. Some have sought finished weapons or technical assistance from existing WMD-possessing states; others have acquired dual-use materials and technology through legitimate channels, and then diverted them to military use; still others have relied on black-market sources to acquire critical materials and technologies unobtainable through legitimate trade channels. When blocked on one front, moreover, most weapon-seeking states have tended to simply shift their efforts to the others.

Nuclear Proliferation

To manufacture nuclear weapons—specifically, fission weapons, as fusion ("hydrogen") weapons are much harder to produce—a proliferator must assemble a wide variety of products and materials. These include the fissile materials used as a nuclear explosive—either highly-enriched uranium (HEU) or weapons-grade plutonium (Pu-239). Because these materials do not exist naturally, weapon-seeking states must also possess the wherewithal to manufacture them. In the case of HEU, this means a capacity for "enriching" natural uranium (which is composed largely of the nonfissile isotope U-238) until it contains 90 percent or more of the fissile isotope U-235; in the case of plutonium, it means a capacity to extract and "reprocess" the Pu-239 residue from uranium fuel rods that have been irradiated in a nuclear reactor. In addition, a proliferator must obtain certain special materials needed to package the nuclear charge in a deliverable weapons device, along with the triggering devices and conventional explosives used to ignite a fissile reaction.[33]

In obtaining these materials (and/or the technology to produce them), some proliferators have been able to rely on the assistance of an existing nuclear power. Israel pursued this approach in the late 1950s by turning to France, which itself was in the initial stages of producing nuclear weapons, for substantial technical support. With the backing of senior leaders, including President Charles de Gaulle, French scientists and engineers helped construct the Israeli reactor and plutonium reprocessing plant at Dimona.[34] French scientists also trained many Israeli nuclear technicians at the French reprocessing plant at Marcoule, and in 1960 may have provided the Israelis with valuable data on the results of their first nuclear test.[35]

Israel itself became a supplier of nuclear weapons technology in the 1970s, when it signed a number of technical exchange agreements with South Africa. According to author Seymour Hersh, these agreements covered several aspects of nuclear weapons development, along with arrangements for a series of joint nuclear weapons tests—three of which reportedly were conducted in 1979 at an offshore site in the Indian Ocean.[36]

Pakistan is also believed to have received considerable assistance from an existing nuclear power, in this case China. According to Reagan administration officials, China assisted in the development of the Pakistani uranium enrichment plant at Kahuta, and also provided Islamabad with the blueprints for a nuclear weapon—relieving the Pakistanis of the need to conduct nuclear tests in order to confirm the validity of their weapon design.[37] The Chinese are also thought to have provided Pakistan with sufficient HEU to produce two nuclear weapons.[38] Although the Chinese have denied that they aided Pakistan in this manner, President Reagan cited such assistance as the reason for delaying an important nuclear trade agreement with China in 1984.[39]

The second proliferation strategy—acquiring key materials under the pretense of engaging in peaceful nuclear efforts—was used successfully by India to acquire a 40-megawatt CIRUS (Canadian–Indian–Reactor–U.S.) research reactor in the late 1950s. This reactor, equipped with heavy water supplied by the United States, was employed by India to produce the plutonium used in its 1974 nuclear test. Although Canada suspended its nuclear assistance program to India after the 1974 test, New Delhi later used the original CIRUS reactor as a model for other reactors employed in its nuclear weapons program.[40]

A somewhat similar strategy was employed by Brazil to acquire key reprocessing and enrichment technology from West Germany. In 1975, Brazil signed an ambitious nuclear power agreement with Bonn that was to entail the construction of up to eight large power reactors, a pilot-scale plutonium reprocessing plant, and a commercial-scale uranium enrichment facility. Under the 1975 agreement, these facilities were all to be placed under nonproliferation "safeguards" (inspection and accounting procedures) in accordance with the NPT. It is widely believed, however, that the Brazilians systematically transferred key technologies and materials from these safeguarded facilities to a parallel, weapons-oriented nuclear program.[41]

The third proliferation strategy—the use of fraud and deception to acquire WMD-related materials not obtainable through legitimate trade channels—has been employed with increasing frequency in recent years as international nonproliferation efforts have made the other two methods more difficult.[42] According to Leonard Spector of the Carnegie Endowment for International Peace, recent investigations have established that "covert nuclear transactions originating in Western Europe and North America . . . [have] played a central role in advancing the nuclear weapons capabilities of a number of developing nations."[43] These transactions range from the smuggling of controlled materials to elaborate schemes involving the formation of seemingly legitimate "front" companies in Western Europe to procure critical items for covert military projects.

By far the most ambitious effort of this sort was conducted by Iraq in the late 1980s. Saddam Hussein, aware that Baghdad would not be allowed access to sensitive nuclear materials with potential military uses through normal trade channels, ordered his technicians to establish a clandestine network of front companies and trading organizations in Europe to procure WMD-related equipment and technology from the West.[44] A single one of these Iraqi-infiltrated firms, Matrix-Churchill Ltd. of Coventry, England, procured over one thousand pieces of equipment for the Iraqi weapons program.[45]

Pakistan has also relied on black-market sources of sensitive materials and technology. According to Spector, Pakistan obtained significant Western technology for its uranium enrichment plant at Kahuta, including an entire facility for converting uranium powder into uranium hexafluoride, the easily gasified material used as feedstock for the gas centrifuge method of U-235 enrichment.[46] Black-market firms also provided the Pakistanis with specialized containers for the handling of uranium hexaflouride, along with 130 metric tons of aluminum for use as centrifuge housings.[47]

Chemical and Biological Weapons Proliferation

Chemical warfare (CW) agents are easier than nuclear weapons to manufacture, requiring only a modern chemical or pharmaceutical industry plus certain commercially available chemical "precursors." Nevertheless, prospective CW proliferators, especially in less-developed countries, have sought to purchase ready-made CW munitions from existing producers, or have turned to foreign suppliers for critical transfers of materials, equipment, and technology.[48]

The Soviet Union is believed to have provided chemical weapons to a number of its overseas allies at the height of the Cold War, including Egypt, Ethiopia, Libya, North Korea, Syria, and Vietnam.[49] In 1989, however, CIA Director William Webster declared that he had no reason to believe that the Soviets were still "supporting proliferation" of CW agents.[50] Several Third World countries have also been charged with transferring chemical weapons to other countries: Egypt, for instance, is believed to have provided a small quantity of CW munitions to Syria in the 1970s, and Iran is reported to have supplied such weapons to Libya.[51]

States attempting to manufacture CW munitions on their own have followed a different route, seeking specialized equipment and know-how from private chemical firms in Western Europe. Egypt, Iran, Iraq, Libya, and Syria all established a significant capacity for chemical weapons production in this manner. According to Webster, "Assistance provided by foreign suppliers, many of whom were fully witting of the intentions of the Middle East countries to produce chemical weapons, has been the key element that has enabled these nations to develop a capability to produce chemical weapons within only a few years."[52]

In at least a few notable cases, prospective proliferators have been able to purchase entire CW facilities from a single supplier. Libya, for instance, obtained the basic materials for its Rabta CW plant from the West German firm Imhausen-Chemie AG. According to the firm's owner, Jurgen Hippensteil-Imhausen (who later pleaded guilty to violations of German export laws), Imhausen-Chemie agreed to supply the plant in 1984 for $150 million.[53] West German chemical firms are also believed to have played a key role in constructing the Iraqi CW plant at Samarra.[54]

Far more common has been the practice of obtaining parts and materials from various companies that may or may not be aware of the possible military implications of such exports, and then combining them on the site into a weapons production facility. Dual-use products normally used in the pharmaceutical and fertilizer industries have been acquired in this manner through ordinary trade channels with a minimum of fuss. Iran, for instance, is thought to have employed this strategy to obtain a wide variety of CW-related products from prominent Western European firms, including Bayer AG and

Lurgi Metallurgie GmbH of Germany and Ciba-Geigy of Switzerland; Syria is believed to have utilized a similar approach in building up its chemical warfare capabilities.[55]

In general, states seeking to develop biological warfare (BW) agents have proceeded along similar lines to those seeking chemical weapons—obtaining dual-use items from a variety of private firms and then assembling them in a BW production facility. Because such equipment is available from many sources and is used in a variety of civilian activities, it is relatively easy for a prospective proliferator to set up facilities for the development and manufacture of BW agents without attracting international notice and disapprobation.[56]

This approach to BW production has been followed by a number of Middle Eastern countries. The most ambitious of these programs was conducted in the late 1980s by Iraq, which reportedly invested some $100 million to establish facilities for the production and testing of candidate BW munitions. According to the United Nations investigators who inspected these facilities after the 1991 Gulf conflict, Iraq was experimenting with the use of several candidate agents, including anthrax, botulin toxin, brucellosis, and tuleramia. No evidence was found, however, that the Iraqis had begun to "weaponize" these agents (that is, to package them in deliverable form as bombs, shells, or missiles).[57] Other suspected proliferators, including Iran, Israel, Libya, and Syria, appear to have proceeded along similar lines, acquiring materials and equipment for the development of BW munitions, but not necessarily advancing to the next stage of weaponization.[58]

Ballistic Missile Proliferation

As in the case of nuclear and chemical proliferation, countries seeking to acquire ballistic missiles have employed a number of strategies to obtain critical know-how and materials. Most missile-seeking states began by buying ready-made missiles, usually Scud-Bs from the Soviet Union or North Korea. At least eight countries have acquired Scuds in this manner: Afghanistan, Egypt, Iran, Iraq, Libya, North

Korea, Syria, and Yemen.[59] The Soviet Union (now Russia) is not known to have exported any Scuds since 1990, when it agreed to abide by the Missile Technology Control Regime, but North Korea continues to sell homemade versions of this 1950s-vintage missile.[60] China has also become a supplier of finished missiles, providing the 2,700-kilometer DF-3 to Saudi Arabia in 1987, and offering the M-9 and M-11 missiles to a number of Middle Eastern and Asian countries in the early 1990s.[61]

The acquisition and modification of existing missiles, space vehicles, and sounding rockets (test rockets sometimes used for scientific experiments) has been another approach employed by missile-seeking states in the Third World. North Korea has proved particularly adept at this approach, producing the 600-kilometer-range Scud-C, an enhanced version of the Scud-B, and an even more advanced version, the 1,000-kilometer NoDong-1.[62] Iraq also produced enhanced versions of the Scud, the al-Hussein, and the al-Abbas. Similarly, the Pakistani Hatf-2 is said to be a militarized version of sounding rockets supplied to Islamabad by Aerospatiale of France, and South Africa's Arniston missile is thought to be a derivative of the Israeli Jericho-II.[63]

Finally, a handful of nations have attempted to develop entirely new missiles of domestic design. Of these, the most successful have been Argentina's Condor-II, India's Prithvi and Agni, Israel's Jericho-I and -II, and Taiwan's Ching Feng and Tien Ma. Even in these cases, however, close investigation generally reveals that the countries involved have relied to one degree or another on imported technology. The Condor-II, for instance, incorporates technology imported from Germany and Italy; the Jericho-I was probably based on a French design; the Agni is thought to incorporate French and German technology; and the Taiwanese missiles are based on U.S. and Israeli designs.[64]

STRATEGIES FOR NONPROLIFERATION: DENIAL AND PREVENTION

Historically, the principal strategy employed by the United States to combat proliferation has been denial and prevention—cutting off the flow of critical materials and technology to weapons-seeking states. To accomplish this, the United States has joined with other states in establishing the various nonproliferation regimes (nuclear, chemical, biological, and missile), and has imposed an assortment of national controls on exports of WMD-related commodities.[65] These efforts have made it more difficult for potential proliferators to obtain critical materials, and may have deterred some states from pursuing WMD altogether; however, as we have seen, the existing denial systems have not prevented the most determined proliferators from acquiring weapons of mass destruction.

Recognizing that the existing nonproliferation regimes have not always been successful in blocking the flow of WMD-related materials to weapons-seeking states, the major powers have sought in recent years to establish new regimes and to tighten the restrictions found in older ones. These efforts have had two basic objectives: to make it harder for proliferators to gain access to WMD-related products, and to increase the onus on those found to be in violation of international nonproliferation restraints. Such endeavors are not expected to stop the spread of dangerous weapons altogether, only to slow the process of proliferation and to increase the number of states participating in nonproliferation regimes.[66]

Much of this effort has been aimed at controlling the transfer of sensitive dual-use commodities to potential proliferators. Computers, scientific instruments, chemical processing equipment, space technology, and so on have many legitimate uses, and have been avidly sought after by the newly industrialized countries (NICs) of the Third World. As might be expected, the older industrialized powers are eager to sell the NICs as many of such products as possible. But many of these items have significant military applications, and such NICs as Argentina, Brazil, China, India, Iran, Israel, South Korea, and

Taiwan have engaged in significant proliferation endeavors. There is an obvious and possibly insoluble tension between the desire to tighten international controls on dual-use items and to permit a commercially lucrative trade in allowable commodities.[67]

In addition to seeking tightened controls on the export of WMD-related materials, U.S. officials have sought to enhance international monitoring of proliferation activities and to stiffen the penalties for those found in violation of established nonproliferation controls. The need for such measures became painfully clear in 1991, when it was discovered that existing regimes had neither prevented the development of WMD in Iraq nor provided an effective means short of war for international counteraction. At the conclusion of the Gulf War, the major powers attempted to remedy their past inaction by establishing the U.N. Special Commission on Iraq, and empowering it (under Security Council Resolution 687) with the power and authority to destroy all Iraqi weapons of mass destruction and WMD production facilities. In addition, steps were taken to enhance the International Atomic Energy Agency's ability to inspect suspect nuclear facilities, and to bring its findings to the attention of the Security Council for possible action, including the imposition of economic sanctions.[68]

Nuclear Nonproliferation

Because each category of WMD is subject to a separate control regime—a legacy of Washington's reluctance to embrace nondiscriminatory controls—these various efforts have proceeded in a somewhat disjointed fashion, with some nonproliferation regimes receiving greater attention than others. In the nuclear area, proposals for modification of the Non-Proliferation Treaty have been stymied by the five declared nuclear states' unwillingness to tinker with an international agreement that grants them extraordinary privileges.[69] Instead, these states have called for a further enhancement of the power and authority of the IAEA and for tighter controls on the transfer of dual-use products to suspected proliferators.

To further restrain the flow of dual-use commodities, the United States and its allies have expanded the range of materials subject to review by the Nuclear Suppliers Group—an association of major industrial powers established in 1976 to regulate nuclear exports in accordance with the NPT. In addition, they have required recipients of critical nuclear commodities to place all their nuclear facilities under so-called full-scope safeguards, that is, periodic inspection by IAEA officials.[70] These measures have closed some of the loopholes in the existing nonproliferation regime, and made it more difficult for proliferators to obtain key items. But American officials continue to worry that other nuclear suppliers, including France and Germany, have not adhered to these controls as strictly as has the United States. Given the importance that other First World suppliers attach to increasing their trade with Third World countries, it remains an open question whether Washington will be able to persuade them to comply fully with more restrictive technology controls.[71]

Problems have also arisen with another major nonproliferation initiative of the post–Gulf War period, the investing of the International Atomic Energy Agency with the authority to inspect suspect nuclear facilities in NPT signatory countries on demand, whether or not these countries have listed these facilities as part of their nuclear infrastructure in required reports to the IAEA. To date, this authority has been put to the test only in North Korea, as part of the IAEA's efforts to inspect suspect facilities at the Yongbyon reactor complex. The result was a major international crisis that to this date remains unresolved. This experience is likely to give the IAEA pause when considering similar inspections in other countries, thereby frustrating U.S. efforts to invest the agency with greater power and authority.[72]

The NPT's original twenty-five-year mandate was to run out in 1995, requiring a vote by member states to keep it in effect. U.S. efforts to extend it indefinitely produced considerable criticism from a number of Third World states, to the effect that insufficient effort had been made by the declared nuclear powers to abolish their nuclear munitions in accordance with Article VI of the Treaty. These critics, led by India, called on the declared nuclear powers to terminate all nuclear testing and to provide evidence of intentions to eliminate their nuclear weapons stockpiles. The United States and its allies were expected to overcome these arguments and secure the treaty's extension, but not without exposing themselves to charges of manipulation and hypocrisy.[73]

Chemical and Biological Nonproliferation

In the chemical weapons area, U.S. efforts to tighten controls on the transfer of CW-related technology and materials have focused on the so-called Australia Group and the recently signed Chemical Weapons Convention. The Australia Group, established in 1984, is an informal association of industrialized states that have agreed to impose uniform controls on the export of precursor chemicals (industrial chemicals used in the production of CW agents) and other CW-related commodities.[74] Following the Persian Gulf War, the United States persuaded other members of the Group to expand the list of chemicals and equipment to be denied to states suspected of producing chemical weapons, and to tighten controls on the export of a wide variety of CW-related materials.[75] Rigorously enforced, these should make it more difficult for prospective proliferators to obtain such materials from major industrial powers. However, the Australia Group lacks any mechanisms for enforcement of its decisions, and there was some concern as to whether all member states would abide by the new rules. To further complicate matters, few of the NICs are members of the Australia Group, allowing chemical firms in these countries to ignore its restrictions.[76]

Efforts to control the spread of chemical munitions will get a boost in 1995, when the Chemical Weapons Convention (CWC) will come into effect. Signatories to this agreement pledge to destroy all CW agents in their possession, to forswear future production of such munitions, and to neither sell nor buy CW agents or production materials. It is hoped that full implementation of the CWC will eliminate many of the problems associated with the Australia Group's controls, because all parties to the agreement (whether or not members of the suppliers' group) will be obliged to impose strict controls on their CW-related chemical exports. In addition, the CWC establishes an implementing body—the Organization for the Prohibition of Chemical Weapons (OPCW)—to conduct inspections and otherwise enforce the terms of the Convention. If ratified and observed by all states with a CW potential—a very big "if"—the CWC will substantially diminish the threat of chemical weapons proliferation.[77]

The control of biological weapons proliferation presents a different set of problems. At present, the only nonproliferation instrument in this field is the 1972 Convention on the Prohibition of the Development, Production, and Stockpiling of Bacteriological and Toxin Weapons and Their Destruction (the "Biological Weapons Convention," or BWC).[78] Although sweeping in its coverage, and supported by many nations, the BWC is not without its shortcomings. For one thing, it permits research on biological agents for "defensive" purposes—a provision that some experts believe is subject to abuse, since agents produced for testing defensive equipment can easily be converted into offensive agents.[79] The BWC also lacks an enforcement arm similar to the IAEA, and has no provision for punishing states that violate its prohibitions.[80]

The United States, which unilaterally decided to eliminate its own BW stockpiles in 1969, has taken steps independent of the BWC to tighten national controls on the export of BW-related products, and has called upon its allies to do likewise. Under the Enhanced Proliferation Control Initiative adopted by President Bush in November 1990, U.S. firms are barred (except under strictly controlled conditions) from exporting a wide variety of microorganisms, toxins, and biological processing equipment to twenty-eight suspect states.[81] Two years later, in December 1992, the Australia Group agreed to adopt similar controls over BW-related exports; as yet, however, not all member states have implemented this decision.[82]

In any case, continuing doubts about the utility of such weapons and the likelihood of a harsh international reaction to any proven case of BW proliferation are likely to deter prospective proliferators from producing large stockpiles of biological weapons. There is some concern, however, that this could change in the early twenty-first century, if BW-seeking states acquire expertise in the rapidly developing field of genetic engineering. Proliferation experts fear that such techniques can be used to develop microorganisms more conducive to offensive military use than the naturally occurring species once considered for this purpose. It might be possible, for instance, to develop biological agents that incubate very rapidly, that are drug- and vaccine-resistant, or that self-destruct after a short period (thereby reducing the risk to friendly forces).[83] So far, there is no clear evidence that any state has proceeded with research along these lines, but the detection of such activities is exceedingly difficult (given that BW research can be easily camouflaged as part of a civilian biotechnology program), and it is possible that one or more countries have commenced secret programs of this sort.

Ballistic Missile Nonproliferation

The major powers have sought to tighten existing controls in the ballistic missile field. For the most part, this has entailed efforts to strengthen the Missile Technology Control Regime. Because the major powers have no desire to eliminate their own weapons capabilities, the MTCR places no restrictions on the missile holdings of member states, instead obliging them to forswear sales of ballistic missiles (with ranges of three hundred kilometers or more) or missile-production technology to nonmembers. The MTCR was first adopted in 1987 by seven major industrial countries—the United States, Britain, Canada, France, Germany, Italy, and Japan—and has been expanded to twenty-five partners, with several other countries, including Russia, China, Brazil, and Israel, agreeing to abide by its provisions.[84]

Because it is not a binding treaty like the NPT, and because responsibility for implementation of its provisions is left to the member states involved, the MTCR has not as yet resulted in a uniform set of nonproliferation controls. In the United States, implementation of MTCR restraints is mandated by the Missile Technology Control

Act of 1990, which also imposes economic sanctions on any foreign firm that is accused of violating the regime. Other adherents to the regime, however, have adopted less stringent national controls than has the United States, and at times have proved more tolerant of missile-related activities by their citizens and corporations.[85]

The MTCR is also limited by the fact that a number of Third World missile producers, including China and North Korea, are not members. During the Bush administration, U.S. officials applied great pressure on China to abide by MTCR restrictions when selling missiles to other countries. Beijing finally agreed to do so in 1991, after the United States promised to lift certain restrictions on high-tech exports to China, but there have been periodic reports that Chinese firms are continuing to provide restricted parts and materials to Iran, Pakistan, and Syria.[86] When such reports were confirmed by U.S. intelligence in 1993, the Clinton administration imposed limited trade sanctions on several of China's missile and space companies; however, this is not believed to have resulted in a complete cutoff of all affected missile exports.[87]

Prevention and denial strategies are useful in curbing some transfers of WMD-related exports to weapons-seeking states, but cannot be relied upon to block all such deliveries; the loopholes in existing controls are too numerous, and the rewards for successfully circumventing them too great. These strategies must therefore be reinforced by other methods if further progress is to be made in the nonproliferation area.

STRATEGIES FOR NONPROLIFERATION: MILITARY PREEMPTION

Recognizing that denial strategies alone cannot stop the spread of weapons of mass destruction, policymakers have begun to consider the use of military force as an "antiproliferation" instrument to destroy the nuclear, chemical, and missile facilities of hostile Third World states. After the Gulf War, officials of both the Bush and

Clinton administrations spoke of the need for an American military capacity to destroy enemy WMD stockpiles in preemptive strikes before they could be used against the United States and its allies.[88]

The debate over preemption inevitably begins with an analysis of the June 1981 Israeli raid on Iraq's nearly completed Osiraq reactor.[89] Claiming that Osiraq would be used to produce nuclear weapons that eventually would be aimed at their country, Israeli leaders defended the raid as a legitimate act of self-defense. "Israel cannot afford the introduction of the nuclear weapon," Defense Minister Ariel Sharon explained a few months later. "For us, it is not a question of a balance of terror but a question of survival."[90] Other governments condemned the Israeli attack, however, asserting that it constituted an unwarranted act of aggression. On this basis, Israel was reprimanded by the U.N. Security Council (under Resolution 487) and barred for three years from participation in the General Conference of the IAEA.[91]

At first, the dispute over the Osiraq raid was confined to questions of its legality under international law, with some experts accepting, others rejecting, Israel's claim that this represented a legitimate act of self-defense. As time went on, the focus of debate shifted to the raid's military effectiveness. Most experts, whatever their position on the legal question, initially considered the raid to have successfully destroyed Iraq's nascent nuclear weapons capability. However, it soon became apparent that the attack had simply intensified Saddam Hussein's determination to acquire nuclear weapons. Within months he ordered the initiation of several new weapons programs; to avoid detection and a repeat of the Osiraq raid they were conducted at underground sites or camouflaged civilian installations.[92] As a result, U.S. intelligence was not fully aware of the Iraqi nuclear program, and many of the facilities committed to this program escaped attack during Operation Desert Storm.[93]

The questionable effectiveness of Desert Storm notwithstanding, many American strategists have continued to view preemptive attacks as a viable and appropriate response to objectionable proliferation activities. This was clearly the intent of Defense Secretary Les

Aspin's 1993 "Defense Counterproliferation Initiative," intended to provide the Pentagon with "offensive" military options in the event that preventive measures failed to stem the flow of WMD capabilities to hostile powers. Specifically, such options were intended to enable Washington to respond "to allied requests for assistance to meet legitimate security needs, by being prepared to seize, disable, or destroy WMD in time of conflict if necessary."[94]

As of this writing, the United States has not carried out preemptive attacks of this type, although there was much discussion of such strikes during the June 1994 crisis over North Korea's nuclear weapons program. It is certain, however, that U.S. military planners have been told to plan for such missions in the expectation that they will someday be ordered to carry them out.

Advocates of preemption argue that the preemptive use of military force can eliminate prospective WMD threats before they become fully operational, at which time U.S. military counteraction in all likelihood would prove far more dangerous and costly. Indeed, Bush administration officials used precisely this argument to justify early military action against Iraq. In a December 1993 appearance before the Senate Armed Services Committee, Secretary Cheney declared, "My own personal view is that it is far better for us to deal with [Saddam Hussein] now" than to do so five or ten years later, "when Saddam has become an even better armed and more threatening regional superpower than he is at present."[95]

However, opponents of preemption assert that the very threat of such action prompts target states to put even greater efforts into hiding, burying, multiplying, and dispersing their WMD facilities— thereby blunting the effectiveness of future preemptive strikes and complicating arms control efforts. This was the ultimate outcome of the 1981 Israeli attack on Iraq, and it is likely to be the result of any future attacks; proliferation expert Leonard Spector believes that preemptive strikes "may simply be unable to achieve the desired objective."[96]

Doubts about the utility of preemptive strikes are particularly strong in the case of proposed raids on North Korea's nuclear facilities. According to Michael Mazarr of the Center for Strategic and International Studies, talk in Washington about such raids undoubtedly spurred the North Koreans to hide their sensitive nuclear materials and equipment in secret, hard-to-spot locations. Even if the right targets could be found, moreover, "U.S. 'smart' bombs might not [be] able to penetrate Korea's granite mountains to reach North Korean bunkers." In sum, air strikes alone cannot "guarantee an end to Pyongyang's nuclear program."[97]

The preemptive use of force against another state's WMD facilities, however "surgical" in character, also entails significant risk of triggering a major regional conflict. As Leonard Spector suggests, most states "seeking to develop nuclear arms already possess significant conventional military power that would allow them to strike back if their nuclear installations were attacked." In the event of a U.S. attack against the North Korean nuclear facilities at Yongbyon, for instance, "the North could easily retaliate by targeting Seoul with Scud missiles," or even by launching an all-out attack on the South."[98]

Another risk attendant on preemptive military strikes is the possible release of nuclear radiation or toxic substances into the atmosphere, contaminating large areas and possibly causing significant civilian casualties. This danger certainly would arise in the case of any attack on functioning nuclear reactors like the North Korean reactor at Yongbyon. Such an attack, Spector suggested, "would be highly likely to have substantial off-site radiological consequences, exposing the attacking state to (1) accusations that it had engaged in unconventional warfare, and (2) substantial international criticism."[99] Similar charges could be raised in the event that attacks on CW or BW facilities resulted in the release of toxic gases or infectious biological agents.[100]

The use of force to resolve disputes over proliferation is also likely to hamper U.S. efforts to increase the participation of Third World countries in the various nonproliferation regimes described above. From a Third World perspective, such regimes are legitimate only to the degree that they treat North and South in an equitable manner.

Any U.S. raid on a rising Third World power would be viewed by many other states as a brazen repudiation of this principle. "As a political message, the notion of [preemptive strikes] is not consonant with a policy seeking to promote global military restraint," arms control expert Janne E. Nolan wrote in 1992. "The idea that a few states have the right to eliminate military capabilities in states of which they disapprove will not help Western credibility in its quest for international acceptance of nonproliferation objectives."[101]

Preemption is not an option, moreover, in the case of nations allied to the United States. No matter how troubled Washington may be by proliferation activities in India, Israel, South Korea, and Taiwan, the existence of formal treaties and diplomatic agreements makes it highly unlikely that U.S. leaders would ever order a preemptive raid against WMD facilities in these countries.

Hence, while there may be some extraordinary circumstances in which military preemption would prove a viable option for U.S. policymakers, the likelihood of such situations arising is exceedingly small, and the risks associated with it substantial. As Janne Nolan put the matter, "Although military options may remain among several instruments that could be used to punish those who violate treaties in extreme cases, they are unlikely to be a long-term or widely applicable solution."[102]

RETHINKING NONPROLIFERATION

That some emerging Third World powers have acquired nuclear, chemical, and biological weapons and the means to deliver them is beyond dispute. These states' acquisition of such munitions will heighten the risk of escalation in future regional conflicts, and prompt other nations to seek WMD of their own. For these reasons, the United States and the larger international community share a strong interest in restraining the flow of sensitive military technologies to prospective proliferators around the world, and in persuading WMD-possessing states to freeze their arsenals and commence the process of disarmament.

For these efforts to succeed, however, the United States must adopt a new approach to nonproliferation. The existing approach, based largely on the denial of critical materials and technologies to weapons-seeking states, clearly is not capable of achieving the desired result. In many respects, current U.S. policy is aimed at preserving a world that no longer exists—a world in which weapons of mass destruction remain the exclusive prerogative of the major powers and no one else. The fact is, however, that a number of Third World countries, including several U.S. allies, have acquired such weapons and are capable of expanding their arsenals through largely indigenous means.

Clearly, to deal effectively with the growing danger posed by the spread of WMD capabilities, the United States must move beyond prophylactic efforts and adopt a comprehensive approach to nonproliferation—one that deals with the arsenals that *are*, not just those that might be in the future. This, in turn, will mean abandoning the favoritism that has diluted past U.S. nonproliferation efforts, as well as Washington's historic preference for discriminatory regimes. More than anything it will mean relating nonproliferation policy to the larger question of U.S. security policy in the post–Cold War era.

Chapter Seven

BEYOND THE ROGUES

Military Doctrine

in a World of Chaos

THE ADOPTION OF the Rogue Doctrine and its incorporation into formal strategic doctrine (via the Bottom-Up Review) represent a stunning victory for the U.S. military establishment. Constructed in haste during the fateful months following the Berlin Wall's collapse, the doctrine assures the military steady funding at near–Cold War levels for an indefinite future. It also provides a rationale for the retention of a large proportion of the high-tech forces once deployed for combat with the Warsaw Pact—forces that many Pentagon officials had feared would be deemed superfluous in the post–Cold War era. Indeed, no outcome could have been more gratifying to the Rogue Doctrine's creators than its current status as the governing rationale of U.S. military policy.

Just as the containment doctrine provided an earlier generation of military officers with a clear, coherent guide to policy formation during forty years of superpower competition, the Rogue Doctrine gives today's officers a strategic compass in an uncertain, post-Soviet environment. It provides a roster of hypothetical enemies, suggests a range of possible combat scenarios, and prescribes various military responses. Even more important, it provides American officers with a credible mission—a *raison d'être*—to fill the void left by the receding Soviet threat.

In justice to history, it should be recalled that the Rogue Doctrine received an enormous boost from the August 1990 Iraqi invasion of Kuwait. From the military's point of view, the doctrine had many attractive features—but it would not have generated the support it did in Congress without the timely emergence of a genuine renegade to lend plausibility to what had been a hastily manufactured concept. Saddam Hussein, not realizing that the U.S. military establishment had just adopted a strategic posture aimed at regimes like his, virtually guaranteed an American military response when he sent his troops into Kuwait. From then on, the concept of rogue regimes with hegemonic aspirations would become an ever more familiar theme in American foreign policy.[1]

The Gulf War not only confirmed the validity of the Rogue Doctrine, but also supplied the preferred strategic template for all future wars. However unique the 1991 U.S.–Iraqi encounter might have appeared to independent analysts, it was anointed by Pentagon officials as *the* model for major regional conflicts. With the preferred model for all future wars in place, the key issue remaining for Pentagon officials was to determine how many "Desert Storm Equivalents" (DSEs) the military should be designed to fight at any one time. While some members of Congress attempted in 1992–93 to limit this number to one and a half, the Pentagon succeeded in setting the number at two, thereby establishing a permanent requirement for a military establishment only slightly smaller than that fielded in the late 1970s and 1980s, when the United States was holding itself ready for global conflict with the Soviet Union. Even if Congress never provides all the funds needed to fully sustain such an establishment, a two-DSE capability will likely remain the Pentagon's ideal standard for military preparedness.

But will this strategy ever be tested again in combat? Nothing is impossible, but the likelihood of another Desert Storm–like engagement with a major regional power like the Iraq of 1990 is rather low. Only North Korea now possesses a military establishment akin to that of Iraq's, and most of the fighting in any future war against the North most likely would be performed by South Koreans, not Americans. Other potential rogue adversaries have smaller and weaker militaries than Saddam Hussein's, and are likely to avoid a head-on clash with American power; or, in the case of China and India, possess much larger forces that could not be easily over-powered through some replication of Operation Desert Storm. The probability of U.S. troops engaging in even *one* replay of Desert Storm appears to be very low; that of a two-DSE scenario, close to zero.[2]

Nevertheless, the two-war, Desert Storm model is likely to govern U.S. military policy for a long time to come. Barring the unlikely emergence of a new superpower, no other posture is so well positioned to elicit ongoing Congressional support, and none is so well designed to satisfy the Pentagon's preference for a high-tech, capital-intensive force. Pentagon officials are thus likely to make every effort to preserve the basic strategic framework of the anti-rogue posture. This will probably remain true whether President Clinton is followed in the White House by a Democrat or a Republican, and regardless of whether the Democrats regain primacy in Congress following the 1996 elections.[3].

America's continuing adherence to the Rogue Doctrine is likely to have profound and long-lasting implications for U.S. society. These implications have received scant attention from government officials, the media, and academic researchers; indeed, rarely has a strategic shift of such significance been sanctioned by civilian policymakers with so little debate and discussion.

Most obvious is the elimination of prospects for a significant re-duction in military spending and the possible redistribution of federal funds to other national priorities. To implement a two-war strategy, the United States would have to spend about $250 billion per year (in 1994 dollars) on "military preparedness," roughly equal to the same amount spent annually on the military during the 1950s, 1960s, and 1970s (excluding peak years of the Korean and Vietnam conflicts).[4] Congress, of course, may try to whittle this amount down a bit and save a billion dollars here or there, but no major reductions will be possible so long as a majority in Congress adheres to the basic logic of the Rogue Doctrine. Attempts to reduce military spending by even a modest amount are likely to be held hostage to Pentagon claims that such action will undermine the two-war strategy, and thereby invite aggressive action by future Iraqs.

Continuing adherence to the Rogue Doctrine will entail a significant risk of precipitous intervention in future regional conflicts. Once U.S. policymakers adopt fixed assumptions regarding the identity of future adversaries, they may be disposed to view any seemingly hostile behavior by those countries as a vital and immediate threat to U.S. security. This has often, in the past, led to the implementation of war plans developed in anticipation of such an encounter. A process of this sort was clearly evident in Washington's reaction to the so-called Tonkin Gulf Incident of August 2–3, 1964, when a number of North Vietnamese torpedo boats allegedly fired on a pair of American destroyers—an action to which President Johnson responded by ordering massive air attacks against North Vietnam and requesting Congressional authorization (via the Gulf of Tonkin Resolution of August 7, 1964) for unlimited military action in the region. This process was also evident in the hasty and excessive U.S. military response to events in Grenada (in 1983) and Panama (in 1989). Washington's current demonization of Third World "rogues" puts U.S. policymakers at risk of similar overreaction to future crises, increasing the likelihood of military intervention in regional disputes that might otherwise be resolved through diplomatic action.

An intimation of this danger was provided by the spring 1994 furor over North Korean nuclear inspections. At the height of the crisis, newspapers and television news shows were full of reports of imminent military preparations for a possible war with North Korea, and some policymakers urged President Clinton to take extreme measures, such as a preemptive strike against North Korean nuclear facilities.[5] Only an eleventh-hour peacemaking visit by former President Jimmy Carter to the North Korean capital, Pyongyang, slowed the rush to war and allowed the negotiating process to get back on track.

There is a possibility of another crisis of this sort occurring whenever a designated "rogue" engages in action that, from Washington's point of view, appears to conform to stereotyped images of "outlaw" behavior. Such action may, of course, constitute a genuine threat to U.S. or allied security, but the tendency to assume the worst about rogues' intentions and, at times of crisis, to move quickly toward a military response may prevent careful appraisal of these states' behavior and discourage the pursuit of diplomatic solutions.

Even if such stereotyped thinking does not result in war, it may poison U.S. relations with Third World countries, and thereby retard future progress on proliferation, environmental protection, human rights, and other vital issues. Because the "rogue" appellation has no fixed content but presumably can be applied to any state, it may be interpreted by some Third World leaders as a blanket indictment of their efforts to diminish their countries' military inferiority, and not just as a description of certain anti-Western regimes. This, in turn, may prompt some states to adopt more belligerent and confrontational stances toward the United States.

Such a process clearly unfolded in 1991, when an American defense contractor, the General Dynamics Corporation (producers of the Tomahawk land-attack cruise missile), provoked a diplomatic clash with India. In a presentation to invited policymakers, company officials—drawing on the sort of anti-rogue thinking that had already become popular in Washington—suggested that the United States might decide to retaliate against a future Indian attack on Pakistan by firing hundreds of Tomahawks at military and industrial sites in India. When news of the presentation made its way into the Indian press, it was widely cited as evidence of an abiding Western inclination to dominate India—a reaction that significantly enhanced the position of those in the Indian military and parliament who favor continued pursuit of nuclear weapons.[6]

Future incidents of this sort, coupled with the generalized use of "rogue state" imagery by American leaders, could produce increased suspicions of and hostility to the United States in the developing world. Such a situation would frustrate U.S. efforts to elicit Third World support for many key initiatives, particularly in the nonproliferation area. Even more serious, it could undermine American efforts to persuade rising powers like India and Iran to abandon their WMD development programs and eliminate their existing stockpiles.

By far the most serious and damaging consequence of the Rogue Doctrine's adoption, however, is its preemption of other strategic postures perhaps more suitable to the post–Cold War security environment. Emerging Third World hegemons may represent a potential peril, but other challenges to global security appear far more threatening, and the measures taken by the United States in accordance with the Pentagon's anti-rogue strategy are not likely to prove helpful in dealing with them. To fully appreciate the implications of the Rogue Doctrine, then, it is necessary to identify the most likely threats to peace and security.

"TECTONIC FORCES" AND THE EMERGING WORLD SECURITY ENVIRONMENT

While no one can produce a detailed guide to future events, analysts have spoken of the "tectonic forces" that are reshaping human society and sharpening conflicts among various groups, tribes, peoples, and states. Like the geological forces that are gradually displacing the world's continental plates, a number of powerful economic, social, and environmental forces are putting great stress on the relationships within, and between, human societies.[7]

Four or five major forces appear to be reshaping human civilization and intensifying intergroup frictions along societal fault lines. These include: (1) the globalization of the market economy, producing increased competition between older and newer centers of capitalist production, and everywhere widening the gap between rich and poor; (2) the diminishing allure of large, multiethnic state systems, and a corresponding increase in the assertion of ethno-nationalist loyalties; (3) the growing worldwide popularity of Western consumer culture, and, in response, a dramatic resurgence of traditional mores and religion; (4) a substantial rise in global population at a time of mounting resource scarcities and deteriorating environmental conditions; and (5) a worldwide loss of faith in the ability of existing state structures to cope successfully with these multiple pressures.[8]

These forces are combining in varied and unpredictable ways to sharpen and intensify preexisting resentments and disputes, often to the breaking point. The result, in all too many cases, has been the outbreak of armed conflict of one sort or another. These include, but are not limited to, the following:

- *Ethnic conflicts* between neighboring groups and tribes that each seek control over a particular piece of territory, as visible in Bosnia, Rwanda, Sri Lanka, the Abkhazia region of Georgia, and Nagorno Karabakh (the Armenian enclave in Azerbaijan).

- *Border and irredentist disputes* between the new nations created from the breakup of large, multiethnic states, such as those between Russia and Ukraine over the Crimea and between Serbia and Croatia over the Krajina region. A very similar dispute, harking back to the partition of India, still engulfs the disputed territory of Kashmir.

- *Nationalist struggles* by peoples long denied statehood, including the Tibetans, the Kurds of Turkey and Iraq, the Palestinians of Israel and the Occupied Territories, the Chechens of Russia, and the Timorese of Indonesian-ruled East Timor.

- *Disputes over the control of vital sources of water or petroleum,* such as the dispute between Egypt and Sudan over control of the Nile River, or between China and its southern neighbors over the Spratly and Paracel archipelagos in the South China Sea (believed to lie astride vast undersea oil reserves).

- *Internal conflict* among groups, tribes, clans, and political factions over the distribution of state power and resources, as visible today in Haiti, Angola, Burundi, Chad, Somalia, Sudan, Afghanistan, Tajikistan, and Yemen.

- *Revolutionary and fundamentalist drives* for state power, as in Peru (the Sendero Luminoso), Cambodia (the Khmer Rouge), the Philippines (the New Peoples Army), Algeria (the Islamic Salvation Front), and Egypt (the Islamic Group).

Such conflicts have generated the greatest amount of bloodshed and trauma in the post–Cold War era, leading in some cases to tens or even hundreds of thousands of deaths while also producing hunger and refugee flows that have repeatedly overwhelmed the world's humanitarian aid capabilities.[9] Although distinct in their particulars, these conflicts all seem to reflect deeper concerns about social and economic security in a world experiencing profound stresses. So long as these pressures continue to bear upon human society, it is likely that similar upheavals will occur in other locations.[10]

However bloody and disheartening, such conflicts may not appear to pose the same sort of threat to U.S. security as the Soviet Union in its prime or the rogues today. Certainly, at least at this stage, they do not appear to threaten "vital" national interests such as the Persian Gulf oilfields or America's major European allies. Such initial impressions may be deceiving, however. A war between India and Pakistan over Kashmir, for instance, could trigger the use of nuclear weapons and/or lead to a major regional conflagration; as might a war between Russia and Ukraine over the Crimea, or between China and its neighbors over the oilfields of the South China Sea. Even a localized war in the former Yugoslavia, whose participants have used only the most basic of conventional weaponry, has produced massive refugee flows with political repercussions throughout Europe. There is also a growing danger that ethnic and internal warfare in the Middle East, the Balkans, or North Africa might spill over into areas seen by Washington as possessing greater strategic significance, such as the Persian Gulf or the Mediterranean, and lead someday to U.S. military intervention.

In the final analysis, however, the greatest threat to American and world security arises not from any one of these conflicts or from any individual belligerent—"rogue" or otherwise—but rather from the potential of smaller wars to escalate into region-wide conflagrations or merge together into a generalized condition of global chaos. However distant the United States may be from the main foci of conflict, such violence, when replicated globally, could disrupt international commerce, destroy access to markets and sources of raw materials, unleash mammoth refugee flows, and otherwise erode what worldwide stability now exists.

The emergence of this global threat, however dimly understood, has left U.S. policymakers uncertain and confused. Because few of these ongoing conflicts appear to threaten vital interests as traditionally understood, and because of the high risk of unintended embroilment in sectarian violence, American officials have been understandably wary of becoming deeply involved; yet, given the magnitude of global violence and the massive refugee flows it has already produced, such wars cannot be ignored altogether. How to deal with these ethnic and sectarian conflicts—which play next to no role in the Rogue Doctrine—has become the most critical foreign policy challenge facing U.S. strategists today.

In responding to these challenges, American policymakers have cobbled together a makeshift policy framework for dealing with ethnic, insurgent, and separatist violence. Intended mainly to avoid U.S. military involvement, this framework calls for heavy reliance on U.N. peacekeeping forces, economic sanctions, high-profile diplomacy, threats, and blackmail of one sort or another. In some cases, most notably in Somalia, the United States has also supplied troops for multinational peace operations. Successes have been few and far between: such efforts failed to still internecine warfare in Somalia, "ethnic cleansing" in Bosnia, or political assassination in Haiti; nor has the world community succeeded in stopping the fighting in Angola, Burma, Georgia, Kashmir, Rwanda, Sudan, and other areas of conflict.

Failure in this regard results in part from the complexity of these conflicts and the lack of adequate support for U.N. peacemaking operations. Each of these conflicts has roots in longstanding ethnic, religious, and political disagreements, and has evolved in such a way as to frustrate international efforts at mediation. But the U.S. role in that general failure of policy also reflects a profound lack of imagination on the part of American policymakers, and the continuing grip of irrelevant strategic concepts—most notably, the two-war posture dictated by the Rogue Doctrine.

To sell Congress on a posture that costs $250 billion a year and entails the maintenance of forces designed for an all-out conflict with the Warsaw Pact, Pentagon officials have little choice but to argue that the challenge posed by Third World hegemons represents the greatest ongoing threat to American national security. Any diversion of significant resources to deal with ethnic and sectarian violence— and other, longer-term dangers—must be portrayed by the Pentagon as undermining U.S. capabilities to deal with the alleged rogue state threat. "We understand the difficulties of ethnic conflict and peace operations," Army Chief of Staff General Gordon R. Sullivan and an aide wrote in 1994. But "we understand as well the need to be ready to fight and win two major regional conflicts. . . . We cannot optimize the force for peace operations at the expense of our ability to fight and win a [regional] war."[11]

So long as this military outlook prevails, and preparations continue for an endless series of regional conflicts with Iraq-like adversaries, the United States is unlikely to develop effective strategies for coping with the threat of global chaos. Instead, hundreds of billions of dollars a year will be spent on high-tech forces and equipment that might be useful for some future replay of Desert Storm, but will be of dubious value in those other types of operations in which American forces are most likely to be engaged. Not only our capital resources but also our intellectual resources will be misallocated in this fashion. Instead of perfecting techniques for peacekeeping operations, international crisis control, and humanitarian relief and rescue, strategists will devote endless time to the further embellishment of the Desert Storm template.

AN ALTERNATIVE STRATEGIC POSTURE

If the United States is to prepare effectively for the most significant threats to its security, it must move quickly to adopt a new strategic posture based on a realistic assessment of the world security environment. Such an assessment would rank global chaos as the greatest future threat, followed by the potential for escalation in regional disputes, the uncontrolled spread of ethnic and sectarian strife, and the prospect of mass migrations from disintegrating states in East Europe, North Africa, and Central America.

In responding to these threats, American security policy should have one overriding goal: amelioration of global discord and violence. This, in turn, entails several secondary objectives: the containment, abatement, and termination of existing conflicts; the negotiated resolution of outstanding disputes between states and peoples; the contraction of international arms flows; the strengthening of international peacemaking institutions; the promotion of social and economic development in war-torn and impoverished societies; and the prevention of further environmental decline in ecologically threatened areas.

Obviously, even under optimal conditions, these objectives could not be achieved by the United States alone. No matter what resources U.S. leaders commit to such efforts, Washington will still require the cooperation of other countries. This is not because the United States is in "decline," as suggested by some pundits, or because it lacks the wealth and energy of an earlier epoch; rather, it is because the causes of conflict are now so complex and so globally intertwined that no nation, no matter how wealthy and powerful, can hope to restore peace and stability in any area without substantial assistance from other countries.

In forging a new security policy, then, America's initial task is to work with other states to strengthen international agencies and institutions and to enhance the world's capacity for multilateral peacemaking. This means, first of all, improving the United Nations' ability to conduct the many critical tasks it has been saddled with over the past fifty years, including its peacekeeping functions, international mediation services, nonproliferation and disarmament activities, refugee assistance, health protection services, and its work for the advancement of human rights. For the U.N. to do a better job in these areas, it will need additional financial resources as well as substantial administrative reform, so that any new resources can be employed in a timely and effective manner.[12]

In bolstering U.N. capabilities, moreover, the primary emphasis should be placed on its mediation and peacemaking activities. The Secretary General should be given additional authority to assume a mediating role in areas of current and potential conflict, and to deploy peacekeeping forces at an early stage of hostilities (so as to preclude the need for larger forces later on). Much thought has been given to this matter by the current Secretary General, Boutros Boutros-Ghali, and by other international policymakers. In his 1992 study *An Agenda for Peace*, Boutros-Ghali laid out a range of proposals for enhanced U.N. peacekeeping operations, including the establishment of a "standby" peacekeeping force for rapid deployment to areas of incipient violence. Many of these proposals require additional refinement before they can be put into practice, but every effort should be made to implement them as quickly as possible.[13]

Because the United Nations cannot be expected to cope with every challenge to international peace and security, and because many problems are best handled at the local and regional level, the United States should also assist in the further development of regional organizations, including the Conference on Security and Cooperation in Europe (CSCE), the Organization of American States (OAS), and the Organization of African Unity (OAU). These organizations should be invested with greater responsibility for the mediation of local disputes, the negotiation of regional arms control and disarmament measures, the protection of human rights, and the promotion of social and economic development. The United States should also assist in establishing such bodies in areas where they do not now exist, including South Asia and the Far East.[14]

The second major task of a new security posture should be to drastically curb the international traffic in conventional armaments. Although most contemporary conflicts are derived from deep-seated fears and animosities that, in many cases, are centuries old, the global abundance of arms makes it easier for belligerents to initiate, sustain, and escalate armed combat against their enemies, and to resist international pressures for a negotiated settlement. This has been particularly evident in Bosnia, where month after month the warring parties have been able to sustain high levels of combat with arms and ammunition secured through a host of illicit and clandestine routes. The ready availability of arms has also helped to sustain fighting in Afghanistan, Angola, Burma, Cambodia, Kashmir, Rwanda, Somalia, and Sri Lanka.[15] Even when these countries are not the intended recipients of arms, the global munitions trade is so diffuse and elastic that large numbers of weapons regularly disappear into black market channels.[16]

The worldwide reach of the arms trade also contributes to the growing violence and destructiveness of contemporary conflicts. Although combatants in these conflicts will turn readily to the most traditional of low-tech weaponry when nothing else is available (as in the bloody massacres in Rwanda in the spring and summer of 1994), the growing international availability of modern aircraft, guided missiles, lightweight artillery, and other such weaponry has dramatically increased the severity of many recent wars. The Iran-Iraq war of 1980–88, for instance, destroyed hundreds of billions of dollars' worth of property and resulted in the death or injury of more than one million people.[17] The growing intensity of conventional warfare is also increasing the danger that WMD-equipped belligerents will employ chemical or nuclear weapons in future wars to avert the apparently imminent defeat of their regular forces.

Despite these dangers, the United States continues to sell large quantities of modern weapons to friendly countries around the world. In 1989–93, for instance, American military firms and the Department of Defense sold $116 billion worth of arms and combat equipment to 160 nations and territories, including 39 in Africa and

38 in South and Central America.[18] In defending these sales, American officials regularly argue that they only deal with "responsible" governments that seek such weaponry for "legitimate defensive purposes."[19] But many of these governments, including Iraq's, have engaged in adventuristic or aggressive behavior, and others have transferred their U.S.-supplied arms to countries not legally entitled to receive them.[20] With so many countries acquiring U.S. weapons, moreover, it is impossible to prevent a certain percentage of these arms from disappearing into black market circles.[21]

However expedient in the short term, American arms sales are contributing to a global glut in military hardware and facilitating the efforts of future belligerents to gear up for war. It is essential, therefore, that the United States work with other arms suppliers to establish new multilateral restraints on the weapons trade. Such curbs, while aimed at a generalized reduction in global arms trafficking, should incorporate tight controls on especially dangerous and destabilizing weapons (for example, cruise missiles and nuclear-capable deep-strike aircraft) and on arms deliveries to areas of conflict.[22] The United States should also take the initiative in launching a global crackdown on black market trafficking, working in conjunction with Interpol and the governments of other affected states to identify, monitor, and apprehend illegal arms dealers. In those countries where the necessary law enforcement capacity is lacking, as in much of the former Soviet Union, technical assistance should be provided by Washington to the appropriate government agencies.[23]

A third key goal of a new security posture should be to bring U.S. and international programs in economic development, population control, and environmental protection in line with efforts to reduce global chaos and violence. Such coordination is essential because of the critical relationship between underdevelopment, environmental decline, and intergroup conflict. Although the precise nature of this relationship is not yet fully understood, researchers are now certain that the rising tide of ethnic and tribal violence can be traced, at least in part, to economic stagnation, explosive population growth, and resource scarcities in environmentally threatened areas. As once viable tilling and grazing lands give out due to overuse, overpopulation, and climatic change, the inhabitants of these lands usually migrate to other areas—often provoking clashes with other ethnic groups and/or contributing to social and economic unrest in already over-crowded Third World urban shantytowns.[24]

To prevent such turmoil, greater efforts are needed to promote sustainable economic development in chronically depressed areas, to protect ecologically fragile regions, and to bring population growth in line with long-term economic growth. Much research and plan-ning has already taken place in each of these areas, but not as part of a larger effort to diminish global violence. Once the connections between these phenomena and intergroup conflict are better under-stood, U.S. aid and development strategies should be geared to con-flict avoidance in areas of potential or recurring violence.[25]

In all of this, a conscious effort should be made to alleviate the global pressures that are now sharpening the divisions between and within human societies. So long as these pressures remain, it will be possible only to mitigate their results, not to eliminate the causes of violence. To accomplish the latter, greater emphasis must be placed on the promotion of authentic, sustainable development in impov-erished areas and on programs to increase economic opportunities for the poor and unemployed. Equally essential are efforts to enhance political participation by unrepresented peoples in local and national government, and to protect the rights of historically disadvantaged minorities. Only through such efforts will it be possible to allay the underlying causes of intergroup friction and reduce the global in-cidence of violent conflict.

Finally, adoption of a new security posture should entail the de-velopment of policies aimed at the main issues addressed in this book: the threat posed by "rogue" regimes in the Third World, the challenge of proliferation, and the U.S. military's role in the post–Cold War era.

COPING WITH THE ROGUES: A STRATEGY OF "MARGINALIZATION"

Any strategy for promoting long-term international security must deal with the threats posed by aggression-minded Third World powers along with all other challenges to global stability; but the response to this threat should be commensurate with the degree of risk it poses, not out of proportion to it. At present, U.S. security policy magnifies the rogue state threat by devoting excessive attention to a handful of isolated and vulnerable regimes. While some of them do pose an elevated risk to regional stability, this danger has often been exaggerated or taken out of the context of regional rivalries in which other states may pose an equal or greater threat.

The adoption of the Rogue Doctrine has prompted American policymakers to invest considerable time and effort in the development of strategies for containing, weakening, and fighting rogue nations. While this might appear to be an appropriate response to a significant danger, it has put these countries on notice that they may be future targets of U.S. military action, and thus may have spurred some of them to bolster their defenses or accelerated their quest for weapons of mass destruction—thereby posing an increased threat to American allies and interests in their vicinity.

At the same time, the Pentagon's policy of identifying certain Third World states as possible enemies may have inspired a certain bravado of the "David and Goliath" variety on the part of these nations' leaders, leading them to eschew compromise and engage in high-risk behavior. There is definite evidence of such behavior in Saddam Hussein's stubborn refusal to withdraw from Kuwait, in Iranian leaders' continuing support of international terrorism, and in North Korea's dogged pursuit of nuclear weapons. Such behavior naturally reinforces American suspicions regarding the intentions of these states' leaders, resulting in an increased risk of U.S. intervention.

To minimize these dangers, the United States should adopt a strategy of rogue state "marginalization"—that is, an effort to diminish these countries' perceived international importance, cut off their access to high-tech commodities, minimize the global media's interest in them, and eliminate any appeal they may have as models for other Third World countries. Without engaging in inflammatory rhetoric, American leaders should strive to minimize the rogues' role in regional and international organizations and otherwise isolate them from the international community. At the same time, Washington should hold out the promise of increased trade, contact, and attention should they agree to abandon their aggressive policies and behave in a more cooperative and peaceful manner.

This approach should be followed with particular vigor in the proliferation arena. Every effort should be made to deny these states access to dual-use materials and know-how that might contribute to their WMD endeavors. Some progress has already been made in this direction by the Bush and Clinton administrations, but further work clearly is needed to close significant loopholes. At the same time, various inducements should be offered to states that renounce WMD activities and agree to abide by international nonproliferation standards—an approach that has shown signs of possible success in negotiations with North Korea.[26]

In sum, the message these states should be given is that they have little to gain by persisting in aggressive or hostile behavior—no accolades or rewards for their "heroic resistance" to "Western imperialism"—and that they would be far better off by if they rejoined the international community on friendly terms. Such an approach would have the added benefit of undercutting the perceived legitimacy of rogue regimes among other states, as well as among their own populations. So long as the rogue regimes are described in Washington as dangerous outlaws that must be countered with the full weight of American power, they will be seen by at least some constituencies as worthy of respect for standing up to the imperial West; if, however, American leaders were to give up their preoccupation with these regimes, they might lose some of their popular legitimacy among their own populations. This, in turn, could pave the way for the emergence of new, less antagonistic forces in these societies or prompt existing leaders to change their ways.

PROMOTING NONPROLIFERATION

In a world of chaos, the overriding goal of nonproliferation and arms control must be to prevent the use of weapons of mass destruction by those states already possessing them. Until now, the United States has focused primarily on prophylactic strategies: preventing non–WMD states in the Third World from acquiring the materials and know-how to produce nuclear, chemical, and biological weapons, and slowing any illicit weapons programs in existing WMD states (especially those considered hostile to the West). While such efforts remain essential, priorities should now shift toward *anti-escalation* strategies: that is, persuading states already possessing nuclear or chemical weapons to freeze their stockpiles, reduce their reliance on WMD, and engage in regional peace and security negotiations aimed at the eventual elimination of such munitions.

—

Switching to such an anti-escalation strategy will require a significant shift in U.S. thinking. Historically, American leaders have expressed greatest concern over the acquisition of WMD capabilities by hostile Third World states such as Iran, Libya, and North Korea, while appearing relatively unperturbed by the growing WMD capabilities of friendly states such as Egypt, India, Israel, South Korea, and Taiwan. Friendly or not, however, these are the states most capable of using weapons of mass destruction in future conflicts, and therefore the ones most deserving of international attention. Because any of these countries could be swept up in a regional conflagration of unpredictable scope and intensity, it is essential that they be brought into the various nonproliferation regimes and persuaded to eliminate their weapons of mass destruction.

To involve these states in vigorous nonproliferation endeavors will not be easy. Most have acquired weapons of mass destruction in the belief—usually realistic—that they face a significant threat from powerful, often WMD–equipped rivals. All feel justified in having done so given the large and diversified WMD arsenals of the traditional powers. Some of these countries also believe that Washington's and Moscow's historic permissiveness regarding the WMD acquisitions of certain favored countries gives them license to proceed in a similar manner—especially if they view themselves as being threatened by one of those states. Washington must address these states' concerns if it hopes to overcome their resistance to future nonproliferation efforts. This, in turn, will require three problematic but essential commitments from American leaders:

- First, the ultimate goal of nonproliferation policy must be a *world free of weapons of mass destruction*, ours included. Although the complete elimination of all such weapons may be a long-term goal, requiring the establishment of new international security structures of a type as yet not discernible, the United States cannot expect other states to give up their weapons of mass destruction unless it agrees, in principle, to give up its own as well. Because Washington has already agreed to eliminate its chemical and biological weapons, this means promising to give up its nuclear weapons and long-range ballistic missiles—or at least demonstrating that it is prepared to make significant strides in this direction.

- Second, nonproliferation measures must *apply equally and uniformly to all WMD-seeking states*, whether or not friends and allies of the United States. Even if it is not possible for the United States to abandon its traditional policies all at once, adoption of this principle is essential for Washington to gain the participation of all WMD-seeking states in future disarmament efforts.

- Third, nonproliferation must be accompanied by *regional peace and security systems* aimed at the amelioration of regional disputes and antagonisms. Weapons-seeking states will not voluntarily abandon their WMD acquisition and development efforts unless they are assured that any threats posed by neighboring states are being alleviated at the same time, and that the major powers, including the United States, are prepared to guarantee full compliance with any agreed-upon regional disarmament schemes.

Once U.S. leaders have announced their commitment to these three principles, it will be possible for Washington to fashion a meaningful and effective strategy for nonproliferation. Such a strategy should proceed on three fronts: (1) strengthening existing nonproliferation regimes through increased participation and compliance by WMD-seeking states; (2) taking the profit out of proliferation; and (3) promoting regional peace and security regimes.

1. Strengthening the Existing Nonproliferation Regimes

Because the existing nonproliferation regimes—the Nuclear Non-Proliferation Treaty (NPT), the Chemical Weapons Convention (CWC), the Biological Weapons Convention (BWC), and the Missile Technology Control Regime (MTCR)—are not likely to be replaced by other measures, it is essential that they be made as inclusive and effective as possible. This means bringing more nonmembers into each, insisting that all signatory parties fully comply with their provisions, and bolstering their capacity for verification and enforcement.[27]

The most important goal, by far, is to involve such major proliferators as India, Israel, North Korea, and Pakistan in these regimes, and to develop acceptable strategies for bringing them into full compliance with their provisions. Although these states have resisted such efforts in the past, they are more likely to prove amenable once U.S. leaders agree to the principles enunciated above and begin to carry them out. With the United States downsizing its own WMD stockpiles and enforcing existing nonproliferation constraints equitably, American leaders will be in a much stronger position to persuade their counterparts in New Delhi, Tel Aviv, Pyongyang, and Islamabad to relinquish their WMD capabilities and to comply with established nonproliferation norms.[28]

Washington must also be prepared to employ a variety of incentives and disincentives—"carrots and sticks"—when approaching nonmembers. As incentives for participation, nonmembers could be offered increased access to economic and technical assistance from the advanced industrial nations, enhanced trade opportunities, and promises of military aid in the event that they are threatened by other WMD-seeking powers. Disincentives, by contrast, could consist of economic and trade sanctions, progressive isolation from the world community, and the denial of military and technical assistance.[29]

Economic incentives and disincentives should also be employed to persuade emerging military producers—especially Argentina, Brazil, China, India, and Israel—to join and adhere to the various technology control groups (the Nuclear Suppliers Group, the Australia Group, the MTCR, and so on). States that agree to comply with these regimes by restricting their exports of WMD-related products should be rewarded with economic and trade benefits, along with increased access to cutting-edge civilian technologies; holdouts should be denied such benefits. A good example of this approach is the Memorandum of Understanding adopted by the United States and Argentina on February 12, 1993, under which Argentina will be permitted access to advanced U.S. technologies in return for a pledge to impose strict nonproliferation controls on its exports of nuclear, chemical, and missile systems.[30] Similar agreements should be signed with such states as Brazil, India, and Israel; at the same time, additional pressure should be brought to bear on China to cease its questionable sales of nuclear and missile technology to Iran, Pakistan, and Syria.

Finally, better mechanisms are needed to monitor suspect proliferation behavior by weapons-seeking states, and to bring international pressure to bear on these states to comply with international nonproliferation restraints. In the nuclear area, this means strengthening the International Atomic Energy Agency and providing it with sufficient staff and funding to carry out its many demanding responsibilities. Similarly, every effort should be made to get the Organization for the Prohibition of Chemical Weapons (OPCW) up and running, and to endow it with the resources it will need to carry out all of the various inspections mandated by the CWC.[31] Finally, to ensure full compliance with the BWC, provision for similar inspections should be agreed to by member parties, and the OPCW or a similar organization should be empowered to carry them out.

2. Taking the Profit Out of Proliferation

Many WMD-seeking states have been aided in their proliferation activities by commercial enterprises in the major supplier countries. These companies have sought to profit from the demand for WMD-related products by supplying suspected proliferators with sensitive dual-use items, knowing that they would probably be diverted to secret military projects. Illicit corporate involvement in WMD technology sales has been especially significant in the chemical weapons area: according to former CIA Director William Webster, assistance provided by foreign suppliers "has been the key element" in the acquisition of CW production capabilities by such states as Iran, Iraq, Libya, and Syria. When asked to explain why Western companies might want to participate in such endeavors, Webster replied: "I can only surmise that greed is the explanation."[32]

Clearly, one way to reduce the threat of proliferation is to eliminate, as far as possible, the element of greed from the proliferation equation. As long as unscrupulous firms or individuals believe that they can benefit from weapons-seeking states' appetite for sensitive commodities without risk or penalty, they will seize every opportunity to circumvent existing restraints on the sale of WMD-related products. If, however, the risks and costs of engaging in such trafficking can be increased substantially, and if the penalties for being found guilty of illegal sales are sufficiently harsh, private entrepreneurs and corporations will be far less likely to seek profit in this fashion. No doubt, some desperate individuals will continue to pursue lucrative sales through black-market channels, but the number doing so will be much fewer and the services they can provide will be far more limited.

Taking the profit out of proliferation is more a national than an international enterprise, although multilateral efforts will be required as well. Each of the major supplier countries will need to adopt tough restrictions on the export of sensitive materials and technology, along with suitable penalties for noncompliance. Improved national and international mechanisms are also needed to monitor suspicious proliferation activities, to track suspicious shipments across international borders, and to identify illicit links between military agencies in WMD-seeking states and private firms in other countries. The United States can assist in these efforts by providing technical assistance in the establishment of appropriate oversight mechanisms, and in the development of the necessary legal and regulatory provisions.

Such help is particularly needed in the case of the successor states to the Soviet Union, several of which, including Russia and Ukraine, possess large reservoirs of nuclear and chemical warfare materials along with well-developed criminal undergrounds and inadequate control systems. Some assistance has already been provided to these states under the Nunn-Lugar program (named for its principal sponsors, Senators Sam Nunn and Richard Lugar), which allocates funds for the safe and secure storage and destruction of ex-Soviet weapons of mass destruction.[33] Recent reports of the smuggling of weapons-grade nuclear materials from Russia to Western Europe suggest, however, that much greater efforts will be needed in this critical area.[34]

3. Promoting Regional Security

Ultimately, it will not be possible to halt the proliferation of weapons of mass destruction so long as there are states with the means and the desire to acquire such capabilities. If these states feel threatened by other well-armed powers in their vicinity, and believe that the possession of WMD will significantly enhance their security, they are unlikely to be swayed by pleas from other states to abide by global nonproliferation constraints. Efforts to slow the pace of WMD proliferation must therefore include initiatives aimed at the demand side of the equation. In particular, future nonproliferation efforts should entail efforts to alleviate the security concerns of Third World powers and help diminish the potential threat to them posed by other states. The best way to accomplish this is through the establishment of regional peace and security systems such as the Conference on Security and Cooperation in Europe (CSCE) that provide for region-wide conflict resolution and arms control under international supervision.[35]

Unfortunately, the development of regional security arrangements has not generally been viewed as a major aspect of the nonproliferation effort. But with the continuing resistance of India, Israel, Pakistan, and other states to participation in existing nonproliferation regimes, it is obvious that the demand side of the proliferation equation requires greater attention. "Improved supplier restrictions will have to be bolstered with efforts to lessen demand for proscribed military activities," nonproliferation expert Janne Nolan observed in 1992. "The developed world must not only control access to weapons technology, but must also simultaneously work to enhance developing states' security [and thereby diminish their appetite for weapons of mass destruction]."[36]

As examples of such efforts, Nolan cited the 1968 Treaty of Tlatelolco, establishing a nuclear-weapons-free zone (NWFZ) in Latin America, and the 1986 Treaty of Rarotonga, creating a NWFZ in the South Pacific area.[37] These, and similar arrangements proposed for other areas, differ from technology-denial systems like the NPT and MTCR in that participating states agree to impose mutual restrictions on their own military activities and to eschew the importation and/or development of certain types of weapons. More important, they provide for the peaceful resolution of intraregional disputes and, in many cases, establish special bodies for dispute resolution, crisis control, and peacekeeping operations.[38]

To reduce the long-term demand for weapons of mass destruction, existing regional security systems should be strengthened as much as possible and used as models for the development of similar systems in other areas. Assuming that the Middle East peace makes genuine progress, and that the Treaty of Tlatelolco is fully ratified by all Latin American countries (including Argentina, Brazil, and Cuba), the most important priority for future action is the initiation of regional security talks in South Asia and the Far East. At present, there is no such process under way in these two areas, despite the fact that key states in these regions are continuing to expand their WMD stockpiles. Major diplomatic efforts therefore should be undertaken by Washington to persuade the nations of these areas to engage in regional security talks and to consider proposals for ending their arms competition.[39]

TOWARD A NEW MILITARY POSTURE

As with every other aspect of foreign policy, U.S. military doctrine must be reconfigured in light of the emerging security challenges of the current era. Because the greatest threat the United States faces today arises from the worldwide proliferation of local conflicts and their potential escalation into regional conflagrations, it is essential that military strategy—like all other components of national policy —be refocused on efforts to prevent, contain, abate, and terminate violent conflicts. In essence, this means developing a military trained and equipped for a wide variety of peacemaking and crisis control activities—including multilateral peacekeeping operations, enforcement of U.N. arms embargoes, and humanitarian aid and rescue— in addition to traditional military activities.

The U.S. military has already conducted many peacekeeping operations in Somalia, Rwanda, Haiti, northern Iraq, the former Yugoslavia, and elsewhere, and is familiar with the tasks and challenges involved. When ordered by the President to engage in such operations, American soldiers have, for the most part, performed with skill and distinction. But this is not what U.S. officers view as their primary mission—namely, the defeat of Iraq-like powers in major regional conflicts of the Desert Storm variety. So long as the military considers implementation of a two-MRC strategy as its top priority, it will not devote the organizational capabilities—and, more important, the leadership and intellectual skills—needed for the successful performance of its peacekeeping and peace-enforcement responsibilities.[40]

For the most part, such responsibilities entail small-unit operations in relatively austere environments with opposition (if any) coming from lightly armed paramilitary or militia-type forces. Such engagements pose challenges very different from those encountered in Operation Desert Storm, and require, in consequence, that American troops be trained and equipped in a different fashion. Instead of relying on massive firepower, as in the Persian Gulf conflict, they must learn to rely on precision, speed, coordination, knowledge of the terrain and the local population, and solid negotiation skills. Superior intelligence-gathering and communications capabilities will still be vital, but heavy weapons will rarely be needed.

To excel at such operations, the military should be transformed from a two-MRC establishment to a crisis control establishment—from a force made up mostly of large, heavily equipped units to one composed primarily of small, lightly equipped units. Every soldier in such a force should receive training in various aspects of peace-keeping and peace-enforcement operations (just as every soldier was once trained to engage in high-intensity combat with the Warsaw Pact), and every officer should be well schooled in the distinctive features of such endeavors. Because peacekeeping is almost always an international activity, moreover, American troops should engage in joint training with those of other nations, and all junior officers should be assigned at least once to a multinational staff or command.

A force organized along these lines would be much smaller and less heavily armed than that mandated by the Bottom-Up Review. It would still incorporate a number of heavy units (perhaps four or five Army divisions) as a hedge against the future emergence of a powerful adversary, but most active Army and Marine Corps units should be relatively compact (battalion and regimental sized), lightly equipped, and ready for rapid assignment to overseas crisis zones. These forces should be assisted by a Navy and Air Force organized along similar lines, with considerable long-range mobility and a capacity to operate out of austere ports and airfields, but with fewer carriers, cruisers, and heavy bombers. Although some new expenses would be generated by such a plan—say, for acquisition of more transport planes and hospital ships—the total cost of the military establishment would decline by a considerable margin.[41]

What will not be needed under a military posture of this sort is a large inventory of intercontinental ballistic missiles, missile-carrying submarines, Stealth bombers, and nuclear warheads. Congress, the Executive Branch, and the American people will have to determine how many of each of these items the United States will require for a residual deterrent force so long as the Russian, China, and other nuclear-armed states continue to deploy some weapons of these types. But with the continuing decline in Russian military capabilities and the growing tempo of U.S.–Russian arms control negotiations, the need is already quite small, and is likely to grow even smaller in the years ahead. Although we cannot yet imagine that need dropping to zero, we should design our military and arms control policies to move us as rapidly as possible in this direction.

By diminishing our own reliance on nuclear weapons and related systems, we achieve another key objective: the advancement of WMD nonproliferation among rising Third World powers. So long as the United States and other traditional powers rest their military posture on the possession of nuclear munitions and ballistic missiles, aspiring hegemons will seek such capabilities as counters to their use by other states, or as tickets of entry into the nuclear and missile clubs. If, however, the United States significantly reduces its stockpile of nuclear weapons and eschews their use as an instrument of war it will be much easier to persuade WMD-seeking powers to abandon their quest for such munitions.[42]

Adoption of a crisis control posture in place of the Pentagon's existing two-MRC strategy will enhance national security in several ways: first, by better equipping American forces to play a significant role in international efforts to contain the threat of global chaos; second, by reducing overall military spending and thereby freeing federal funds for the reconstruction of America's educational and industrial infrastructure; and third, by facilitating American efforts to promote international nonproliferation. Equally important, it will liberate U.S. strategists from the "tunnel vision" induced by rigid adherence to faulty military doctrine, and enable them to develop responses to the greatest dangers facing the United States.

Once the new military posture has been adopted, a major priority for U.S. military leaders will be to develop, test, and evaluate new and innovative plans and tactics for international peacemaking and crisis control in the changing and chaotic world of the twenty-first century. Unlike the sham exercise conducted by Defense Secretary Les Aspin and his staff in 1993, this effort should entail a genuine "bottom-up review," intended to reconsider every aspect of military planning in light of the altered character of the global security environment. Analysts from every sector of American society should be invited to participate in this review, and the American public should have ample opportunity to debate its outcome.

Ultimately, military doctrine is only useful when it serves to prepare the armed forces for coping with the most likely threats to national security. The two-war, anti-rogue posture developed by Pentagon officials at the Cold War's end is conceivably useful in meeting some low-probability threats, but largely irrelevant to the larger spectrum of global security risks. In a world of chaos, such negligence is an invitation to disaster. Only by discarding the two-war strategy and adopting a more realistic posture can we ensure that American forces will be adequately prepared for the challenges of the coming century.

CHAPTER ONE

1. Quoted in Thomas L. Friedman, "U.S. Enthusiastic, but Has Concerns," *New York Times*, November 11, 1989.

2. From transcript of speech by Les Aspin at Georgetown University, Washington, D.C., September 2, 1993.

3. Gaddis Smith, "What Role for America?" *Current History*, April 1993, pp. 150–51.

4. International Institute for Strategic Studies, *The Military Balance 1989–1990* (London: Brassey's, 1989), pp. 16–27. (Hereinafter cited as IISS, *The Military Balance 19xx–19xx.*)

5. Smith, "What Role for America," p. 151.

6. Quoted in Patrick E. Tylor, "New Pentagon 'Guidance' Cites Soviet Threat in Third World," *Washington Post*, February 13, 1990.

7. From transcript of press conference at the Department of Defense, Washington, D.C., September 1, 1993.

8. For examples of this literature, see Robert B. Reich, *The Next American Frontier* (New York: Times Books, 1983); Robert B. Reich and Ira C. Magaziner, *Minding America's Business: The Decline and Rise of the American Economy* (New York: Harcourt Brace Jovanovich, 1982); Bruce R. Scott and

George C. Lodge, eds., *U.S. Competitiveness in the World Economy* (Boston: Harvard Business School Press, 1985); Lester C. Thurow, *The Zero-Sum Solution: Building a World-Class American Economy* (New York: Simon and Schuster, 1985); Laura Tyson and John Zysman, *American Industry in International Competition* (Ithaca: Cornell University Press, 1983).

9. Paul Kennedy, *The Rise and Fall of the Great Powers* (New York: Random House, 1987). See also Kennedy, "The (Relative) Decline of America," *Atlantic Monthly*, August 1987, pp. 29–38.

10. See, for instance, "Does America Need an Army," *U.S. News and World Report*, December 11, 1989, pp. 22–30.

11. See R. Jeffrey Smith, "Arms Cuts Gain Favor as Anxieties Ebb," *Washington Post*, May 8, 1989.

12. See David E. Rosenbaum, "Pentagon Spending Could Be Cut in Half," *New York Times*, December 13, 1989.

13. Quoted in Ibid.

14. Quoted in Tom Kenworthy and Molly Moore, "Democrats Gird to Lower Boom on Military Budget," *Washington Post*, January 14, 1990.

15. Ibid.

16. See Smith, "Arms Cuts Gain Favor."

17. U.S. Department of Defense, *Annual Report to the Congress*, Fiscal Year 1991 (Washington, D.C., January 1990), p. 1. (Hereinafter cited as DoD, *Annual Report FYxx.*)

18. From the "Defense Guidance Document for Fiscal Years 1992–97," as cited in Taylor, "New Pentagon 'Guidance.'" Cheney's continued emphasis on the Soviet threat is confirmed by an internal Pentagon study of strategic planning during this crucial period. See Lorna S. Jaffe, *The Development of the Base Force 1989–1992* (Washington, D.C.: Joint History Office, Office of the Chairman of the Joint Chiefs of Staff, 1993), pp. 18, 20.

19. See, for instance, Michael R. Gordon and Bernard E. Trainor, "Army, Facing Cuts, Reported Seeking to Reshape Itself," *New York Times*, December 12, 1989.

20. Jaffe, *The Development of the Base Force*, pp. 2–11.

21. Ibid., pp. 11–21. See also U.S. General Accounting Office, *Force Structure: Issues Involving the Base Force*, Report no. GAO/NSIAD-93-65 (Washington, D.C., January 1993), p. 15. (Hereinafter cited as GAO, *Force Structure.*) This account is based on interviews conducted by GAO investigators with officials of the U.S. Joint Staff and former staff members of the National Security Council.

22. "General Powell believed that . . . U.S. forces structure would have to be based on what it would take for the United States to be perceived as a superpower." Ibid. See also Jaffe, *The Development of the Base Force*, pp. 11, 22–23.

23. Quoted in Bob Woodward, "The Conversion of Gen. Powell," *Washington Post*, December 21, 1989.

24. For discussion, see GAO, *Force Structure*, pp. 15–18.

25. A. M. Gray, "Defense Policy for the 1990s," *Marine Corps Gazette*, May 1990, p. 18. For a similar approach, see Senator John McCain, "The Need for Strategy in the New Postwar Era," *Armed Forces Journal*, January 1990, pp. 43–47. "The U.S. may not be the 'world's policeman,' " Senator McCain wrote, but, in the face of growing Third World instability, "its power projection forces will remain the free world's insurance policy" (p. 46).

26. For background on such operations, see Michael T. Klare and Peter Kornbluh, eds., *Low-Intensity Warfare* (New York: Pantheon, 1988). For background on counterinsurgency strategy and tactics, see Douglas Blaufarb, *The Counterinsurgency Era* (New York: Free Press, 1977).

27. Larry D. Welch, "Global Reach in a Non-Tranquil World," *Sea Power*, April 1990, p. 50.

28. Senator Sam Nunn, "Defense Budget Blanks," prepared statement before the U.S. Senate, Washington, D.C., March 22, 1990 (mimeo), pp. 1–2. For a discussion of the impact of the Nunn speech on senior military officers, see Jaffe, *Development of the Base Force*, pp. 28–29.

29. George P. Shultz, "New Realities and New Ways of Thinking," *Foreign Affairs*, Spring 1985, pp. 706–707. For an elaboration of this theme, see Jeane J. Kirkpatrick, *The Reagan Doctrine and U.S. Foreign Policy* (Washington, D.C.: Heritage Foundation, 1985).

30. U.S. Department of Defense, Defense Security Assistance Agency, *Foreign Military Sales, Foreign Military Construction Sales, and Military Assistance Facts*, as of September 30, 1990 (Washington, D.C., n.d.).

31. For discussion of this point, see Gerard C. Smith and Helena Cobban, "A Blind Eye to Nuclear Proliferation," *Foreign Affairs* 68:4 (Summer 1989), pp. 53–70.

32. IISS, *The Military Balance 1989–1990* and *The Military Balance 1974–1975*.

33. See Leonard S. Spector, *Nuclear Proliferation Today* (New York: Vintage Books, 1984); *The New Nuclear Nations* (New York: Vintage Books, 1985); *Going Nuclear* (Cambridge, MA: Ballinger, 1987); *The Undeclared Bomb* (Cambridge, MA: Ballinger, 1988); *Nuclear Ambitions* (Boulder, CO: Westview Press, 1990).

34. U.S. Commission on Integrated Long-Term Strategy, *Discriminate Deterrence* (Washington, D.C.: U.S. Government Printing Office, 1988), p. 9.

35. Ibid., p. 10.

36. Thus, while the total "military capital stock" (the value of weapons plus military structures and bases) of the Soviet Union was predicted to rise by 46 percent between 1990 and 2010, the total stock of China was expected to rise by 225 percent and that of India by 210 percent. U.S. Commission

on Integrated Long-Term Strategy, Future Security Environment Working Group, *The Future Security Environment* (Washington, D.C., October 1988), p. 25.

37. Ibid., p. 24.

38. Ibid., p. 67.

39. Debra von Opstal and Andrew C. Goldberg, *Meeting the Mavericks: Regional Challengers for the Next President*, Significant Issues Series, vol. X, no. 7 (Washington, D.C.: Center for Strategic and International Studies, 1988), p. xiii.

40. Ibid., p. 4.

41. Remarks of William Webster before the Council on Foreign Relations, Washington, D.C., December 2, 1988 (CIA text).

42. Remarks by William H. Webster before the Town Hall of Los Angeles, California, March 30, 1989 (CIA text). See also coverage of Webster's remarks in the *New York Times*, March 31, 1989.

43. See U.S. Congress, Senate, Committee on Governmental Affairs, *Global Spread of Chemical and Biological Weapons*, Hearings, 101st Cong., 1st Ses. (Washington, D.C.: U.S. Government Printing Office, 1990). (Hereinafter cited as SCGA, *Global Spread.*) See also U.S. Congress, House, Committee on Foreign Affairs, Subcommittee on Arms Control, *Missile Proliferation: The Need for Controls*, Hearings, 101st Cong., 1st Ses. (Washington, D.C.: U.S. Government Printing Office, 1990).

44. U.S. Department of the Army, *Trained and Ready in an Era of Change, the Posture of the U.S. Army*, Fiscal Year 1991 (Washington, D.C.: 1990), chap. 1, pp. 1, 6.

45. "Today, around the globe, developing countries are armed with 'First World Weapons.' " Statement by Admiral Carlisle A. H. Trost before the House Appropriations Committee, Washington, D.C., February 22, 1990 (mimeo), p. 4.

46. Carl E. Vuono, "Versatile, Deployable, and Lethal: The Strategic Army in the 1990s and Beyond," *Sea Power*, April 1990, pp. 59–61.

47. U.S. Army, *Trained and Ready in an Era of Change*, chap. 1, pp. 2–4.

48. For example, the Chief of Naval Operations, Admiral Carlisle A. H. Trost, made this statement in April 1990: "The proliferation of sophisticated weapons among nations which have resources to pay cash, or have credit with an agreeable supplier, is affecting regional stability in many parts of the world. In turn, a growing threat is posed to American lives, American property, and vital economic and political interests overseas." Moreover, "our concern is worsened by the race in some countries to develop chemical and biological agents to put in the warheads of their missiles. And we have seen that the will exists in some of these countries to use such weapons against not only their neighbors, but even their own citizens." Trost, "The Dangerous Crossroads," *Sea Power*, April 1990, pp. 69–70, 75.

49. Anthony Lake, "Confronting Backlash States," *Foreign Affairs* 73:2 (March/April 1994), pp. 45–46.

50. "Terrorism: The Challenge to the Democracies," speech by George Shultz before the Jonathan Institute, Washington, D.C., June 24, 1984, Current Policy No. 589 (U.S. Department of State). See also his speech before the Park Avenue Synagogue in New York City, October 25, 1984, Current Policy No. 629 (U.S. Department of State).

51. Address by President Reagan before the American Bar Association, Washington, D.C., July 8, 1985, Current Policy No. 721 (U.S. Department of State).

52. For discussion, see: Noam Chomsky, *The Cult of Terrorism* (Boston: South End Press, 1988); Richard Falk, *Revolutionaries and Functionaries* (New York: E. P. Dutton, 1988); Richard E. Rubenstein, *Alchemists of Revolution* (New York: Basic Books, 1987).

53. Statement by Secretary of State-Designate James A. Baker before the Senate Foreign Relations Committee, Washington, D.C., January 17, 1989, Current Policy No. 1146 (U.S. Department of State).

54. Echoing this theme, President Bush observed in 1990: "Inevitably, high-tech weapons will fall into the hands of those whose hatred of America and contempt for civilized norms is well-known." From speech before the Commonwealth Club of San Francisco, February 7, 1990.

55. See the opening remarks by Nunn, Glenn, and other prominent senators, in SCGA, *Global Spread*, pp. 1–10, 119–26.

56. Jaffe, *Development of the Base Force*, pp. 28–35.

57. See GAO, *Force Structure*.

58. U.S. Department of Defense, *National Military Strategy of the United States* (Washington, D.C.: January 1992), pp. 9–10.

59. See statement by Powell before the House Budget Committee, Washington, D.C., February 5, 1992 (mimeo). For background and discussion, see GAO, *Force Structure*; Michael Gordon, "Military Services Propose Slashes in Existing Forces," *New York Times*, May 12, 1990; Gordon, "Cheney Gives Plan to Reduce Forces by 25% in 5 Years," *New York Times*, June 20, 1990; Jaffe, *Development of the Base Force*, pp. 21, 26–27, 33–35; John D. Morrocco, "New Pentagon Strategy Shifts Focus from Europe to Regional Conflicts," *Aviation Week and Space Technology*, August 13, 1990, pp. 25–27.

60. GAO, *Force Structure*. See also DoD, *Annual Report FY92*, esp. pp. 61–81.

61. The terms "New Strategy" and "Regional Defense Strategy" were used, and the strategy itself described, by Secretary Cheney in his testimony before the House Foreign Affairs Committee on March 18, 1991, and the House Budget Committee on February 5, 1992. The strategy is further described by Cheney in U.S. Department of Defense, *Annual Report to the Congress*, Fiscal Year 1994 (Washington, D.C.: January 1993), pp. 1–13.

62. From text in DoD, *Annual Report FY92*, pp. 131–32.

63. Carl E. Vuono, "National Strategy and the Army of the 1990s," *Parameters*, Summer 1991, p. 12.

CHAPTER TWO

1. For background on these developments, see Bob Woodward, *The Commanders* (New York: Simon and Schuster, 1991), pp. 205–22.

2. For background on this exercise, see H. Norman Schwarzkopf, *It Doesn't Take a Hero* (New York: Bantam Books, 1992), pp. 288–89, 291–92.

3. U.S. Department of Defense, *Conduct of the Persian Gulf War*, Final Report to Congress (Washington, D.C.: U.S. Government Printing Office, April 1992), p. 351. (Hereinafter cited as DoD, *Gulf War Final Report*.) For background on this planning effort, see ibid., pp. 349–51.

4. Joseph Albright, "Army Mastermind Stays Ahead of the 'Game,' " *The Atlanta Constitution*, October 25, 1990. For additional background on this effort, see DoD, *Gulf War Final Report*, pp. 349–51; U.S. Congress, House Armed Services Committee, *Defense for a New Era: Lessons of the Persian Gulf War* (Washington, D.C.: U.S. Government Printing Office, 1992), pp. 83–84.

5. Statement by Dick Cheney before the House Foreign Affairs Committee, Washington, D.C., March 4, 1992 (mimeo), p. 8.

6. For discussion on the Pentagon's planning assumptions with regard to such conflicts, see U.S. Joint Chiefs of Staff, *Joint Net Military Assessment 1991* (Washington, D.C., March 1991), chap. 9.

7. See transcript of meeting released by Iraq, in Micah L. Sifry and Christopher Cerf, eds., *The Gulf War Reader: History, Documents, Opinions* (New York: Times Books/Random House, 1991), pp. 128–30.

8. For discussion, see Jeffrey Record, *Hollow Victory: A Contrary View of the Gulf War* (Washington, D.C.: Brassey's U.S., 1993), pp. 30–34.

9. From White House press conference, August 5, 1990, as transcribed in *New York Times*, August 6, 1990.

10. Address to the National Convention of the Veterans of Foreign Wars, Baltimore, Md., August 20, 1990, as transcribed in Current Policy No. 1294 (U.S. Department of State).

11. U.S. Congress, Senate, Committee on Armed Services, *Crisis in the Persian Gulf Region*, Hearings, 101st Cong., 2d Ses. (Washington, D.C.: U.S. Government Printing Office, 1990), p. 13. (Hereinafter cited as SASC, *Crisis in the Gulf*.)

12. See DoD, *Gulf War Final Report*, pp. 65–67; Woodward, *The Commanders*, pp. 247–54, 303–307, 318–20.

13. For data on U.S. and allied military capabilities in the Gulf, see DoD, *Gulf War Final Report*, pp. 81–86, 107–12, 184, 232–37. For discussion of allied and Iraqi troops strength, and the controversy surrounding these numbers, see Record, *Hollow Victory*, pp. 78–82.

14. IISS, *The Military Balance 1989–1990*, pp. 101–102.

15. DoD, *Gulf War Final Report*, pp. 13–15.

16. The description of Iraq as having the world's sixth largest army appears in Defense Secretary Cheney's testimony before the Senate Armed Services Committee, December 2, 1990. See SASC, *Crisis in the Gulf*, p. 643. According to the IISS, larger armies were possessed by the Soviet Union, China, India, Vietnam, and North Korea. See IISS, *The Military Balance 1989–1990*.

17. SASC, *Crisis in the Gulf*, p. 18.

18. Ibid., p. 41.

19. For discussion, see Lawrence Freedman and Efraim Karsh, "How Kuwait Was Won," *International Security* 16:2 (Fall 1991), pp. 12–13.

20. See Record, *Hollow Victory*, pp. 63–64.

21. See International Institute of Strategic Studies, "War in the Middle East," *Strategic Survey 1990–1991* (London: Brassey's U.K., 1991), pp. 63–65. (Hereinafter cited as IISS, *Strategic Survey 90–91*.)

22. For discussion, see Freedman and Karsh, "How Kuwait Was Won," pp. 13–14.

23. "Thanksgiving Day Address to U.S. Forces in Saudi Arabia," Dhahran, Saudi Arabia, November 22, 1990, as transcribed in *U.S. Department of State Dispatch*, November 26, 1990, p. 279.

24. For background on these events, see Anthony H. Cordesman and Abraham R. Wagner, *The Lessons of Modern War*, vol. 2, the Iran-Iraq War (Boulder, CO.: Westview Press, 1991), pp. 10–36, 76–156; Stephen C. Pelletiere and Douglas V. Johnson II, *Lessons Learned: The Iran-Iraq War* (Carlisle, PA.: U.S. Army War College, 1991), pp. 7–12, 27–29.

25. Former CIA official Edward Juchniewicz, as quoted in William Scott Malone, "Like Playing Poker with Our Cards Face Up: How the U.S. Gave Its Secrets to Saddam Hussein," *Washington Post National Weekly Edition*, November 11–17, 1991, p. 22.

26. On U.S. food aid, see Alan Friedman, *Spider's Web: The Secret History of How the White House Illegally Armed Iraq* (New York: Bantam, 1993), pp. 94–107. See also the *New York Times*, August 13, 1990, and April 27, 1992; *Washington Post*, September 16, 1990, and April 2 and September 5, 1991; *Los Angeles Times*, February 13, 1991; *Chicago Tribune*, April 10, 1991; *Wall Street Journal*, March 1, 1991.

Many of these CCC-backed credits were awarded by the Atlanta branch of Italy's state-owned Banca Nazionale del Lavoro (BNL), which later went on to provide Iraq with billions of dollars of unsecured loans—funds that were used by Baghdad to purchase tools and materials employed in the production of arms. On August 4, 1989, the head of the BNL-Atlanta office, Christopher Drogoul, was indicted in Atlanta for improper banking operations. Drogoul eventually pleaded guilty to a number of illicit transactions, with much accompanying speculation in Congress and the press as to whether Bush administration officials knew of the illicit BNL loans prior to 1989 and deliberately chose to allow them to proceed. For a thorough history of the case, see Friedman, *Spider's Web*, esp. chaps. 7, 8, 12, 14.

On technology transfers, see Friedman, *Spider's Web*, p. 37; *Los Angeles Times*, February 13, 1991.

27. See Friedman, *Spider's Web*, pp. 27, 31, 36, 41, 51, 167–68; Bob Woodward, *Veil: The Secret Wars of the CIA, 1981–1987* (New York: Pocket Books, 1988), pp. 517, 556. See also *Washington Post*, December 15, 1986; *New York Times*, December 16, 1986, and January 27, 1992.

28. Friedman, *Spider's Web*, p. 17. See also *New York Times*, January 27 and April 21, 1992; *Los Angeles Times*, March 8 and April 18, 1992.

29. For background on these activities, see Kenneth R. Timmerman, *The Death Lobby: How the West Armed Iraq* (Boston: Houghton Mifflin, 1991).

30. For discussion, see ibid., esp. chaps. 7, 9–12, 14–15.

31. Ibid., pp. 103–12, 131–32, 133–34, 148.

32. SCGA, *Global Spread*, p. 12. For additional background on Iraqi chemical weapons capabilities, see DoD, *Gulf War Final Report*, p. 15.

33. Mike Eisenstadt, *"The Sword of the Arabs": Iraq's Strategic Weapons* (Washington, D.C.: Washington Institute for Near East Policy, 1990), pp. 6–7. See also *New York Times*, July 31 and November 11, 1991.

34. For discussion, see DoD, *Gulf War Final Report*, pp. 640–45.

35. Ibid., p. 640. In any case, the Iraqis chose—for reasons not yet fully determined—to eschew the use of chemical weapons in the 1991 war. When asked, at the end of Desert Storm, why he thought the Iraqis did not use CW munitions, General Schwarzkopf responded: "Number one, we destroyed their artillery. We went after their artillery big time . . . and that's how they would have delivered their chemical weapons, either that or by air, and we all know what happened to their air. . . . There's other people who are speculating that the reason why they didn't use chemical weapons is because they're afraid that if they use chemical weapons there would be nuclear retaliation. There's other people that speculate that they didn't use their chemical weapons because their chemical weapons degraded, and because of the damage that we did to their chemical weapon production facilities, they were unable to upgrade the chemicals within their weapons as a result of that degradation. That's one of the reasons, among others, why we went after their chemical production facilities early on in this

campaign." From the transcript of a press conference at U.S. headquarters, Riyadh, Saudi Arabia, February 27, 1991, as published in the *New York Times*, February 28, 1991.

36. Cordesman and Wagner, *Lessons of Modern War*, pp. 495–500.

37. See Timmerman, *The Death Lobby*, pp. 149–60.

38. Janne E. Nolan, *Trappings of Power: Ballistic Missiles in the Third World* (Washington, D.C.: Brookings Institution, 1991), pp. 52–58. See also Timmerman, *The Death Lobby*, pp. 250–56.

39. W. Seth Carus and Joseph S. Bermudez, Jr., "Iraq's *Al-Husayn* Missile Programme," *Jane's Soviet Intelligence Review*, May 1990, pp. 204–209. The Iraqis immediately began firing these missiles at the Iranian capital, provoking fresh missile strikes by Iran and launching what came to be called the "War of the Cities." While the Iraqi missile strikes did not produce large numbers of casualties, they did instill great fear among Iranian civilians— several million of whom reportedly fled Teheran in the spring of 1988— and thus weakened Iran's will to continue the war. See Cordesman and Wagner, *Lessons of Modern War*, pp. 363–68, 499–503.

40. Nolan, *Trappings of Power*, pp. 55–56.

41. For discussion, see W. Seth Carus, "Iraq: A Threatening New Superpower," *Movement*, December 1989, pp. 51–52; Carus and Bermudez, "Iraq's *Al-Husayn* Missile Programme"; Timmerman, *The Death Lobby*, pp. 157–60, 251–56.

42. See Record, *Hollow Victory*, pp. 66–67.

43. The former estimate was by National Security Adviser Brent Scowcroft, speaking on "This Week with David Brinkley," November 25, 1990; the latter by Secretary Cheney, speaking on "Face the Nation," November 25, 1990. For complete texts of their comments, see SASC, *Crisis in the Gulf*, pp. 595–604.

44. See Spector, *Nuclear Ambitions*, pp. 186–88.

45. For background, see Eisenstadt, *"The Sword of the Arabs"*; Gary Milhollin, "Building Saddam Hussein's Bomb," *New York Times Magazine*, March 8, 1992, pp. 30–36; Jeffrey Smith and Glenn Frankel, "Too Close for Comfort," *Washington Post National Weekly Edition*, October 21–27, 1991, pp. 9–11; Spector, *Nuclear Ambitions*, pp. 187–202.

46. For background on Iraq's nuclear weapons programs, see the following four articles by David Albright and Mark Hibbs in the *Bulletin of the Atomic Scientists*: "Iraq and the Bomb: Were They Even Close?" March 1991, pp. 16–25; "Iraq's Nuclear Hide-and-Seek," September 1991, pp. 14–23; "Iraq's Bomb: Blueprints and Artifacts," January/February 1992, pp. 14–23; and "Iraq's Shop-Till-You-Drop Nuclear Program," April 1992, pp. 27–37. See also Milhollin, "Building Saddam Hussein's Bomb"; Smith and Frankel, "Too Close for Comfort"; Spector, *Nuclear Ambitions*, pp. 186–202;

New York Times, July 9, August 6, September 27, and October 8, 10, and 22, 1991, and February 13, 1992.

47. See sources in n. 46.

48. See sources in n. 46 and Timmerman, *The Death Lobby*, pp. 270–300.

49. DoD, *Gulf War Final Report*, pp. 15, 639–46.

50. U.S. Department of Defense, *Conduct of the Persian Gulf Conflict*, Interim Report to Congress (Washington, D.C., July 1991), Pt. 2, p. 6. (Hereinafter cited as DoD, *Gulf War Interim Report*.) For elaboration of the targeting philosophy for Operation Desert Storm, see DoD, *Gulf War Final Report*, pp. 95–98.

51. SASC, *Crisis in the Gulf*, pp. 663–64. See also Freedman and Karsh, "How Kuwait Was Won," pp. 15–24.

52. For discussion, see Lawrence Freedman, "Escalators and Quagmires: Expectations and the Use of Force," *International Affairs*, January 1991, pp. 15–32.

53. Quoted in *New York Times*, August 25, 1990. A similar view was expressed by General Jimmie V. Adams of the Air Force in an interview in *Air Force* magazine: "I think we learned a lot of lessons in Vietnam, and one of them is that gradualism doesn't work. We hope that if we are allowed to inflict pain [against the Iraqis], we would be allowed to inflict it rapidly and with an overwhelming capability. . . ." (January 1992, p. 70.)

54. See Woodward, *The Commanders*, pp. 303–307, 318–20.

55. From the opening statement by Bush at a White House press conference, Washington, D.C., November 30, 1990, as transcribed in *U.S. Department of State Dispatch*, December 3, 1990, p. 296.

56. DoD, *Gulf War Final Report*, p. 70.

57. DoD, *Annual Report FY90*, p. 47.

58. See Michael T. Klare, "NATO's Improved Conventional Weapons," *Technology Review*, May–June 1985, pp. 35–40, 73.

59. For discussion, see Robert J. Berens, "Competitive Strategies," *National Defense*, October 1989, pp. 29–33; Tim Carrington, "Defense Debate: Some Pentagon Hands Push a New Strategy Reflecting War Game," *Wall Street Journal*, December 20, 1988.

60. DoD, *Annual Report FY90*, pp. 47–48. For discussion, see Klare, "NATO's Improved Conventional Weapons," pp. 34–40, 73; Bernard W. Rogers, "ACE Attack of Warsaw Pact Follow-on Forces," *Military Technology*, May 1983, pp. 39–50; Stockholm International Peace Research Institute, *SIPRI Yearbook 1984* (London: Taylor and Francis, 1984), pp. 293–301. (Hereinafter cited as SIPRI, *SIPRI Yearbook 19xx*.)

61. U.S. Army, *Weapons Systems 1991* (Washington, D.C.: Department of the Army, 1991), pp. 69–70, 91–92.

62. For discussion, see Paul F. Walker and Eric Stambler, "And the Dirty Little Weapons," *Bulletin of the Atomic Scientists*, May 1991, pp. 21–24.

63. DoD, *Gulf War Final Report*, pp. 752–54.

64. Walker and Stambler, "Dirty Little Weapons," p. 24.

65. DoD, *Gulf War Interim Report*, Pt. 2, p. 4.

66. DoD, *Gulf War Final Report*, p. 92.

67. See James P. Coyne, "Plan of Attack," *Air Force*, April 1992, pp. 40–46.

68. DoD, *Gulf War Final Report*, p. 92.

69. DoD, *Gulf War Interim Report*, Pt. 2, p. 6.

70. DoD, *Gulf War Final Report*, p. 394.

71. Record, *Hollow Victory*, p. 94.

72. For discussion, see Freedman and Karsh, "How Kuwait Was Won," pp. 11–12, 22; IISS, *Strategic Survey 90–91*, pp. 93–94.

73. For discussion, see Record, *Hollow Victory*, pp. 87–101.

74. DoD, *Gulf War Final Report*, p. 114.

75. Ibid., p. 119.

76. Ibid., pp. 114–24.

77. Ibid., p. 118.

78. Ibid., pp. 114–30.

79. From transcript of Powell's briefing in the *New York Times*, January 24, 1991.

80. See DoD, *Gulf War Final Report*, pp. 154–56.

81. Ibid., pp. 130–44.

82. Quoted in the *New York Times*, March 4, 1991. According to analysts at the International Institute for Strategic Studies in London, "The morale of the Iraqi troops, always low because of a lack of decent leadership, training or a desire to fight, was further sapped by the awesome bombardment they were forced to withstand. They surrendered in droves, and in relief." IISS, *Strategic Survey 1990–91*, p. 49.

83. DoD, *Gulf War Final Report*, pp. 752–53.

84. Walker and Stambler, "Dirty Little Weapons."

85. Quoted in "Getting Blown to Bits in the Dark," *Toronto Globe and Mail*, February 25, 1991.

86. DoD, *Gulf War Final Report*, p. 140.

87. Ibid., pp. 142–43.

88. "The land war was a race between the coalition's determination to destroy as much as possible of the Iraqi military capability and Saddam's awareness of the requirement to accept all U.N. resolutions unequivocally." Freedman and Karsh, "How Kuwait Was Won," p. 34.

89. The "turkey shoot" remark was cited in the *Washington Post*, February 27, 1991.

90. Schwarzkopf's remarks were quoted in the *New York Times* for March 27, 1991. Additional remarks by Schwarzkopf, Cheney, and Bush on this matter were published in the *Washington Post* for March 28, 1991. For

analysis of this affair, see Patrick E. Tyler, "General's Account of Gulf War's End Disputed by Bush," *New York Times*, March 28, 1991; Michael R. Gordon and Bernard E. Trainor,"How Iraq Escaped to Threaten Kuwait Again," *New York Times*, October 23, 1994.

91. DoD, *Gulf War Final Report*, p. 294.

92. "Allies Shoot Down 42 Iraqi Aircraft," *Aviation Week and Space Technology*, March 11, 1991, p. 22.

93. DoD, *Gulf War Final Report*, pp. 148–59.

94. From the transcript in *U.S. Department of State Dispatch*, March 11, 1991, p. 161.

95. Radio speech to U.S. forces in the Persian Gulf, March 2, 1991, as transcribed in *U.S. Department of State Dispatch*, March 11, 1991, p. 164.

96. Statement before the House Foreign Affairs Committee, Washington, D.C., March 19, 1991 (mimeo), p. 7.

97. Ibid.

CHAPTER THREE

1. The House Armed Services Committee report was published as Representatives Les Aspin and William Dickinson, *Defense for a New Era: Lessons of the Persian Gulf War* (Washington, D.C.: U.S. Government Printing Office, 1992). (Hereinafter cited as HASC, *Defense for a New Era*.)

2. See James Blackwell, Michael J. Mazarr, and Don M. Snider, *The Gulf War: Military Lessons Learned*, Interim Report of the CSIS Study Group on Lessons Learned from the Gulf War (Washington, D.C.: Center for Strategic and International Studies, July 1991). See also IISS, *Strategic Survey 90–91*, pp. 49–98; Lieutenant Colonel Jeffrey McCausland, *The Gulf Conflict: A Military Analysis*, IISS Adelphi Paper no. 282 (London: Brassey's, 1993); Lawrence Freedman and Efraim Karsh, *The Gulf Conflict 1990–1991* (Princeton: Princeton University Press, 1993).

3. DoD, *Gulf War Final Report*, p. xvi.

4. Quoted in HASC, *Defense for a New Era*, p. 3.

5. Prominent among these critical studies are Record, *Hollow Victory*.

6. DoD, *Gulf War Final Report*, p. xx.

7. It is true that a number of these systems were first used during the December 1989 invasion of Panama, but that can hardly be considered a genuine war in that U.S. forces were not confronted by a determined and well-equipped adversary.

8. The nature and specific Gulf War applications of these and other systems is described in DoD, *Gulf War Final Report*, Appendix T.

9. Ibid., p. xx.

10. Some analysts have argued, however, that the definition of "collateral damage" should be broadened to include long-lasting effects on the civilian population caused by the destruction of power plants, electrical distribution systems, and other facilities upon whose continued functioning a modern urban society depends. During the Gulf War, U.S. aircraft seeking to damage Iraq's communications, air defense, and logistical infrastructure often struck such facilities, cutting off power to water treatment plants, hospitals, food production and storage facilities, and other vital installations. As a consequence, an unknown but substantial number of Iraqi civilians died or became ill from drinking untreated water, eating spoiled food, or from malnutrition and infection. Such effects, according to Greenpeace, should be viewed as collateral damage from U.S. air and missile strikes. See David Evans, "Study: 'Hyperwar' Devastated Iraq," *Chicago Tribune*, May 29, 1991. See also William M. Arkin, et al., *On Impact: Modern Warfare and the Environment* (Washington, D.C.: Greenpeace, May 1991).

11. On the U.S. advantage in surveillance, intelligence-collection, and "battlefield management," see Blackwell, et al., *The Gulf War*, pp. 13–14.

12. Steve Coll and William Branigan, "U.S. Scrambled to Shape View of 'Highway of Death,' *Washington Post*, March 11, 1991. See also Donatella Lorch, "7 Miles of Carnage Mark Road Iraqis Used to Flee," *New York Times*, March 4, 1991; Randall Richard, " 'Like Fish in a Barrel,' U.S. Pilots Say," *Washington Post*, February 27, 1991. For a photograph of the image of fleeing Iraqi vehicles produced by the JSTARS radar, see *Aviation Week and Space Technology*, March 25, 1991, p. 27.

13. McCausland, *The Gulf Conflict*, p. 56.

14. Statement before the House Budget Committee, Washington, D.C., February 5, 1994 (mimeo), p. 17.

15. Michael Wines, "Extravaganza on the Mall Hails Troops Today," *New York Times*, June 8, 1991; Michael Wines, "Parade Unfurls Symbols of Patriotism in the Capital," *New York Times*, June 9, 1991.

16. Quoted in John D. Morrocco, "Looming Budget Cuts Threaten Future of Key High-Tech Weapons," *Aviation Week and Space Technology*, April 22, 1991, p. 66.

17. On the Tomahawk, see Eric H. Arnett, "Awestruck Press Does Tomahawk PR," *Bulletin of the Atomic Scientists*, April 1991, pp. 7–8; Eric H. Arnett, "Truth and Tomahawks," *Bulletin of the Atomic Scientists*, July/August 1992, pp. 3–4. On the F-117A, see Barton Gellman, "Gulf Weapons' Accuracy Downgraded," *Washington Post*, April 10, 1992.

18. Quoted in John Conyers, Jr., "The Patriot Myth: Caveat Emptor," *Arms Control Today*, November 1992, p. 3.

19. Ben Sherwood, "The Blip Seen 'Round the World," *Washington Post*, September 22, 1982. See also Conyers, "The Patriot Myth," pp. 3–4.

20. For a devastating critique of Patriot effectiveness in the Gulf, see

Theodore A. Postal, "Lessons of the Gulf War Experience with Patriot," *International Security*, Winter 1991/92, pp. 119–71. Postal, a physicist and former Pentagon science adviser, examined film clips and other material on Patriot operations during the Gulf War and concluded that few, if any, of the Patriots fired in Israel resulted in the successful interception of incoming Scud missiles. See William J. Broad, "Critic of Patriot Missile Says It Was 'Almost Total Failure' in War," *New York Times*, January 9, 1992; John Aloysius Farrell, "MIT Physicist Says Patriot Failed in Gulf," *Boston Globe*, January 24, 1992.

21. Conyers, "The Patriot Myth," p. 3.

22. The Department of Defense, in its preliminary report on the war, noted a number of significant "shortcomings" in the intelligence area: "Joint intelligence architecture may need further refinement"; "BDA [battle damage assessment] was difficult and slow, especially for determining the need to restrike targets"; "procedures for secondary imagery dissemination may require improvement"; "Broad area, all-weather, search/surveillance systems are required to improve the intelligence available to tactical commanders." DoD, *Gulf War Interim Report*, Pt. 14, p. 3. For further discussion, see Colonel David H. Hackworth, "The Lessons of the Gulf War," *Newsweek*, June 24, 1991, pp. 22–24; and Molly Moore, "War Exposed Rivalries, Weaknesses in Military," *Washington Post*, June 10, 1991.

23. HASC, *Defense for a New Era*, p. ix.

24. Ibid., p. 23. See also Moore, "War Exposed Rivalries."

25. For discussion, see McCausland, *The Gulf Conflict*, pp. 34–35; Record, *Hollow Victory*, pp. 66–67.

26. See, for instance, "Tactical Bombing of Iraqi Forces Outstripped Value of Strategic Hits, Analyst Contends," *Aviation Week and Space Technology*, January 27, 1992, pp. 62–63. The analyst in question, William Arkin of Greenpeace, examined bombing damage in Iraq and spoke with many Iraqi military officials. See also IISS, *Strategic Survey 90–91*, pp. 69–70.

27. Quoted in John D. Morrocco, "Beware of 'Lessons' from the Gulf in Shaping the U.S. Military," *Aviation Week and Space Technology*, December 24, 1990, p. 32.

28. For discussion, see Freedman and Karsh, "How Kuwait Was Won," pp. 13–15, 27–28; Jeffrey Record, "Why the Air War Worked," *Armed Forces Journal*, April 1991, pp. 44–45.

29. For further discussion of this point, see Blackwell, et al., *The Gulf War*, pp. 27–28.

30. DoD, *Gulf War Final Report*, p. xxi.

31. HASC, *Defense for a New Era*, p. 7.

32. For discussion, see David Callahan, "Air Power Comes of Age," *Technology Review*, August/September 1994, pp. 62–70; Eliot A. Cohen, "The

Mystique of U.S. Air Power," *Foreign Affairs* 73:1 (January/February 1994), pp. 109–24. Record, *Hollow Victory*, pp. 106–109.

33. DoD, *Gulf War Final Report*, p. 150. Although useful in degrading the effectiveness of Iraqi military installations, these attacks also cut off power to Iraqi hospitals and water treatment plants, causing considerable hardship (and some sickness and death) among Iraq's civilian population. Accordingly, this particular aspect of the U.S. air campaign has come in for some degree of criticism. See Cohen, "The Mystique of Air Power," p. 123; Michael R. Gordon, "Pentagon Cites Problems with Gulf War Effort," *New York Times*, February 23, 1992.

34. According to the Pentagon's history of the war, allied aircraft carried out some 500 sorties against Iraqi oil facilities, dropping about 1,200 tons of bombs to cripple the national refining and distribution system. By using "smart bombs" with pinpoint accuracy, these aircraft damaged approximately 80 percent of Iraq's refining capacity. "For about half the bomb load dropped on one typical refinery in Germany during World War II, the Coalition effectively stopped all Iraqi refined fuels production." DoD, *Gulf War Final Report*, pp. 157–58.

35. Ibid., pp. 133–44.

36. HASC, *Defense for a New Era*, p. 7. See also: IISS, *Strategic Survey 90–91*, p. 70.

37. Whether air power alone could have prevailed in the Gulf will never be known; the Bush administration chose to proceed with the ground campaign, Operation Desert Sabre, even though Iraq was showing signs of capitulating to the Coalition's demands. On February 15, four weeks after the air war commenced, Saddam Hussein told Soviet envoy Yevgeni Primakov that he would abide by U.N. Security Council Resolution 660 and withdraw from Kuwait if certain conditions were met; one week later, after a series of meetings between Soviet and Iraqi officials, Hussein agreed to abandon most of these conditions. For a brief moment it appeared that a ground campaign would not be needed to secure Iraqi compliance with U.N. demands, but on February 22 President Bush issued a 24–hour ultimatum demanding that Hussein immediately agree to the terms of Resolution 660 without reservations, and, when Hussein failed to respond, the ground war began as planned on February 24. Freedman and Karsh, *The Gulf Conflict*, pp. 374–85.

38. McCausland, *The Gulf Conflict*, p. 63.

39. From the transcript in the *New York Times*, March 7, 1991.

40. See Paul Lewis, "U.N. Aides Discover Arms Center Concealed by Iraq," *New York Times*, October 8, 1991. See also *Washington Post*, August 8, 1991; *New York Times*, 10, 1991.

41. For discussion, see Jeffrey Record, "The Air War Missed Its Biggest

Target," *Baltimore Sun*, November 21, 1991. See also McCausland, *The Gulf Conflict*, pp. 63–64; Record, *Hollow Victory*, pp. 64–68.

42. According to the Department of Defense, a key goal of the air campaign was to "isolate and incapacitate the Iraqi regime" through attacks on "leadership command facilities, electricity production facilities that power military and military-related industrial systems, and command, control, and communications systems." DoD, *Gulf War Interim Report*, Pt. 2, p. 6. See also Coyne, "Plan of Attack."

43. For discussion, see IISS, *Strategic Survey 90–91*, p. 69; "Tactical Bombing of Iraqi Forces," p. 62.

44. Stewart M. Powell, "Friendly Fire," *Air Force*, December 1991, pp. 58–63. See also Douglas Johl, "War Analysts Delving into What Went Wrong," *Los Angeles Times*, March 24, 1991.

45. See DoD, *Gulf War Interim Report*, Pt. 17, p. 3; Powell, "Friendly Fire," p. 63; Eric Schmitt, "U.S. Seeks to Cut Accidental War Death," *New York Times*, December 9, 1991.

46. The problem of distinguishing friend from foe when flying at high speeds was again demonstrated in April 1994 when U.S. F-15 fighters mistakenly shot down two American UH-60 helicopters over a Kurdish enclave in northern Iraq, killing 26 people. According to press accounts of the incident, the F-15 pilots involved thought that the UH-60s were Russian-built Iraqi Mi-24 "Hind" helicopters. See Eric Schmitt, "Copter Deaths: Pentagon Finds Human Failure," *New York Times*, July 1, 1994.

47. Record, *Hollow Victory*, pp. 107, 117.

48. Quoted in Rick Atkinson, "U.S. to Rely on Air Strikes if War Erupts," *Washington Post*, September 16, 1990.

49. For a discussion of the reaction to Dugan's comments among other senior officers, see Woodward, *The Commanders*, pp. 290–96.

50. Edward N. Luttwak, "Getting Stuck in the Sand," *Washington Post National Weekly Edition*, November 19–25, 1990.

51. SASC, *Crisis in the Gulf*, pp. 662–63.

52. Ibid., p. 663.

53. For more on this operation, see DoD, *Gulf War Final Report*, pp. 247–48; McCausland, pp. 41–42.

54. DoD, *Gulf War Final Report*, p. xxii.

55. From U.S. Department of Defense, *Joint Warfare of the U.S. Armed Forces*, Joint Publication 1 (1991), as extracted in "Molding the Joint Fighting Force," *Defense/92*, March/April 1992, p. 21.

56. For early signs of such wrangling, see Jason Glashow and Robert Holzer, "USAF Aggressively Guns for Roles," *Defense News*, September 12–18, 1994, p. 7; David A. Fulghum, "USAF Clashes with Navy, Army over Roles," *Aviation Week and Space Technology*, October 31, 1994, pp. 25–27.

57. DoD, *Gulf War Final Report*, pp. 393–94.

58. Testimony before the House Budget Committee, Washington, D.C., February 5, 1992 (mimeo), p. 22.

59. SASC, *Crisis in the Gulf*, p. 668.

60. Ibid.

61. DoD, *Annual Report 1992*, p. 93. For further discussion of these supply operations, see DoD, *Gulf War Final Report*, Appendixes E and F.

62. For discussion, see Blackwell, et al., *The Gulf War*, pp. 2–3, 7, 33–34; Record, *Hollow Victory*, pp. 73–76.

63. Under Secretary of Defense Frank Kendall, quoted in *Aviation Week and Space Technology*, April 22, 1991, p. 40.

64. "It was only because there was, in the event, ample time to allow for the necessary logistic build-up, that there were no serious logistic problems" in the Gulf, the International Institute for Strategic Studies observed in 1991. "Had the timescale been more demanding, it would have been a different story." Hence, "the real lesson of the war was that in normal circumstances the logistic lift capability for out-of-area operations was almost certainly inadequate." IISS, *Strategic Survey 90–91*, p. 96. For further discussion, see Blackwell, et al., *The Gulf War*, pp. 33–35.

65. DoD, *Annual Report FY93*, p. 99.

66. Ibid., pp. 94–99. See also "Mobility: Future Protection," *Defense/92*, March/April 1992, pp. 29–32.

67. In his first statement on the crisis, on August 8, 1990, Bush listed four basic objectives that would govern U.S. policy in the Gulf: the complete withdrawal of Iraqi forces from Kuwait, the restoration of the original Kuwaiti regime, the protection of vital U.S. security interests in the Gulf, and the safety of all U.S. citizens trapped in the region. Address by the President from the White House, August 8, 1990 (White House Press Office transcript).

68. From press conferences in Kennebunkport, ME, August 11, 1990, as transcribed in the *New York Times*, August 12, 1990.

69. Address by the President to a Joint Session of Congress, Washington, D.C., September 11, 1990 (White House Press Office transcript).

70. For background and discussion, see Freedman and Karsh, *The Gulf Conflict*, pp. 410–25. See also McCausland, *The Gulf Conflict*, pp. 54–55.

71. See Powell's testimony before the House Budget Committee, Washington, D.C., February 5, 1992.

72. See Woodward, *The Commanders*, pp. 240–46, 254–59, 263–73.

73. See Record, *Hollow Victory*, pp. 73–76.

74. DoD, *Gulf War Final Report*, pp. 50–53, 112, 237, 487–521.

75. For discussion, see Freedman and Karsh, *The Gulf Conflict*, pp. 95–127.

76. DoD, *Gulf War Final Report*, p. 634.

77. Blackwell, et al., *The Gulf War*, p. 8.

78. Vuono, "National Strategy and the Army of the 1990s," p. 10.

79. For discussion of these odds, see Record, *Hollow Victory*, pp. 78–79.

80. Blackwell, et al., *The Gulf War*, p. 21.

81. Andrew F. Krepinevich, *The Bottom-Up Review: An Assessment* (Washington, D.C.: Defense Budget Project, 1994), p. 29.

82. For discussion of this concept, see CSIS Study Group on the MTR, *The Military Technical Revolution: A Structural Framework* (Washington, D.C.: Center for Strategic and International Studies, March 1993).

83. For discussion, see Deborah Shapley, "The Army's New Fighting Doctrine," *New York Times Magazine*, November 28, 1982, pp. 37 ff; Michael R. Gordon, "The Army's 'Air-Land Battle' Doctrine Worries Allies, Upsets the Air Force," *National Journal*, June 18, 1983, pp. 1274–77.

84. This offensive, the Pentagon later noted, "employed the strength in AirLand Battle Doctrine, including agility, depth, synchronization of combat power, initiative, and sustainment of the force." DoD, *Gulf War Interim Report*, Pt. 2, p. 7.

85. U.S. Army Training and Doctrine Command, *Airland Operations* (Ft. Monroe,VA., 1991), p. 13.

86. Another description of "non-linear warfare" is provided by James Blackwell and his associates at the Center for Strategic and International Studies. As a result of advances in long-range, precision-guided weaponry, "modern armies are looking at concepts of nonlinear warfare in which smaller, fast moving, more independent units maneuver around a battlefield, coalesce to attack enemy formations, then melt away into smaller component units less vulnerable to [the enemy's] smart weapons. As in war at sea, the focus will not so much be on seizing territory as on destroying enemy combat forces." *The Gulf War*, p. 11.

87. U.S. Department of the Army, Field Manual 100-5, *Operations* (Washington, D.C., June 1993), p. vi.

88. Ibid., chap. 6, p. 16.

89. Lieutenant Colonel David F. Melcher, "The United States Army: A Strategic Force for the Post-Containment Era," paper presented at the Third Annual Strategy Conference, U.S. Army War College, Carlisle Barracks, PA, February 13–14, 1992, pp. 6–7.

90. For further articulation of such a battlefield, see Thomas E. Ricks, "How Wars Are Fought Will Change Radically, Pentagon Planner Says," *Wall Street Journal*, July 15, 1994.

91. Quoted in Barton Gellman, "Army's New Doctrine Manual Sees High-Tech, Distant Battles," *Washington Post*, June 15, 1993. For discussion of this point, see General Gordon R, Sullivan and Colonel James M. Dubik, "War in the Information Age," *Military Review*, April 1994, pp. 46–62.

CHAPTER FOUR

1. For summaries of this document and background discussion, see Patrick E. Tyler, "Pentagon Imagines New Enemies to Fight in Post-Cold War Era," *New York Times*, February 17, 1992; Barton Gellman, "Pentagon War Scenario Spotlights Russia," *Washington Post*, February 20, 1992; Gellman, "Pentagon Says War Scenario Doesn't Reflect or Predict U.S. Policy," *Washington Post*, February 21, 1992.

2. See sources cited in n. 1 and Barton Gellman, "Debate Over Military's Future Escalates into a War of Scenarios," *Washington Post*, February 26, 1992; Eric Schmitt, "Some Senators See Little Risk of War," *New York Times*, February 21, 1992.

3. Quoted in Schmitt, "Senators See Little Risk of War."

4. See Gellman, "Debate Over Military's Future."

5. Quoted in the *Washington Post*, February 21, 1992.

6. For summary of this document and discussion, see Patrick E. Tyler, "U.S. Strategy Plan Calls for Insuring No Rivals Develop," *New York Times*, March 8, 1992.

7. From the excerpts published in the *New York Times*, March 8, 1992.

8. Ibid.

9. Quoted in Barton Gellman, "Keeping the U.S. First," *Washington Post*, March 11, 1992.

10. Quoted in Patrick E. Tyler, "Lone Superpower Plan: Ammunition for Critics," *New York Times*, March 10, 1992.

11. Ibid.

12. Peter Tarnoff, "Why Must U.S. Take the Role of the World's Peace Monitor?" *Newsday*, March 18, 1992.

13. "America Only," *New York Times*, March 10, 1994.

14. Pentagon spokesperson Pete Williams, quoted in Tyler, "Lone Superpower Plan."

15. See comments by unidentified official in Gellman, "Keeping the U.S. First."

16. For summary of this document and discussion, see Patrick E. Tyler, "Pentagon Drops Goal of Blocking New Superpowers," *New York Times*, May 24, 1992.

17. Representative Les Aspin, *An Approach to Sizing American Conventional Forces for the Post-Soviet Era: Four Illustrative Options* (Washington, D.C.: House Armed Services Committee, February 25, 1992), pp. 6, 13–17. (Hereinafter cited as Aspin, *Four Options.*)

18. Ibid., pp. 20–23.

19. Ibid., p. 21 and charts 4, 7. See also Patrick E. Tyler, "Top Congress-

man Seeks Deeper Cuts in Military Budget," *New York Times*, February 24, 1992.

20. For discussion, see John T. Correll, "The Base Plan Meets Option C," *Air Force*, June 1992, pp. 15–17; Gellman, "War of Scenarios."

21. Gellman, "War of Scenarios."

22. See, for instance, Correll, "The Base Force Meets Option C."

23. See Donna Cassata, "House OKs Defense Budget with SDI, B-2 Intact," *Baltimore Sun*, June 6, 1992; Dunbar Lockwood, "House Approves Military Budget Leaving Major Programs Intact," *Arms Control Today*, June 1992, pp. 19, 28.

24. From Clinton's speech at Georgetown University on December 12, 1991, as published in "A Democrat Lays Out His Plan," *Harvard International Review*, Summer 1992, p. 28.

25. See Governor Bill Clinton and Senator Al Gore, *Putting People First* (New York: Times Books, 1992), pp. 129–39. Under "National Security," Clinton and Gore include a section on "A Technological Edge," in which they state that we must "maintain our ability to compete with Europe and Japan in emerging technologies like biotechnology, superconductors, and computer-integrated manufacturing."

26. Samuel R. Berger and Janne E. Nolan, "Overview: Military and Foreign Policy," in Mark Green, ed., *Changing America: Blueprints for the New Administration* (New York: Newmarket Press, 1992), pp. 177, 179.

27. For discussion, see David C. Morrison, "Over Here," *National Journal*, February 6, 1993, pp. 326–30.

28. Les Aspin, "The First Post-Cold War Defense Program," *Defense/93*, no. 2 (1993), pp. 2–3.

29. Remarks by Les Aspin at the National Defense University, Washington, D.C., March 25, 1993 (Department of Defense News Release).

30. Ibid.

31. For discussion, see Barton Gellman and John Lancaster, "U.S. May Drop 2-War Preparedness," *Washington Post*, June 17, 1993; Michael R. Gordon, "Cuts Force Review of War Strategies," *New York Times*, May 30, 1993; Eric Schmitt, "Pentagon Is Ready with a Plan for a Leaner, Versatile Military," *New York Times*, June 12, 1993. See also Callahan, "Air Power Comes of Age," p. 69.

32. Unidentified personnel quoted in Gellman and Lancaster, "U.S. May Drop 2-War Preparedness."

33. From "Carriers for Force 2001," as cited in Eric Schmitt, "Top Navy Officer Criticizes Plan to Cut Carriers," *New York Times*, June 19, 1993.

34. Remarks by Les Aspin at the U.S. Air Force Senior Statesman Symposium, Andrews Air Force Base, Md., June 24, 1993 (U.S. Department of Defense, mimeo), p. 1. See also John Lancaster, "Aspin Opts for Winning 2 Wars—Not 1½—at Once," *The Washington Post*, June 25, 1993; David

Callahan, "Saving Defense Dollars," *Foreign Policy*, Fall 1994, pp. 107–108.

35. Michael R. Gordon, "Pentagon Seeks to Reduce Cuts in Carrier Fleet," *New York Times*, August 11, 1993.

36. Department of Defense news conference, The Pentagon, Washington, D.C., September 1, 1993 (U.S. Department of Defense transcript).

37. Les Aspin, *Bottom-Up Review, Force Structure Excerpts* (U.S. Department of Defense, September 1, 1993), pp. 1, 5. (Hereinafter cited as Aspin, *Bottom-Up Review.*)

38. News conference, September 1, 1993.

39. Aspin, *Bottom-Up Review*, pp. 5–6.

40. Ibid., p. 17. For discussion, see Michael R. Gordon, "Military Plan Would Cut Forces but Have Them Ready for 2 Wars," *New York Times*, September 2, 1993; John Lancaster, "Pentagon Issues Plan for Future," *Washington Post*, September 2, 1993; Thomas E. Ricks, "Military Unveils Plan to Reshape Armed Forces," *Wall Street Journal*, September 2, 1993.

41. Aspin, *Bottom-Up Review*, pp. 7–9.

42. Ibid., p. 10.

43. Ibid., p. 9.

44. See Glenn W. Goodman, Jr., "Fire and Forget," *Armed Forces Journal*, August 1994, pp. 36–39. For background, see U.S. Department of Defense, *Program Acquisition Costs by Weapons System*, Fiscal Year 1993 (Washington, D.C., January 29, 1992), pp. 42, 90, 93.

45. Aspin, *Bottom-Up Review*, p. 9. See also DoD, *Annual Report 1994*, pp. 16–17.

46. Ibid., p. 12. See also Ricks, "Military Unveils Plan."

47. U.S. Department of Defense, *Report on the Bottom-Up Review* (Washington, D.C.: October 1993), p. 6. These measures were spelled out further in a "Defense Counterproliferation Initiative" announced by Secretary Aspin on December 7, 1993, in a speech before the Committee on International Security and Arms Control of the National Academy of Sciences in Washington, D.C. For text of this talk, see "The Defense Counterproliferation Initiative," *Defense/94*, no. 1 (1994), pp. 28–31. See also DoD, *Annual Report 1994*, pp. 34–50.

48. See R. W. Apple, Jr., "Wounded in Policy Wars," *New York Times*, December 16, 1993; Bruce B. Auster, "Caught in the Crossfire," *U.S. News and World Report*, December 6, 1993, pp. 30–31; John Barry, et al., "The Collapse of Les Aspin," *Newsweek*, December 27, 1993, pp. 23–25; Thomas L. Friedman, "Others Tottered Earlier, but Aspin Fell," *New York Times*, December 17, 1993; Barton Gellman and R. Jeffrey Smith, "Hesitant by Design," *Washington Post*, November 14, 1993.

49. From statement at White House press conference, December 15, 1993, as cited in *New York Times*, December 16, 1993.

50. From transcript of opening statement by Perry at Confirmation Hear-

ing, Senate Armed Services Committee, Washington, D.C., February 2, 1994, as recorded by Federal News Service.

51. See Tony Capaccio, "Panetta: Match of Bottom-Up Forces, Dollars Is a 'Tight One,' " *Defense Week*, February 8, 1994, p. 1; Michael Gordon, "Pentagon Fights Budget Officials over $50 Billion," *New York Times*, December 10, 1993; Michael Gordon, "Pentagon's Budget Gap Is Narrowed to $31 Billion," *New York Times*, December 18, 1993; John Lancaster, "Aspin Says 5-Year Strategy Requires $50 Billion More," *Washington Post*, December 11, 1993; Lancaster, "Pentagon Spending Gap Revised to $31 Billion," *Washington Post*, December 18, 1993; John D. Morrocco, "Defense Budget May Be Up to $150 Billion Short," *Aviation Week and Space Technology*, August 8, 1994, p. 24.

52. John D. Morrocco, "USAF Bomber Force Could Drop to 100," *Aviation Week and Space Technology*, December 13/30, 1993, pp. 28–29.

53. See David A. Fulghum and John D. Morrocco, "Deutch Demands Cuts, Services Scramble Anew," *Aviation Week and Space Technology*, August 24, 1994, pp. 22–24; John Lancaster, "Army Challenges Clinton Defense Cuts as Security Threat," *Washington Post*, November 13, 1993; Lancaster, "Army Study Warns of Possible Equipment Shortages," *Washington Post*, December 14, 1993; John D. Morrocco, "U.S. Facing Shortfalls in Two-War Strategy," *Aviation Week and Space Technology*, May 2, 1994, p. 59.

54. Aspin, *Bottom-Up Review*, p. 5.

55. See Callahan, "Saving Defense Dollars," pp. 102–10. See also testimony by Carl J. Conetta of the Project on Defense Alternatives before the House Committee on Armed Services, Washington, D.C., March 10, 1994 (mimeo), p. 6.

56. Andrew F. Krepinevich, *The Bottom-Up Review: An Assessment* (Washington, D.C.: Defense Budget Project, 1994), p. 50.

57. Ibid., pp. 26, 41–44. See also Committee for National Security, *The Bottom-Up Review: Exaggerated Threats and Undervalued Allies?* (Washington, D.C.: n.d.).

58. For discussion, see Callahan, "Saving Defense Dollars," pp. 111–12.

59. IISS, *The Military Balance 89–90*, p. 16. For total warhead numbers, see "Estimated Nuclear Stockpiles 1945–1993," *Bulletin of the Atomic Scientists*, December 1993, p. 57.

60. "U.S. Strategic Nuclear Forces, End of 1992," *Bulletin of the Atomic Scientists*, January/February 1993, p. 57.

61. See "Past and Projected Strategic Nuclear Forces," Arms Control Association Fact Sheet, Washington, D.C., September 3, 1992. See also *SIPRI Yearbook 1992*, pp. 13–92.

62. Les Aspin, *Annual Report of the Secretary of Defense to the President and the Congress, January 1994* (Washington, D.C.: U.S. Government Printing Office, 1994), pp. 57–58. See also Dunbar Lockwood, "Pentagon Begins

Policy Review of Post-Cold War Nuclear Strategy," *Arms Control Today*, December 1993, pp. 23, 27.

63. See Center for Defense Information, "Nuclear Weapons After the Cold War: Too Many, Too Costly, Too Dangerous," *Defense Monitor* 22:1 (1993), entire.

64. See R. Jeffrey Smith, "U.S. Urged to Cut 50% of A-Arms," *Washington Post*, January 6, 1992.

65. Thomas C. Reed and Michael O. Wheeler, *The Role of Nuclear Weapons in the New World Order*, December 1991 (mimeo), pp. iii, iv, 19, 26.

66. As quoted in Smith, "U.S. Urged to Cut 50%."

67. Ibid.

68. Thomas F. Ramos, "The Future of Theater Nuclear Weapons," *Strategic Review*, Fall 1991, pp. 41–47.

69. Thomas W. Dowler and Joseph S. Howard II, "Countering the Threat of the Well-Armed Tyrant: A Modest Proposal for Small Nuclear Weapons," *Strategic Review*, Fall 1991, pp. 34–40.

70. See Paul Quinn-Judge, "U.S., Russia Strategists See Place for 'Mini-nukes," *Boston Globe*, July 12, 1993; Mark Thompson, "A Push for 'Mini-Nukes Research," *Philadelphia Inquirer*, June 17, 1993. See also William Arkin and Robert S. Norris, "Tinynukes for Mini Minds," *Bulletin of the Atomic Scientists*, April 1992, pp. 24–25.

71. "Mr. Perry's Backward Nuclear Policy," editorial, *New York Times*, March 24, 1994.

72. Perry's denial was offered in a letter to the editor of the *New York Times* that appeared in the March 31, 1994, issue. For discussion of this question, see Jon B. Wolfstahl and Dunbar Lockwood, "Pentagon Report Provides Glimpse into Future Nuclear Policies, Forces," *Arms Control Today*, April 1994, p. 21.

73. *A National Security Strategy of Engagement and Enlargement* (Washington, D.C.: The White House, July 1994), p. 12.

74. U.S. Department of Defense, *Nuclear Posture Review* (Washington, D.C., September 1994). See also R. Jeffrey Smith, "Clinton Decides to Retain Bush Nuclear Arms Policy," *Washington Post*, September 22, 1994; Jon B. Wolfstahl, "New Nuclear Posture Review Shows Little Change in Policies," *Arms Control Today*, November 1994, pp. 27, 32.

75. Address to the U.N. General Assembly, New York, N.Y., September 27, 1993, as transcribed in *U.S. Department of State Dispatch*, September 27, 1993, p. 651.

76. News conference, Little Rock, Ark., November 12, 1992, as transcribed in *New York Times*, November 13, 1993.

77. Statement before the Senate Foreign Relations Committee, Washington, D.C., January 13, 1993, as transcribed in *U.S. Department of State Dispatch*, January 25, 1993, p. 47.

78. Address by Bill Clinton before the National Assembly of Korea, Seoul, South Korea, July 10, 1993, as transcribed in *U.S. Department of State Dispatch*, July 19, 1993, p. 510.

79. Ibid.

80. As quoted in *Washington Post*, July 12, 1993.

81. Anthony Lake, "From Containment to Enlargement," address at the School of Advanced International Studies, Johns Hopkins University, Washington, D.C., September 21, 1993, as transcribed in *U.S. Department of State Dispatch*, September 27, 1993, pp. 661–62.

82. Patrick E. Tyler, "No Chemical Arms Aboard China Ship," *New York Times*, September 6, 1993.

83. Statement before the Senate Foreign Relations Committee, Washington, D.C., March 22, 1994, as transcribed in *U.S. Department of State Dispatch*, April 4, 1994, p. 183.

84. See Douglas Jehl, "U.S. Is Pressing Sanctions for North Korea," *New York Times*, June 11, 1994; Michael R. Gordon, "White House Asks Global Sanctions on North Koreans," *New York Times*, June 3, 1994; David E. Sanger, "North Korea Foils Efforts to Halt Its Nuclear Plans," *New York Times*, May 29, 1994; Sanger, "North Korea Quits Atom Agency in Wider Rift with U.S. and U.N.," *New York Times*, June 14, 1994; Paul Shin, "N. Korea Repeats Threat of War over Sanctions by U.N.," *Washington Times*, June 7, 1994; R. Jeffrey Smith, "N. Korea Defies Atomic Energy Agency," *Washington Post*, May 15, 1994.

85. Richard N. Haass, "Keep the Heat on North Korea," *New York Times*, June 17, 1994.

86. "The time for temporizing is over," suggested former NSC Director Brent Scowcroft in June 1994. In pursuing U.S. objectives, "we [must] make clear to Pyongyang that we will not be intimidated by its threats and will not be paralyzed by the possibility of war." Brent Scowcroft, writing in *Washington Post*, June 15, 1994.

87. See, for example, Charles Krauthammer, "Get Ready for War," *Washington Post*, June 3, 1994; William Safire, "Korean Conflict II?" *New York Times*, June 9, 1994.

CHAPTER FIVE

1. Statement before the House Armed Services Committee, Washington, D.C., March 19, 1991 (mimeo), pp. 7–8.

2. Carl E. Vuono, "Building the Army of Tomorrow," *Sea Power*, April 1991, pp. 40–41.

3. Aspin, *Bottom-Up Review*, p. 1.

4. Lake, "Confronting Backlash States," pp. 45–46.

5. The Joint Chiefs of Staff in 1992 identified Iran, Iraq, and North Korea as "specific threats for which we must maintain forces." In addition, they identified Cuba, Iran, Iraq, Libya, and Syria as "state sponsors of terrorism." U.S. Joint Chiefs of Staff, *1992 Joint Military Net Assessment* (Washington, D.C.: August 11, 1992), chap. 1, pp. 8, 11. (Hereinafter cited as JCS, *JMNA 1992.*) Similarly, the Chairman of the JCS, General John M. Shalikashvili, told the House Armed Services Committee on February 22, 1994, that "there are still identifiable regional threats like North Korea, Iran, Iraq, Libya, and others" that must be defended against. And, in a 1994 "World Wide Threat Briefing" to the House Armed Services Committee, Joseph S. Nye of the National Intelligence Council listed Cuba, Iran, Iraq, Libya, and North Korea as "hostile states."

6. "In planning military forces for the future," the Joint Chiefs of Staff explained in their 1992 military posture statement, "we must look to regions where potential aggressors have the motive and capability to employ military coercion or actual force against their neighbors." JCS, *JMNA 1992*, chap. 1, p. 9.

7. Ibid.

8. The data for these assessments are drawn from newspaper accounts, government reports, and the publications of such organizations as the International Institute of Strategic Studies (IISS) and the Stockholm International Peace Research Institute (SIPRI). Other sources include Spector, *Nuclear Ambitions;* Kenneth R. Timmerman, *Weapons of Mass Destruction: The Cases of Iran, Syria, and Libya* (Los Angeles: Simon Wiesenthal Center, 1992). Information is current as of mid-1994.

9. According to a January 1994 statement by CIA Director James Woolsey, "We believe that North Korea could already have produced enough plutonium for at least one nuclear weapon." From opening statement before the Senate Select Committee on Intelligence, Washington, D.C., January 24, 1994 (mimeo), p. 6. Similarly, in February 1994, Secretary of Defense designate William Perry testified that "we understand that [the North Koreans] may have achieved some small quantity of plutonium out of the earlier operation of one of their smaller reactors, and that it is possible that they could make one or even two [nuclear] devices, perhaps even nuclear bombs, with this small amount of plutonium." From transcript by Federal News Service of confirmation hearing before the Senate Armed Services Committee, Washington, D.C., February 2, 1994.

10. One such call for preemptive action was made by former NSC official Richard N. Haass in "Keep the Heat on North Korea." The "sea of fire" remark was made at a meeting between North and South Korean representatives at Panmunjon on March 19, 1994. See R. Jeffrey Smith and Ann

Devroy, "U.S. Backs Maneuvers in S. Korea," *Washington Post*, March 20, 1994.

11. See Don Oberdorfer, "The Remilitarized Zone," *Washington Post*, May 1, 1994; T. R. Reid, "North Korea Warns of 'Brink of War,' " *Washington Post*, March 23, 1994; R. Jeffrey Smith, "Perry Sharply Warns North Korea," *Washington Post*, March 31, 1994.

12. As cited in "Evans-Novak Political Report," April 5, 1994.

13. For discussion, see Bruce Cumings, "Spring Thaw for Korea's Cold War?" *Bulletin of the Atomic Scientists*, April 1992, pp. 14–23; John Curtis Perry, "Dateline North Korea: A Communist Holdout," *Foreign Policy*, no. 80 (Fall 1990), pp. 172–91.

14. IISS, *The Military Balance 93–94*, pp. 159–62. See also William J. Taylor, Jr., "East Asia and the Pacific: The North Korean Military Threat and U.S. Responses," in U.S. General Accounting Office (GAO), *Papers Prepared for GAO Conference on Worldwide Military Threats, April 1992* (Washington, D.C.: GAO, 1992), pp. 105–107.

15. For discussion, see Barton Gellman, "Trepidation at Root of U.S. Korea Policy," *Washington Post*, December 12, 1993; Michael R. Gordon, "Pentagon Studies Plans to Bolster U.S.–Korea Forces," *New York Times*, December 2, 1993; Michael R. Gordon and David E. Sanger, "North Korea's Huge Military Spurs New Strategy for South," *New York Times*, February 6, 1994; Jim Mann, "Scenarios for a 2nd Korean War Grim for U.S., South," *Los Angeles Times*, February 22, 1994.

16. News briefing, The Pentagon, December 14, 1993, as transcribed in U.S. Department of Defense, *Defense Issues* 8:72 (Washington, D.C., n.d.), p. 1.

17. For discussion, see Gellman, "Trepidation at Root of U.S. Korea Policy"; Mann, "Scenarios for a 2nd Korean War."

18. As quoted in Mann, "Scenarios for a 2nd Korean War." According to one report, U.S. military officials estimate that an all-out war between North and South would produce as many as 400,000 U.S. and South Korean troop fatalities. See Gilbert A. Lewthwaite, "40 Years of Planning to Keep Seoul Free," *Baltimore Sun*, June 14, 1994.

19. See Robin Bulman, "Koreas Sign Declaration Banning Nuclear Arms," *Washington Post*, January 1, 1992; Dan Oberdorfer, "U.S. Welcomes Korea's Nuclear Accord," *Washington Post*, January 2, 1992.

20. For background on North Korea's nuclear program, see Spector, *Nuclear Ambitions*, pp. 118–40.

21. For discussion, see David Albright, "How Much Plutonium Does North Korea Have?" *Bulletin of the Atomic Scientists*, September/October 1994, pp. 46–53; Joseph H. Bermudez, Jr., "North Korea's Nuclear Programme," *Jane's Intelligence Review*, September 1991, pp. 404–11; Andrew Mack,

"North Korea and the Bomb," *Foreign Policy*, no. 83 (Summer 1991), pp. 87–104.

22. See David E. Sanger, "North Korea Plan on Fueling A-Bomb May Be Confirmed," *New York Times*, June 15, 1992; Jon B. Wolfsthal, "IAEA Conducts First Inspection of North Korean Nuclear Facilities," *Arms Control Today*, June 1992, p. 22; Sheryl WuDunn, "North Korea Site Has A-Bomb Hints," *New York Times*, May 18, 1992.

23. See Albright, "How Much Plutonium?" pp. 46–48; David E. Sanger, "In Reversal, North Korea Bars Nuclear Inspectors," *New York Times*, February 9, 1993; Sanger, "Atom Agency Said to Issue Demand to North Korea," *New York Times*, February 11, 1993; Sanger, "Atomic Energy Agency Asks U.N. to Move Against North Koreans," *New York Times*, April 2, 1993. For further background, see summary of presentation by Jon B. Wolfsthal of the Arms Control Association in "The Continuing North Korean Nuclear Crisis," *Arms Control Today*, June 1994, pp. 18–20.

24. See Sanger, "Atomic Energy Agency Asks U.N. to Move Against North Koreans"; R. Jeffrey Smith, "N. Korea Quitting Arms Pact," *Washington Post*, March 12, 1993.

25. See Albright, "How Much Plutonium?" pp. 48, 50; Michael R. Gordon, "U.S. Cancels Talks with North Korea over Atom Inspections," *New York Times*, March 17, 1994; David E. Sanger, "North Korea Said to Block Taking of Radioactive Samples from Site," *New York Times*, March 16, 1994; Sanger, "North Korea Foils Efforts to Halt its Nuclear Plans," *New York Times*, May 29, 1994; Sanger, "North Korea Quits Atom Agency in Wider Rift with U.S. and U.N.," *New York Times*, June 14, 1994; R. Jeffrey Smith and Julia Preston, "Nuclear Watchdog Says N. Korea Steps Up Fuel Rod Withdrawal," *Washington Post*, May 28, 1994; R. Jeffrey Smith, "N. Korea Defies Atomic Energy Agency," *Washington Post*, May 15, 1994. See also Wolfsthal interview, "The Continuing North Korean Crisis."

26. See Ann Devroy and Julia Preston, "U.S. to Seek Sanctions on North Korea," *Washington Post*, June 3, 1994; Michael R. Gordon, "White House Asks Global Sanctions on North Koreans," *New York Times*, June 3, 1994; R. Jeffrey Smith, "U.S. Plans to Seek North Korea Sanctions," *Washington Post*, June 1, 1994.

27. See Michael R. Gordon, "Clinton May Add G.I.'s in Korea While Remaining Open to Talks," *New York Times*, June 17, 1994; Paul Shin, "N. Korea Repeats Threat of War over Sanctions by U.N.," *Washington Times*, June 7, 1994.

28. Michael R. Gordon, "Back from Korea, Carter Declares the Crisis Is Over," *New York Times*, June 20, 1994.

29. Robert S. Greenberger, "Clinton Says North Korea Agreed to Freeze Its Nuclear Program," *Wall Street Journal*, June 23, 1994; Douglas Jehl, "Clinton Finds North Koreans Really May Be Ready to Talk," *New York*

Times, June 27, 1994; Ruth Marcus and R. Jeffrey Smith, "North Korea Confirms Freeze; U.S. Agrees to Resume Talks," *Washington Post*, June 23, 1994; Jon B. Wolfstahl, "N. Korea Freezes Nuclear Program in Exchange for Talks with U.S.," *Arms Control Today*, July/August 1994, pp. 20, 25.

30. See Alan Riding, "U.S. and North Korea Agree to Build on Nuclear Accord," *New York Times*, October 18, 1994; David E. Sanger,"Clinton Approves Plan to Give Aid to North Koreans," *New York Times*, October 19, 1994; R. Jeffrey Smith, "N. Korea, U.S. Reach Nuclear Accord," *Washington Post*, October 18, 1994; Jon B. Wolfstahl, "U.S., Pyongyang Reach Accord on North's Nuclear Program," *Arms Control Today*, November 1994, pp. 25, 32. See also R. Jeffrey Smith, "N. Korea Accord: A Troubling Precedent?" *Washington Post*, October 20, 1994.

31. U.S. Defense Intelligence Agency (DIA), *North Korea: The Foundations for Military Strength* (Washington, D.C.: DIA, 1991), pp. 60–62.

32. See Eric Schmitt, "North Korea Delivers to Iran," *New York Times*, March 18, 1992, describing a shipment of Scud missiles to Iran (for delivery to Syria). See also statement by Bermudez before the House Committee on Foreign Affairs, Subcommittee on International Security, September 14, 1993, pp. 2–3, 5–9.

33. See statement by Bermudez, September 14, 1993, pp. 2–3. See also Paul Beaver, "Nodong-1 Details Fuel New Fears in Asia," *Jane's Defence Weekly*, January 15, 1994, p. 4; David E. Sanger, "Missile is Tested by North Koreans," *New York Times*, June 13, 1993; R. Jeffrey Smith, "CIA Confirms North Korea's New Missiles," *Washington Post*, March 18, 1994.

34. See Robert E. Greenberger, "North Korea's Missile Sales in Mideast, Along with Nuclear Issue, Raise Concern," *Wall Street Journal*, July 19, 1993; David Wright and Timur Kadyshev, "The North Korean Missile Program: How Advanced Is It?" *Arms Control Today*, April 1994, pp. 9–12.

35. For discussion see Jim Mann, "N. Korea Succession 'Not Falling into Place,' " *Los Angeles Times*, August 19, 1994; Andrew Pollack, "North Korea Said to Dip into Rice Reserves to Bar Unrest," *New York Times*, July 18, 1994; James Sterngold, "New Wrinkle in Korea Issue: Who Is in Charge in the North?" *New York Times*, August 25, 1994.

36. Lake, "Confronting Backlash States," p. 52.

37. According to CIA Director James Woolsey, "Iran remains determined to maintain its implacable hostility, to eliminate any opposition to its rule, and to undermine our security interests and those of our friends and allies in the region." Moreover, "We are especially concerned that Iran continues to develop its ambitious multibillion dollar military modernization program and to pursue development of weapons of mass destruction." From statement before the Senate Select Committee on Intelligence, January 25, 1994.

38. See, for instance, Thomas L. Friedman, "U.S. to Counter Iran in Central Asia," *New York Times*, February 6, 1992; Chris Hedges, "Iran Is

Riling Its Gulf Neighbors, Pressing Claim to 3 Disputed Isles," *New York Times*, September 13, 1992; Youseef M. Ibrahim, "Iran Shifting Its Attention from Lebanon to Sudan," *New York Times*, December 13, 1991; Ibrahim, "Iran Upsets Algeria by Backing Muslims," *New York Times*, January 19, 1992; Ibrahim, "Dispute over Gulf Islands Worsens Iran-Arab Ties," *New York Times*, October 4, 1992; Ibrahim, "Rebounding Iranians Are Striving for Regional Leadership in Gulf," *New York Times*, November 7, 1992; Ibrahim, "Arabs Raise a Nervous Cry over Iranian Militancy," *New York Times*, December 21, 1992; Douglas Jehl, "Iran-Backed Terrorists Are Growing More Aggressive, U.S. Warns," *New York Times*, March 18, 1993; Jehl, "Egypt Warns CIA Chief on Iran-Backed Terror," *New York Times*, April 19, 1993.

39. See Tim Weiner, "Iran and Allies Are Suspected in Bomb Wave," *New York Times*, July 29, 1994.

40. Lake, "Confronting Backlash States," pp. 52, 55.

41. See Elaine Sciolino, "Iran's Problems Raising Doubts of Peril to U.S.," *New York Times*, July 5, 1994; R. Jeffrey Smith, "Gates Warns of Iranian Arms Drive," *Washington Post*, March 28, 1992.

42. SIPRI, *SIPRI Yearbook 1994*, p. 526. See also Michael R. Gordon, "Russia Selling Submarines to Teheran's Navy," *New York Times*, September 24, 1992; Robert Holzer and Neil Munro, "Iran Speeds Rearming Process," *Defense News*, February 17, 1992, pp. 1, 52; Jack Nelson, "Arms Buildup Making Iran Top Gulf Power," *Los Angeles Times*, January 7, 1992; Claude van England, "Iran Steps Up Arms Purchases to Prop Military," *Christian Science Monitor*, April 20, 1992; "Iran Buys Anti-Ship Missiles," *Arms Control Today*, June 1993, p. 35.

43. For discussion, see Callahan, "Saving Defense Dollars," p. 107.

44. Testimony before House Banking Committee, May 8, 1992, p. 9.

45. See Elaine Sciolino, "CIA Says Iran Makes Progress on Atom Arms," *New York Times*, November 30, 1992; R. Jeffrey Smith, "Officials Say Iran Is Seeking Nuclear Weapons Capability," *Washington Post*, October 30, 1991; Smith, "China-Iran Tie Long Known," *Washington Post*, October 31, 1991.

46. See David Albright and Mark Hibbs, "Spotlight Shifts to Iran," *Bulletin of the Atomic Scientists*, March 1992, pp. 9–11; Leonard S. Spector, "Nuclear Proliferation in the Middle East," *Orbis* 36:2 (Spring 1992), pp. 186–89; Timmerman, *Weapons of Mass Destruction*, pp. 43–44.

47. According to a 1993 statement by CIA Director James Woolsey, "Iran will take at least 8 to 10 years to produce its own nuclear weapons, perhaps fewer years if it receives critical foreign assistance for its development effort." U.S. Congress, Senate, Committee on Governmental Affairs, *Proliferation Threats of the 1990's*, Hearing, 103d Cong., 1st Ses., February 24, 1993, p. 13. (Hereinafter cited as SCGA, *Proliferation Threats*.)

48. According to the CIA, "Iraq has an active chemical weapons program

and has been producing chemical weapons at a steadily increasing rate since 1984. Iran has produced at least several hundred tons of blister, choking, and blood agents." Ibid. p. 185. See also SIPRI, *SIPRI Yearbook 1994*, pp. 326–27.

49. On Iran's missile capabilities, see statement by Bermudez, September 14, 1993, pp. 5–7. See also Douglas Jehl, "Iran Is Reported Acquiring Missiles," *New York Times*, April 8, 1993; Timmerman, *Weapons of Mass Destruction*, pp. 20–38.

50. For discussion, see Chris Hedges, "Islamic Hard–Liners Said to Gain Ground in Iran," *New York Times*, August 3, 1994; Sciolino, "Iran's Problems Raising Doubts"; Edward G. Shirley, "The Iran Policy Trap," *Foreign Policy*, no. 96 (Fall 1994), pp. 75–93.

51. On the question of hidden military capabilities, see Robert Gates' testimony to the House Banking Committee on May 8, 1992.

52. DoD, *Gulf War Final Report*, p. 294. Another 109 combat planes were flown to Iran during the war and later confiscated by the Iranian military.

53. IISS, *The Military Balance 92–93*, pp. 100–11.

54. These are the terms set by U.N. Security Council 687. For text of this agreement, see *U.S. Department of State Dispatch*, April 8, 1991, pp. 234–39.

55. See "Status of Iraqi Compliance with U.N. Resolutions," letter from George Bush to leaders of the U.S. Congress, November 16, 1992, in *U.S. Department of State Dispatch*, November 23, 1992, pp. 841–42. See also "Nuclear Situation in Iraq," statement by Assistant Secretary of State Robert L. Gallucci before the House Foreign Affairs Committee, June 29, 1993, as published in *U.S. Department of State Dispatch*, July 5, 1993, pp. 483–84.

56. For discussion, see Gallucci, "Nuclear Situation In Iraq"; Spector, "Nuclear Proliferation in the Middle East," pp. 181–86.

57. Jon B. Wolfsthal, "Allied Forces Bomb Iraq to Force Compliance with Demands," *Arms Control Today*, January/February 1993, pp. 21, 30.

58. Quoted in *New York Times*, October 11, 1994.

59. On the U.S. and British charges regarding the Lockerbie bombing, see Andrew Rosenthal, "U.S. Accuses Libya as 2 Are Charged in Pan Am Bombing," *New York Times*, November 15, 1991. For text of U.N. Security Council Resolution 748 of March 31, 1992, imposing sanctions on Libya, see *U.S. Department of State Dispatch*, April 6, 1992, pp. 268–69.

60. For discussion, see George Lardner, Jr., and John M. Goshko, "Libya's Terrorist Training Camps," *Washington Post*, February 27, 1992; Clifford Krauss, "Qaddafi Plays Quietly, but He's Still in the Game," *New York Times*, March 17, 1991.

61. IISS, *The Military Balance 93–94*, pp. 122–23.

62. For an account of these endeavors, see Spector, *Nuclear Ambitions*, pp. 175–79; Timmerman, *Weapons of Mass Destruction*, pp. 88–90.

63. See data supplied by the Central Intelligence Agency in SCGA, *Pro-*

liferation Threats, p. 188. See also Elaine Sciolino, "U.S. Agents Say Libya Is Adding and Hiding Chemical Weapons," *New York Times*, January 22, 1992; SIPRI, *SIPRI Yearbook 1994*, p. 327; Timmerman, *Weapons of Mass Destruction*, pp. 80–82.

64. Statement by Bermudez, September 14, 1993, pp. 7–8.

65. Chris Hedges, "Gaddafi Reported to Quash Army Revolt," *New York Times*, October 23, 1993.

66. For discussion, see Volker Perthes, "Incremental Change in Syria," *Current History*, January 1993, pp. 23–26; John Yemma, "U.S.–Syria Alliance Is an Uneasy One," *Boston Globe*, January 27, 1991.

67. IISS, *The Military Balance 93–94*, pp. 129–31.

68. Timmerman, *Weapons of Mass Destruction*, pp. 59–61. See also the 1989 testimony of William Webster (then Director of the CIA) and W. Seth Carus before the Permanent Investigations of the U.S. Senate, in SCGA, *Global Spread*, pp. 12, 61.

69. See Timmerman, *Weapons of Mass Destruction*, p. 60; statement by Bermudez, September 14, 1993, pp. 8–9.

70. See Steven Greenhouse, "U.S. Says It Is Pleased Syrians Are Acting to Limit Terrorism," *New York Times*, May 1, 1994; Elaine Sciolino, "U.S. Assures Damascus on Commitment to Peace," *New York Times*, November 16, 1993; Sciolino, "U.S. Plans to Ease Sanctions on Syria in Peace Gesture," *New York Times*, December 7, 1993. On President Clinton's 1994 meeting with Assad in Damascus, see Douglas Jehl, "Clinton Reports Progress in Talks in Syrian Capital," *New York Times*, October 28, 1994.

71. For background on these states' nuclear programs, see Spector, *Nuclear Ambitions;* on their chemical weapons program, see SCGA, *Global Spread*. For background on their conventional arms production capabilities, see U.S. Congress, Office of Technology Assessment, *Global Arms Trade* (Washington, D.C.: 1991). (Hereinafter cited as OTA, *Global Arms Trade*.)

72. For discussion of China's global role, see Barber M. Conable, Jr., and David M. Lampton, "China: The Coming Power," *Foreign Affairs* 71:5 (Winter 1992–93), pp. 133–49; Denny Roy, "Hegemon on the Horizon?" *International Security* 19:1 (Summer 1994), pp. 149–68; David Shambaugh, "China's Security Policy in the Post–Cold War Era," *Survival*, 34:2 (Summer 1992), pp. 88–106.

73. For an inventory of Chinese nuclear capabilities, see Dunbar Lockwood, "The Status of U.S., Russian, and Chinese Nuclear Forces in Northeast Asia," *Arms Control Today*, November 1994, pp. 23–24; Robert S. Norris, Andrew S. Burrows, and Richard W. Fieldhouse, *The Nuclear Weapons Databook, Volume V: British, French, and Chinese Nuclear Weapons* (Boulder, CO: Westview Press, 1994), pp. 324–97.

74. See D. Banerjee, "New Generation Weapons Behind China's Nuclear Test," *Business Times*, November 27, 1993; Jim Mann, "China Upgrading

Nuclear Arms, Experts Say," *Los Angeles Times*, November 9, 1993; SIPRI, *SIPRI Yearbook 1994*, pp. 304–306; Lena H. Sun, "Atomic Test Carried Out by China," *Washington Post*, October 6, 1993; Patrick E. Tyler, "China Explodes H-Bomb Underground as Test," *New York Times*, June 11, 1994; Tyler,"As China Upgrades Its Nuclear Arsenal, It Debates Need for Guns vs. Butter," *New York Times*, October 26, 1994.

75. Samuel S. Kim, "China as a Regional Power," *Current History*, September 1992, p. 248.

76. See Paul Godwin and John J. Schulz, "Arming the Dragon for the 21st Century: China's Defense Modernization Program," *Arms Control Today*, December 1993, pp. 3–8; Nicholas D. Kristof, "Experts Fret over Reach of China's Air Force," *New York Times*, August 23, 1992; Kristof, "China Builds Its Military Muscle, Making Some Neighbors Nervous," *New York Times*, January 11, 1993; "Chinese Navy to Expand," *Washington Times*, January 12, 1993.

77. See David A. Fulghum, "China Seeks to Build MiG-31," *Aviation Week and Space Technology*, October 5, 1992, pp. 27–29; Michael R. Gordon, "Moscow is Selling Weapons to China, U.S. Officials Say," *New York Times*, October 18, 1992; Jim Mann, "Russia Boosting China's Arsenal," *Los Angeles Times*, November 30, 1992.

78. See William Branigin, "As China Builds Arsenal and Bases, Asians Wary of 'Rogue in the Region,' " *Los Angeles Times*, March 31, 1993; Leszek Buszynski, "ASEAN Security Dilemmas," *Survival*, 34:4 (Winter 1992–93), pp. 91–94; Kim, "China as a Regional Power," pp. 247–52; Philip Shenon, "China Sends Warships to Vietnam Oil Site," *New York Times*, July 21, 1994; "South China Sea: Treacherous Shoals," *Far Eastern Economic Review*, August 13, 1992, pp. 14–17; Sheila Tefft, "China's Army Looms over Asia," *Christian Science Monitor*, August 10, 1994.

79. Shirley A. Kan, *Chinese Missile and Nuclear Proliferation: Issues for Congress*, CRS Issue Brief (Washington, D.C.: Congressional Research Service, November 16, 1992).

80. Ibid., pp. 7–8. See also: Spector, "Nuclear Proliferation in the Middle East," pp. 188–92; Timmerman, *Weapons of Mass Destruction*, pp. 43–44, 75–76.

81. See Bill Gertz, "Pakistan–China Deal for Missiles Exposed," *Washington Times*, September 7, 1994; Douglas Jehl, "China Breaking Missile Pledge, U.S. Aides Say," *New York Times*, May 6, 1993; Kan, *Chinese Missile and Nuclear Proliferation*, pp. 2–5; John Wilson Lewis and Hua Di, "China's Ballistic Missile Programs," *International Security* 17:2 (Fall 1992), pp. 5–50; R. Jeffrey Smith and Thomas W. Lippman, "Pakistan M-11 Funding Is Reported," *Washington Post*, September 8, 1994.

82. See Kan, *Chinese Missile and Nuclear Proliferation*, pp. 3–4; Timmerman, *Weapons of Mass Destruction*, pp. 24–27, 69–71.

83. Steven A. Holmes, "U.S. Determines China Violated Pact on Missiles," *New York Times*, August 25, 1993; Jon B. Wolfsthal, "U.S. Imposes Sanctions over China's Missile Transfers," *Arms Control Today*, September 1993, p. 27.

84. According to CIA Director James Woolsey: "We are closely monitoring China's military modernization, as well as its attempts to export extremely potent weapons technology into some of the more unstable regions of the world such as the Middle East." From statement before the Senate Select Committee on Intelligence, January 25, 1994 (mimeo), p. 10. See also "China and Arms: Worry Lingers," *Los Angeles Times*, October 6, 1994.

85. Elaine Sciolino, "U.S. and Chinese Reach Agreement on Missile Export," *New York Times*, October 5, 1994; Jon B. Wolfstahl,"U.S., China Reach Accord on MTCR, Fissile Cutoff Issues," *Arms Control Today*, November 1994, p. 28.

86. U.S. Defense Security Assistance Agency, *Foreign Military Sales, Foreign Military Construction Sales, and Military Assistance Facts*, as of September 30, 1992 (Washington, D.C.: n.d.), pp. 3, 11, 55. Includes sales through the U.S. Government's Foreign Military Sales program and direct sales by U.S. firms through the Commercial Sales program. (Hereinafter cited as DSAA, *FMS Facts 19xx*.)

87. See Nolan, *Trappings of Power*, pp. 53–55.

88. Philip Shenon, "U.S. Accuse 2 Egyptian Colonels in Plot to Smuggle Missile Material," *New York Times*, June 25, 1988; Patrick E. Tyler, "High Link Seen in Cairo Spy Case," *Washington Post*, August 20, 1988.

89. See See Chris Hedges, "As Islamic Groups Thunder, Egypt Grows More Nervous," *New York Times*, November 12, 1992; Hedges, "Frustrations Blaze a Path for Egypt's Fundamentalists," *New York Times*, December 6, 1992; Hedges, "As Egypt Votes on Mubarak, He Faces Rising Peril," *New York Times*, October 4, 1993; Hedges, "Egypt Loses Ground, to Muslim Militants and Fear," *New York Times*, February 11, 1994; Youssef M. Ibrahim, "Egypt Fights Militant Islam with More of the Same," *New York Times*, August 18, 1993; Robert D. Kaplan,"Eaten from Within," *Atlantic Monthly*, November 1994, pp. 26–43; William E. Schmidt, "A Deluge of Foreign Assistance Fails to Revive Egypt's Stricken Economy," *New York Times*, October 17, 1993; Peter Waldman, "A Disgruntled Arms and Mounting Unrest Face Egyptian Regime," *Wall Street Journal*, June 14, 1993.

90. See IISS, *The Military Balance 93–94*, pp. 113–14. On Egypt's chemical warfare capabilities, see SCGA, *Global Spread*, p. 283.

91. For an inventory of India's military capabilities, see IISS, *The Military Balance 93–94*, pp. 138–40. For discussion, see Mohammed Ayoob, "India in South Asia: The Quest for Regional Dominance," *World Policy Journal*

7:1 (Winter 1989–90), pp. 107–33. On India's military-industrial complex, see SIPRI, *SIPRI Yearbook 1994*, pp. 243–65.

92. See Praful Bidwai, "India's Passage to Washington," *The Nation*, January 20, 1992, pp. 47–49; Ajoy Bose, "U.S. to Replace Soviet Union as India's Military Ally," *The Guardian*, January 22, 1992; Sanjoy Hazarika, "India Moving Toward Closer Relations with U.S.," *New York Times*, March 15, 1992.

93. Spector, *Nuclear Ambitions*, pp. 63–88. See also Carnegie Endowment for International Peace, Nuclear Non-Proliferation Project, "Nuclear Proliferation Status Report, July 1992" (mimeo), p. 3.

94. See Steve Coll, "India Tests Controversial Agni Missile," *Washington Post*, May 30, 1992; Sanjoy Hazarika, "India Successfully Tests a Medium–Range Missile," *New York Times*, May 31, 1992; Nolan, *Trappings of Power*, pp. 40–48; SCGA, *Proliferation Threats*, pp. 186–87; Spector, *Nuclear Ambitions*, pp. 74–76.

95. For discussion, see Seymour M. Hersh, "On the Nuclear Edge," *The New Yorker*, March 29, 1993, pp. 56–73.

96. See John F. Burns, "India Rejects U.S. Bid for Nuclear Pact with Pakistan," *New York Times*, March 28, 1994; Steve Coll, "U.S. Nuclear Diplomacy in South Asia Faces Obstacles," *Washington Post*, February 8, 1992; Barbara Crossette, "India Is Pressed on Atom Project," *New York Times*, February 12, 1992; Edward A. Gargan, "Diplomats Are Edgy as India Stubbornly Builds Its Nuclear Arsenal," *New York Times*, January 21, 1992; Thomas W. Lippman, "U.S. Efforts to Curb Nuclear Weapons in Peril as India Insists on Limits for China," *New York Times*, July 7, 1994.

97. Barbara Crossette, "Russia's Rocket Deal with India Leads U.S. to Impose Trade Bans," *New York Times*, May 12, 1992; R. Jeffrey Smith, "U.S. Imposes Sanctions Against Russian, Indian Concerns over Rocket Deal," *Washington Post*, May 12, 1992.

98. See Mohammed Ayoob, "Dateline India: The Deepening Crisis," *Foreign Policy*, no. 85 (Winter 1991–1992), pp. 166–84; Edward A. Gargan, "Hindus Now Demanding the Leadership of India," *New York Times*, January 24, 1993; Bernard Weinraub, "Hindu Nationalists' Power Solidifies," *New York Times*, June 17, 1991.

99. See Gargan, "Hindus Now Demanding." Gargan quotes BJP Vice President Kavel Ratna Malkani as saying: "We should go nuclear and sign the NPT as a nuclear weapons state." In this manner, "The whole world will recognize us by our power."

100. DSAA, *FMS Facts 1990*, pp. 33, 69.

101. For background on Pakistan's nuclear weapons program, see Spector, *Nuclear Ambitions*, pp. 89–111. See also David Albright and Mark Hibbs, "Pakistan's Bomb: Out of the Closet," *Bulletin of the Atomic Scientists*, July/August 1992, pp. 38–43; SCGA, *Proliferation Threats*, p. 187.

102. Bob Drogin, "U.S. Officials Reportedly Conclude That Pakistan Has a Nuclear Bomb," *Los Angeles Times*, October 24, 1990; Michael R. Gordon, "End to Pakistan Aid Is Sought over Nuclear Issue," *New York Times*, September 25, 1990. For discussion, see Hersh, "On the Nuclear Edge"; Smith and Cobban, "A Blind Eye to Nuclear Proliferation," pp. 57–59; Spector, *Nuclear Ambitions*, pp. 93–109.

103. See Edward A. Gargan, "Bhutto Stands by Nuclear Program," *New York Times*, October 21, 1993; "Pakistani Is Rebuked on A-Bomb Remark," *New York Times*, August 25, 1994.

104. John Ward Anderson, "Pakistan Rebuffs U.S. on A-Bomb," *Washington Post*, April 8, 1994.

105. See R. Jeffrey Smith, "U.S. Reports Chinese Missile Launchers Sighted in Pakistan," *Washington Post*, April 6, 1991; Smith and Lippman, "Pakistan M-11 Funding Is Reported." Pakistan will produce the Chinese K-8 jet trainer at Kamra, and may begin assembly of F-7P jet fighters. See "Embargo on Pakistan F-16s Sparks Self-Sufficiency," *Aviation Week and Space Technology*, October 19, 1992, p. 47.

106. DSAA, *FMS Facts 1992*, pp. 31, 71.

107. According to the International Institute of Strategic Studies, the South Korean military has some 633,000 active-duty troops, most of whom serve in the army. Equipment holdings include some 1,800 tanks, 2,000 armored infantry fighting vehicles, 4,400 heavy artillery pieces, and 445 combat aircraft. IISS, *The Military Balance 93–94*, pp. 161–62.

108. Spector, *Nuclear Ambitions*, p. 122. See also Paul Shin, "U.S. Said to Stop South Korea's Nuke Bomb Plans," *Washington Times*, March 29, 1994.

109. See Eric Nadler, "North Korea's Nuclear Neighbors," *The Nation*, July 4, 1994, pp. 17–19.

110. See Merrill Goozner, "Koreas Ask Why as Japan Pushes Nuclear Program," *Chicago Tribune*, June 29, 1994; David E. Sanger, "Wary of North Korea, Seoul Debates Building Atomic Bomb," *New York Times*, March 19, 1993.

111. According to the International Institute of Strategic Studies, the RoC military has 442,000 active-duty troops and 1.66 million reserves; equipment holdings include 530 tanks, 484 combat aircraft, and 37 major combat ships. IISS, *The Military Balance 93–94*, pp. 168–69.

112. SIPRI, *SIPRI Yearbook 1994*, pp. 541–42.

113. See Barbara Amouyal, "Taiwan Aims for Military Self Sufficiency by 2000," *Defense News*, October 15, 1990, pp. 1, 82; Anthony Leung, "Fortress Formosa—In Defence of Taiwan," *Military Technology*, August 1990, pp. 19–30; OTA, *Global Arms Trade*, pp. 170–73.

114. Spector, *Nuclear Ambitions*, p. 60.

115. See Lincoln Kaye, "Atomic Intentions," *Far Eastern Economic Review*, May 3, 1990, p. 9.

116. See Elisa D. Harris, "Chemical Weapons Proliferation," in Aspen Strategy Group, *New Threats: Responding to the Proliferation of Nuclear, Chemical, and Delivery Capabilities in the Third World* (Lanham, MD: University Press of America, 1990), p. 71 and note 7; Robert Karniol, "Taiwan's Space and Missile Programs," *International Defense Review*, August 1989, pp. 1077–78.

117. According to the International Institute of Strategic Studies, the Turkish military in 1993 possessed some 4,835 tanks, 4,550 heavy artillery pieces, and several hundred combat aircraft. IISS, *The Military Balance 93–94*, pp. 60–62.

118. See SIPRI, *SIPRI Yearbook 1993*, pp. 495–96.

119. Ibid., pp. 496–97.

120. Ibid., pp. 521–32.

121. See Robert S. Greenberger,"Turkey, Stalwart Ally in Gulf War, Is Asserting Its Independence from U.S.," *Wall Street Journal*, October 3, 1994; Norman Kempster, "Angered Turks May Halt Use of Air Base," *Los Angeles Times*, January 29, 1993.

122. In 1993, for instance, Prime Minister Tansu Ciller warned that Turkey would not "sit with its arms crossed" if the Armenians continued their "aggression" against Azerbaijanis, who are ethnic kin to the Turks. See Serge Schmemann, "Turkey Holds Talks on Caucasus War," *New York Times*, September 10, 1993. See also "Turkey's Military Said Eager to Fight," *Washington Times*, September 7, 1994.

123. See Spector, *Nuclear Ambitions*, pp. 223–63.

124. See John R. Redick, "Latin America's Emerging Non-Proliferation Consensus," *Arms Control Today*, March 1994, pp. 3–9; Leonard S. Spector, "Repentant Nuclear Proliferants," *Foreign Policy*, no. 88 (Fall 1992), pp. 26–27.

125. On Indonesia's military-industrial efforts, see OTA, *Global Arms Trade*, pp. 168–70.

126. Aspin, *Bottom-Up Review*, p. 5.

127. See Callahan, "Saving Defense Dollars," pp. 109–10. On South Korea's military proficiency, see William W. Kaufmann and John D. Steinbruner, *Decisions for Defense: Prospects for a New Order* (Washington, D.C.: Brookings Institution, 1991), pp. 45–46.

128. On this point, see the declassified CIA report entitled "Prospects for the Worldwide Development of Ballistic Missile Threats to the Continental United States," provided to Representative Ronald Dellums in November 1993. See also Lora Lumpe, Lisbeth Gronlund, and David C. Wright, "Third World Missiles Fall Short," *Bulletin of the Atomic Scientists*, March 1992, pp. 30–37.

129. As suggested by William Kaufmann and John Steinbruner of the Brookings Institution, "it is not easy to find a substitute [for Iraq] with the same capabilities and intentions." Various Third World states—Iran, Syria, Libya, and so on—can, of course, be viewed as possible adversaries. But "the likelihood seems rather low for the next ten years that any one of them could or would want to replace Iraq—especially after the awesome, if excessive, display of U.S. military power [in Operation Desert Storm]." Kaufmann and Steinbruner, *Decisions for Defense*, p. 44.

CHAPTER SIX

1. Les Aspin, "The Defense Counterproliferation Initiative," summary of remarks given before the National Academy of Sciences Committee on International Security and Arms Control, Washington, D.C., December 7, 1993, as published in *Defense/94*, no. 1 (1994), p. 29.

2. Warren Christopher, "The Strategic Priorities of American Foreign Policy," statement before the Senate Foreign Relations Committee, Washington, D.C., November 4, 1993, as published in *U.S. Department of State Dispatch*, November 22, 1993, p. 800.

3. In "Confronting Backlash States," National Security Adviser Anthony Lake wrote that the "outlaw" and "backlash" states "exhibit a chronic inability to engage constructively with the outside world," as demonstrated, most particularly, by their pursuit of weapons of mass destruction (p. 46).

4. "There are still too many nations who seem determined to . . . develop a nuclear weapon or a biological or chemical weapon," President Clinton declared in 1993. "It is a mistake, and we should try to contain it and stop it." Statement at Los Alamos High School, Los Alamos, N.M., May 17, 1993 (White House Press Office transcript, mimeo), p. 4.

5. For a description of these regimes, see Zachary S. Davis, *Nonproliferation Regimes: Policies to Control the Spread of Nuclear, Chemical, and Biological Weapons and Missiles* (Washington, D.C.: U.S. Library of Congress, Congressional Research Service, February 18, 1993).

6. In his 1992 report to Congress, for instance, Secretary of Defense Dick Cheney indicated that the United States "may require advanced [military] systems to deal with the proliferation of weapons of mass destruction—*to destroy them before they are used* [or] to discourage others from contemplating their use" (emphasis added). DoD, *Annual Report FY93*, p. 6.

7. Address to the U.N. General Assembly, New York City, September 27, 1993, as published in *U.S. Department of State Dispatch*, September 27, 1993, p. 651.

8. For discussion, see Smith and Cobban, "A Blind Eye to Nuclear Proliferation."

9. For discussion of the tensions in U.S. foreign policy between nonproliferation and containment, see U.S. Congress, Office of Technology Assessment, *Proliferation of Weapons of Mass Destruction: Assessing the Risks*, Report OTA-ISC-559 (Washington, D.C.: U.S. Government Printing Office, August 1993), pp. 25–26. (Hereinafter cited as OTA, *Proliferation of WMD*.) See also Peter A. Clausen, *Nonproliferation and the National Interest* (New York: HarperCollins College Publishers, 1993, chap. 5).

10. For discussion, see Terry Deibel, "Hidden Commitments," *Foreign Policy*, no. 67 (Summer 1987), pp. 46–63; Michael T. Klare, "Subterranean Alliances: America's Global Proxy Network," *Journal of International Affairs* 43:1 (Summer/Fall 1983), pp. 97–118; Stephen W. Walt, *The Origins of Alliances* (Ithaca: Cornell University Press, 1987).

11. For discussion of this sort of "reverse dependency," see Deibel, "Hidden Commitments"; Walt, *The Origins of Alliances*, especially pp. 236–41.

12. For discussion, see Clausen, *Nonproliferation and the National Interest*, pp. 164–71; Hersh, "On the Nuclear Edge," pp. 56–73; Smith and Cobban, "A Blind Eye to Nuclear Proliferation," pp. 57–59; Spector, *The Undeclared Bomb*, pp. 125–42, 474–80; Spector, *Nuclear Ambitions*, pp. 91–110.

13. For discussion, see Clausen, *Nonproliferation and the National Interest*, pp. 108–14, 116–21; Hersh, *The Sampson Option;* Smith and Cobban, "A Blind Eye to Nuclear Proliferation," pp. 59–65.

14. For discussion, see Clausen, *Nonproliferation and the National Interest*, pp. 101–107, 121–24; Richard P. Cronin, "India and Pakistan," in Snyder and Wells, *Limiting Nuclear Proliferation*, pp. 79–80.

15. Statement of Rear Admiral Thomas A. Brooks, Director of Naval Intelligence, Before the Seapower, Strategic, and Critical Materials Subcommittee of the House Armed Services Committee, Washington, D.C., March 7, 1991 (mimeo), p. 58.

16. The skewed U.S. position on proliferation is evident, for example, in the statement delivered by CIA Director James Woolsey before the Senate Governmental Affairs Committee on February 24, 1993. Billed as a comprehensive overview of the proliferation problem, the statement devoted 23 lines of text to Iran, 30 to North Korea, and 38 to Iraq, while India and Pakistan were allotted only 19 between them and Egypt, Israel, South Korea, and Taiwan, none.

17. For background on the various regimes and their provisions, see Davis, *Nonproliferation Regimes*.

18. For discussion, see Wolfgang K. H. Panofsky and George Bunn, "The Doctrine of the Nuclear-Weapon States and the Future of Proliferation," *Arms Control Today*, July/August 1994, pp. 3–9.

19. For an articulation of critical Third World views on proliferation, see

Shireen M. Mazari, "Nuclear Weapons and Structures of Conflict in the Developing World," in W. Thomas Wander and Eric H. Arnett, eds., *The Proliferation of Advanced Weaponry: Technology, Motivations, and Responses* (Washington, D.C.: American Association for the Advancement of Science, 1992), pp. 43–51; C. Raja Mohan and K. Subrahmanyam, "High-Technology Weapons in the Developing World," in Eric H. Arnett, ed., *New Technologies for Security and Arms Control* (Washington, D.C.: American Association for the Advancement of Science, 1989), pp. 229–37.

20. For discussion, see Nolan, *Trappings of Power*, chap. 1.

21. Quoted in *Arms Control Today*, May 1992, p. 18.

22. For an excellent survey of this struggle throughout history, see William H. McNeill, *The Pursuit of Power* (Chicago: University of Chicago Press, 1982).

23. Speaking of the desire of these states to acquire ballistic missiles, for instance, W. Thomas Wander of the American Association for the Advancement of Science wrote: "Politically, the possession and especially the production of ballistic missiles are important symbols of a nation's status. Including ballistic missiles in one's arsenals indicates to a country's foes and, importantly, to its own people that it belongs to a select group of nations that can produce or operate some of the world's most technologically sophisticated weapons and that it will arm its military forces with the best technology available to it." Wander, "The Proliferation of Ballistic Missiles," in Wander and Arnett, *The Proliferation of Advanced Weaponry*, p. 76.

24. For discussion of CW proliferator motives, see W. Seth Carus, "Why Chemical Weapons Proliferate: Military and Political Perceptions," in Arnett, *New Technologies*, pp. 279–85.

25. For further discussion of proliferator motives, see the essays in Part III ("Why Nations Buy, Build, and Sell Arms") in Wander and Arnett, *The Proliferation of Advanced Weaponry*. See also the essays by Mushahid Hussain and Shireen Mazari in same volume.

26. For discussion of the tension between commercial interests and nonproliferation objectives in U.S. foreign policy, see OTA, *Proliferation of WMD*, pp. 26–28.

27. See Stuart Auerbach, "1.5 Billion in U.S. Sales to Iraq," *Washington Post*, March 11, 1991; Michael Wines, "U.S. Tells of Prewar Technology Sales to Iraq," *New York Times*, March 12, 1991. See also Henry Weinstein and William C. Rempel, "Iraq Arms: Big Help from U.S.," *Los Angeles Times*, February 13, 1991; U.S. General Accounting Office, *Iraq: U.S. Military Items Exported or Transferred to Iraq in the 1980s* (Washington, D.C.: General Accounting Office, February 1994).

28. See Keith Bradsher, "Report Links German Companies and Scud Parts," *New York Times*, December 8, 1991; Milhollin, "Building Saddam's Bomb"; Milhollin, "Iraq's Bomb—an Update," *New York Times*, April 26,

1993; R. Jeffrey Smith and Marc Fisher, "German Firms Primed Iraq's War Machine," *Washington Post*, July 23, 1992; R. Jeffrey Smith, "13 Firms Named as Sources of Nuclear Items for Iraq," *Washington Post*, December 12, 1991; R. Jeffrey Smith, "Dozens of U.S. Exports Went to Iraqi Arms Projects," *Washington Post*, July 22, 1992.

29. For a review of current U.S. controls over the export of technology, see Lynn E. Davis, "Export Controls and Non-proliferation in the Post-Cold War World," statement before the Subcommittee on International Finance and Monetary Policy of the Senate Banking, Housing, and Urban Affairs Committee, Washington, D.C., February 24, 1994, as published in *U.S. Department of State Dispatch*, March 14, 1994, pp. 149–52. For a critical response, see Jon B. Wolfstahl, "Administration's Export Act Proposal Rankles Industry, Control Advocates," *Arms Control Today*, April 1994, p. 24.

30. See Steve Coll, "Stolen Plutonium Linked to Arms Lab," *Washington Post*, August 17, 1994; Craig R. Whitney, "Germans Seize 3d Atom Sample, Smuggled by Plane from Russia," *New York Times*, August 14, 1994; Whitney, "Germans Suspect Russian Military in Plutonium Sale," *New York Times*, August 16, 1994.

31. See William J. Broad, "U.S. Energy Chief Sees Russian Security as Lax," *New York Times*, August 18, 1994; Broad, "A Smuggling Boom Brings Calls for Tighter Nuclear Safeguards," *New York Times*, August 21, 1994; Michael R. Gordon and Matthew L. Wald, "Russian Controls on Bomb Material Are Leaky," *New York Times*, August 18, 1994.

32. Sources for this discussion include Spector, *Nuclear Ambitions*; Spector, "Nuclear Proliferation Status Report, July 1992" (Carnegie Endowment for International Peace); Spector, "Nuclear Proliferation in the Middle East."

Sources on chemical and biological weapons include "Chemical Weapons in the Middle East," *Arms Control Today*, May 1991, pp. 26–27; Elisa D. Harris, "Chemical Weapons Proliferation," in Aspen Strategy Group, *New Threats: Responding to the Proliferation of Nuclear, Chemical, and Biological Capabilities in the Third World* (Lanham, MD.: Aspen Institute and University Press of America, 1990), pp. 70–75; OTA, *Proliferation of WMD*, p. 65; SCGA, *Global Spread* (especially testimony by Elisa Harris and W. Seth Carus); Statement of Rear Admiral Brooks, March 7, 1991, pp. 56–59; Timmerman, *Weapons of Mass Destruction*, pp. 27–38, 59–69, 80–82 (on Iran, Syria, and Libya).

Sources on ballistic missiles include Lora Lumpe, et al., "Third World Missiles Fall Short"; "Missile and Space Launch Capabilities of Selected Countries," *Proliferation Review*, Winter 1994, pp. 96–99; Janne D. Nolan and Albert D. Wheelon, "Third World Ballistic Missiles," *Scientific American*, August 1990, pp. 34–40; SIPRI, *SIPRI Yearbook 1990*, pp. 287–317; SIPRI, *SIPRI Yearbook 1991*, pp. 317–43; Timmerman, *Weapons of Mass Destruction*, pp. 20–27, 69–73, 82–83 (on Iran, Syria, and Libya).

33. For background on the production of nuclear weapons, see David Albright, "A Proliferation Primer," *Bulletin of the Atomic Scientists*, June 1993, pp. 14–23; OTA, *Proliferation of WMD*, pp. 33–36; Spector, *Nuclear Ambitions*, Appendixes A and B.

34. Hersh, *The Sampson Option*, pp. 36–40, 59–65, 68–70.

35. Ibid., p. 30. See also Spector, *Nuclear Ambitions*, p. 152.

36. Hersh, *The Sampson Option*, pp. 263–68, 271–83.

37. See Kan, *Chinese Missile and Nuclear Proliferation*, p. 6; Spector, *Nuclear Ambitions*, p. 93.

38. Kan, *Chinese Missile and Nuclear Proliferation*, p. 6, based on information supplied to *Washington Post* on May 12, 1991, by University of Wisconsin law professor Gary Milhollin.

39. See Leslie H. Gelb, "Pakistan Links Peril U.S.-China Nuclear Pact," *New York Times*, June 22, 1984; Gelb, "Peking Said to Balk at Nuclear Pledges," *New York Times*, June 23, 1984.

40. See Clausen, *Nonproliferation and the National Interest*, pp. 101–107; Cronin, "India and Pakistan," pp. 62–63.

41. Spector, *Nuclear Ambitions*, pp. 40, 251–54.

42. For discussion, see Spector, *Nuclear Ambitions*, pp. 29–42.

43. Ibid., p. 31.

44. See Albright and Hibbs, "Iraq's Shop-Till-You-Drop Nuclear Program," pp. 27–37; Glenn Frankel, "How Saddam Built His War Machine," *Washington Post*, September 17, 1990. See also Jeff Gerth, "Iraqi Agents and Fronts Listed by U.S.," *New York Times*, April 2, 1991.

45. Albright and Hibbs, "Iraq's Shop-Till-You-Drop Nuclear Program," p. 35. For more on Matrix-Churchill, see Timmerman, *The Death Lobby*, pp. 271–72, 280–83, 286, 327, 332, 341, 352.

46. Spector, *Nuclear Ambitions*, pp. 34, 91.

47. Ibid., p. 34–35.

48. For background on CW agents and their manufacture, see OTA, *Proliferation of WMD*, pp. 36–38, 46–50.

49. Harris, "Chemical Weapons Proliferation," p. 74.

50. SCGA, *Global Spread*, p. 20.

51. Ibid. See also Michael R. Gordon and Stephen Engelberg, "Egypt Accused of Big Advance in Gas for War," *New York Times*, March 10, 1989; Elaine Sciolino, "U.S. Sends 2,000 Gas Masks to the Chadians," *New York Times*, September 25, 1987.

52. SCGA, *Global Spread*, p. 11.

53. Ferdinand Protzman, "German Confesses on Libyan Plant," *New York Times*, June 14, 1990; Serge Schmemann, "German Is Charged in Libyan Case," *New York Times*, March 23, 1990.

54. Smith and Fisher, "German Firms Primed Iraq's War Machine." See also Timmerman, *The Death Lobby*, pp. 110–12.

55. On Iraq, see Timmerman, *Weapons of Mass Destruction*, pp. 34–37. On Syria, see ibid., pp. 61–68.

56. For background on BW munitions and their production, see OTA, *Proliferation of WMD*, pp. 38–40, 46–50.

57. John M. Goshko and Trevor Rowe, "U.N. Panel Describes Iraq's Anthrax Threat," *Washington Post*, August 15, 1991. See also Bill Gertz, "Biological Arms Elude Inspectors," *Washington Times*, April 21, 1991; Susan Wright, "Prospects for Biological Disarmament in the 1990s," *Transnational Law and Contemporary Problems* 2:2 (Fall 1992), pp. 467–69.

58. See Wright, "Prospects for Biological Disarmament," pp. 466–71.

59. See "Missile and Space Launch Capabilities of Selected Countries," pp. 96–99; Nolan and Wheelan, "Third World Ballistic Missiles."

60. On North Korean Scud sales, see statement Bermudez, September 14, 1993, pp. 2–3. See also Peter Hayes, "The Two Koreas and the International Missile Trade," in William C. Potter and Harlan W. Jencks, eds., *The International Missile Bazaar* (Boulder, CO: Westview, 1994), pp. 147–51.

61. Hua Di, "China's Case: Ballistic Missile Proliferation," in Potter and Jencks, *The International Missile Bazaar*, pp. 163–80; Kan, *Chinese Missile and Nuclear Proliferation*, pp. 2–5. See also Holmes, "U.S. Determines China Violated Pact on Missiles."

62. For background, see Hayes, "The Two Koreas," pp. 130–34.

63. For background on Pakistan's missile development, see Cameron Binkley, "Pakistan's Ballistic Missile Development: The Sword of Islam?" in Potter and Jencks, *The International Missile Bazaar*, pp. 75–98; on the Arniston, see *SIPRI Yearbook 1991*, pp. 331–32.

64. On the Condor-II, see Carus, *Ballistic Missiles in the Third World*, p. 22; Nolan, *Trappings of Power*, p. 53–54. On the Jericho, see SIPRI, *SIPRI Yearbook 1990*, p. 299. On the Agni, see Gary Milhollin, "India's Missiles—with a Little Help from Our Friends," *Bulletin of the Atomic Scientists*, November 1989, pp. 31–35; Nolan, *Trappings of Power*, pp. 40–46. On Taiwan's missiles, see SIPRI, *SIPRI Yearbook 1990*, p. 307.

65. For a description of these measures, see Davis, *Nonproliferation Regimes*.

66. For background on these measures, see "Nonproliferation Efforts Bolstered," Statement released by the President, the White House, Washington, D.C., July 13, 1992, as published in *U.S. Department of State Dispatch*, July 20, 1992, pp. 569–71.

67. For discussion of this tension, see OTA, *Proliferation of WMD*, pp. 26–28.

68. See Lawrence Scheinman, "Nuclear Safeguards and Non–Proliferation in a Changing World Order," *Security Dialogue* 23:4 (1992), pp. 37–

50. See also "Non–proliferation Efforts Bolstered," *U.S. Department of Dispatch*, July 20, 1992, pp. 569–71.

69. For text and interpretation of the NPT, see U.S. Arms Control and Disarmament Agency (ACDA), *Arms Control and Disarmament Agreements*, 1990 ed. (Washington, D.C.: ACDA, 1990), pp. 89–106. For background on the establishment of the NPT, see Clausen, *Nonproliferation and the National Interest*, chap. 4.

70. For background on this organization, see Davis, *Nonproliferation Regimes*, pp. 14–16; Spector, *Nuclear Ambitions*, pp. 433–36.

71. See Scheinman, "Nuclear Safeguards and Non–Proliferation," pp. 44–45.

72. Ibid., pp. 43–44.

73. For discussion, see James Leonard, "Strengthening the Treaty on the Non–Proliferation of Nuclear Weapons," *Transnational Law and Contemporary Problems* 2:2 (Fall 1992), pp. 385–98.

74. Davis, *Nonproliferation Regimes*, pp. 31–32.

75. Stuart Auerbach, "19 Nations Back U.S. Plan for Chemical Arms Curbs," *Washington Post*, May 31, 1991. See also SIPRI, *SIPRI Yearbook 1994*, pp. 319–20.

76. Indeed, both India and China have already been accused of such transgressions. In one such case, United Phosphorous Co. of Bombay was charged with supplying Syria with 45 tons of trimethyl phosphate, a precursor substance for nerve agents. Jackson Diehl, "India to Investigate Chemical Shipment," *Washington Post*, September 22, 1992. In another case, China was accused of shipping thiodiglycol, a precursor for mustard gas, to Iran. Patrick E. Tyler, "No Chemical Arms Aboard China Ship," *New York Times*, September 6, 1993.

77. For discussion of the CWC, see Jay Brin, "Ending the Scourge of Chemical Weapons," *Technology Review*, April 1993, pp. 30–40; James F. Leonard, "Rolling Back Chemical Proliferation," *Arms Control Today*, October 1992, pp. 13–18; Amy E. Smithson, "Chemical Weapons: The End of the Beginning," *Bulletin of the Atomic Scientists*, October 1992, pp. 36–40.

78. For text and interpretation of the BWC, see ACDA, *Arms Control and Disarmament Agreements*, pp. 129–41.

79. For discussion, see Wright, "Prospects for Biological Disarmament," pp. 456–65; Susan Wright, ed., *Preventing a Biological Arms Race* (Cambridge: MIT Press, 1990), chaps. 6–8.

80. For discussion, see GAO, *Efforts to Ban Biological Weapons*, pp. 14–28; Jonathan B. Tucker, "The Future of Biological Warfare," in Wander and Arnett, *The Proliferation of Advanced Weaponry*, pp. 59–60; Susan Wright, "Biowar Treaty in Danger," *Bulletin of the Atomic Scientists*, September 1991, pp. 36–40; Wright, "Prospects for Biological Disarmament," pp. 473–84.

81. For a list of controlled materials, suspect states, and licensing pro-

cedures under the EPCI, see GAO, *Efforts to Ban Biological Weapons*, pp. 29–30, 59–61.

82. Ibid., pp. 35–36.

83. For discussion, see Tucker, "The Future of Biological Warfare," pp. 62–65.

84. For background on the MTCR, see Davis, *Nonproliferation Regimes*, pp. 42–44; Stanford University, Center for International Security and Arms Control (CISAC), *Assessing Ballistic Missile Proliferation and Its Control* (Stanford: CISAC, 1991), pp. 119–23.

85. See CISAC, *Assessing Ballistic Missile Proliferation*, p. 122; U.S. General Accounting Office (GAO), *Arms Control: U.S. Efforts to Control the Transfer of Nuclear-Capable Missile Technology*, Report GAO/NSIAD-90-176 (Washington, D.C.: GAO, June 1990), pp. 17–18.

86. See Di, "China's Case," pp. 168–71; Steven A. Holmes, "China Denies Violating Pact by Selling Arms to Pakistan," *New York Times*, July 26, 1993; Kan, *Chinese Missile and Nuclear Proliferation*, pp. 3–5.

87. See Holmes, "U.S. Determines China Violated Pact"; Wolfsthal, "U.S. Imposes Sanctions over China's Missile Transfers."

88. See statement by Defense Secretary Cheney cited in n. 6, above. In his confirmation statement to the Senate Foreign Relations Committee, Warren Christopher observed, "We must work assiduously with other nations to discourage proliferation through improved intelligence, export controls, incentives, sanctions, and even force when necessary." From text of presentation in *U.S. Department of State Dispatch*, January 25, 1993, p. 47.

89. For background, see Jed C. Snyder, "Iraq," in Snyder and Wells, *Limiting Nuclear Proliferation*, pp. 19–28.

90. Foreign Broadcast Information Service, *Middle East and North Africa*, December 18, 1981, pp. I–17.

91. For discussion, see Snyder, "Iraq," pp. 22–24.

92. For discussion, see Spector, *Nuclear Ambitions*, pp. 188, 191–92.

93. See Lewis, "U.N. Aides Discover Arms Center Concealed by Iraq"; Record, *Hollow Victory*, pp. 64–66; R. Jeffrey Smith, "Grim Lessons for the World in Iraq's Secret Nuclear Program," *Washington Post National Weekly Edition*, August 19–25, 1991, pp. 22–23.

94. DoD, *Annual Report FY95*, p. 38.

95. Testimony, December 3, 1990, as transcribed in SASC, *Crisis in the Gulf*, p. 650.

96. Leonard Spector, "Deterring Regional Threats from Weapons Proliferation," in Gary L. Guertner, ed., *The Search for Strategy* (Westport, CT: Greenwood Press, in association with the Strategic Studies Institute of the U.S. Army War College, 1993), pp. 226–27.

97. Michael J. Mazarr, "Lessons of the North Korean Crisis," *Arms Control Today*, July/August 1993, p. 9.

98. Spector, "Deterring Regional Threats," p. 226.

99. Ibid., p. 227.

100. For a discussion of this risk, see Jiri Matousek, "The Release in War of Dangerous Substances from Chemical Facilities," in Arthur Westing, ed., *Environmental Hazards of War* (London: Sage Publications, 1990), pp. 30–37.

101. Nolan, "Proliferation and International Security: An Overview," in Wander and Arnett, *The Proliferation of Advanced Weaponry*, p. 9.

102. Ibid.

CHAPTER SEVEN

1. According to one survey, the use of the terms "rogue nation," "rogue state," and "rogue regime" in major newspapers and journals increased by more than 1500 percent between 1990 and 1993. "Citations to Rogue Nation, Rogue State, or Rogue Regime," *Proliferation Watch*, Senate Committee on Governmental Affairs, March–April 1994, p. 2.

2. For further discussion of this point, see Paul Bracken, "The Military After Next," *Washington Quarterly* 16:4 (Autumn 1993), pp. 157–74; Callahan, "Saving Defense Dollars," pp. 107–10; Krepinevich, *The Bottom-Up Review*, esp. pp. 11–19, 41–44; Philip Morrison, Kosta Tsipis, and Jerome Wiesner, "The Future of American Defense," *Scientific American*, February 1994, pp. 38–45.

3. In 1994, Senator John Glenn of Ohio wrote that " 'Rogue mania' is sweeping the nation . . . [uniting] Democrat and Republican, liberal and conservative." "The Proliferation of Rogues," *Proliferation Watch*, March–April 1994, p. 1.

4. Steven Kosiak, *Analysis of the Fiscal Year 1994 Defense Budget Request* (Washington, D.C.: Defense Budget Project, April 14, 1993), Table 3. Figures are for annual Budget Authority, and include all National Security (federal budget category 050) items.

5. See, for instance, Charles Krauthammer, "Get Ready for War," *Washington Post*, June 3, 1994; William Safire, "Korean Conflict II?" *New York Times*, June 9, 1994.

6. See David C. Morrison, "Phony War Scenario Stirs India," *National Journal*, April 6, 1991, pp. 804–806.

7. For discussion of the tectonic concept as applied to human societies in the post–Cold War era, see John Lewis Gaddis, "Tectonics, History, and the End of the Cold War (Columbus, OH: Occasional Paper from the Mershon Center of Ohio State University, 1992).

8. For discussion of these points, see Thomas Homer-Dixon, Jeffrey Bout-

well, and George Rathjens, "Environmental Change and Violent Conflict," *Scientific American*, February 1993, pp. 38–45; Samuel P. Huntington, "The Clash of Civilizations?" *Foreign Affairs*, Summer 1993, pp. 22–49; Michael T. Klare, "The New Challenges to Global Security," *Current History*, April 1993, pp. 166–61; Nicholas X. Rizopolous, ed., *Sea Changes: American Foreign Policy in a World Transformed* (New York: Council on Foreign Relations Press, 1990); Myron Wiener, "Peoples and States in a New Ethnic Order?" *Third World Quarterly* 13:2 (1992), pp. 317–33.

9. See Peter Wallensteen and Karin Axell, "Armed Conflict at the End of the Cold War, 1989–92," *Journal of Peace Research* 30:3 (1993), pp. 331–46. For background on each of these conflicts, see the annual survey of "major armed conflicts" in the *SIPRI Yearbook*. On refugee flows, see John Darnton, "U.N. Faces Refugee Crisis that Never Ends," *New York Times*, August 8, 1994.

10. For discussion, see Pierre Hassner, "Beyond Nationalism and Internationalism: Ethnicity and World Order," *Survival* 35:2 (Summer 1993), pp. 49–65; Donald L. Horowitz, "Ethnic and Nationalist Conflict," in Michael T. Klare and Daniel Thomas, *World Security: Challenges for a New Century*, 2nd ed. (New York: St. Martin's Press, 1994), pp. 175–87; Ronald K. McMullen and Augustus Richard Norton, "Somalia and Other Adventures for the 1990s," *Current History*, April 1993, pp. 169–74;

11. Gordon R. Sullivan and Andrew B. Twomey, "The Challenges of Peace," *Parameters*, Autumn 1994, p. 6.

12. For elaboration on these points, see Robert C. Johansen, "Building Security: The Need for Strengthened International Institutions," in Klare and Thomas, *World Security*, pp. 372–97. See also SIPRI, *SIPRI Yearbook 1994*, pp. 19–25.

13. Boutros Boutros-Ghali, *An Agenda for Peace* (New York: United Nations, 1992). See also SIPRI, *SIPRI Yearbook 1994*, pp. 14–19.

14. See ibid., pp. 43–51.

15. See Jeffrey Boutwell, Michael Klare, and Laura Reed, eds., *Lethal Commerce: The Global Trade in Small Arms and Light Weapons* (Cambridge: American Academy of Arts and Sciences, 1994); Aaron Karp, "Arming Ethnic Conflict," *Arms Control Today*, September 1993, pp. 8–13; Daniel N. Nelson, "Ancient Enmities, Modern Guns," *Bulletin of the Atomic Scientists*, December 1993, pp. 21–27; Christopher Smith, "Light Weapons: The Forgotten Dimension of the International Arms Trade," in *Brassey's Defence Yearbook 1994* (London: Brassey's U.K., 1994), pp. 271–84. For a detailed study on arms sales to Rwanda, see Human Rights Watch Arms Project, *Arming Rwanda* (New York and Washington: Human Rights Watch, January 1994).

16. For discussion, see "The Covert Arms Trade," *The Economist*, February 12, 1994, pp. 21–23; Michael T. Klare, "The Thriving Black Market for

Weapons," *Bulletin of the Atomic Scientists*, April 1988, pp. 16–24. See also U.S. Congress, Senate, Committee on Governmental Affairs, Permanent Subcommittee on Investigations, *Arms Trafficking, Mercenaries and Drug Cartels*, Hearing, 102d Cong., 1st Ses. (Washington, D.C.: U.S. Government Printing Office, 1991).

17. See "High Costs of the Persian Gulf War," U.S. Arms Control and Disarmament Agency, *World Military Expenditures and Arms Transfers 1988* (Washington, D.C.: U.S. Government Printing Office, 1989), pp. 21–23.

18. DSAA, *Military Sales Facts 1993*. For background on U.S. arms export policies, see William D. Hartung, *And Weapons for All* (New York: HarperCollins, 1994).

19. In testimony before the House Foreign Affairs Committee on November 10, 1993, Undersecretary of State Lynn Davis commented on U.S. arms sales policy in the Middle East as follows: "Arms sales are appropriate to responsible allies, and that is where our sales have been going in the follow-on to the Gulf War, to allay the insecurities in the Middle East and the Gulf. . . ." Asked whether Washington could credibly ask other arms suppliers to restrain their sales when the United States is selling so many weapons to its clients, Davis responded, "We can have credibility by the fact that the [arms] transfers that we are making are for legitimate security reasons." Quoted in *Arms Sales Monitor*, Federation of American Scientists, July 30, 1994, p. 2.

20. See, for example, Thomas L. Friedman, "U.S. Says Saudi Arabia Sent U.S.–Made Arms to Iraq and 2 Other Nations," *New York Times*, April 21, 1992.

21. See Klare, "The Thriving Black Market for Weapons"; Edward J. Laurance, "Political Implications of Illegal Arms Exports from the United States," *Political Science Quarterly* 102:3 (1992), pp. 109–40.

22. For elaboration of such proposals, see Michael T. Klare, "Gaining Control: Building a Comprehensive Arms Restraint System," *Arms Control Today*, June 1991, pp. 9–13.

23. For further discussion of such proposals, see Klare, "The Thriving Black Market for Weapons," pp. 23–24.

24. For discussion, see Thomas Homer-Dixon, "Environmental Scarcity and Violent Conflict: Evidence from Cases," *International Security* 19:1 (Summer 1994), pp. 5–40; Jessica Tuchman Mathews, "The Environment and International Security," in Klare and Thomas, *World Security*, pp. 274–89; Dennis Pirages, "Demographic Change and Ecological Insecurity," in ibid., pp. 314–31.

25. For discussion of this problem, see Homer-Dixon, "Environmental Scarcity and Intergroup Conflict," pp. 306–310. See also World Bank, *Development and the Environment*, World Development Report 1992 (Washington, D.C.: World Bank, 1992).

26. For discussion, see Michael J. Mazarr, "Lessons of the North Korean Crisis," *Arms Control Today*, July/August 1993, pp. 8–12.

27. For discussion, see Jacqueline R. Smith and Lewis A. Dunn, "The Main Proliferation Risks," *Transnational Law and Contemporary Problems* 2:2 (Fall 1992), pp. 331–56.

28. For discussion, see ibid., pp. 343–54. See also Leonard, "Strengthening the Treaty on the Non–Proliferation of Nuclear Weapons."

29. For discussion, see OTA, *Proliferation of WMD*, pp. 93–104.

30. See Nathaniel C. Nash, "Argentina Signs Technology Pact," *New York Times*, February 13, 1993.

31. For discussion, see Paul Doty, "Policy Issues in Chemical Weapons Control," in Aspen Strategy Group, *New Threats*, pp. 143–62; Kyle Olson, "Feasibility of a Chemical Weapons Regime," in Aspen Strategy Group, *New Threats*, pp. 129–41; Roberts, "Controlling Chemical Weapons," pp. 446–51.

32. SCGA, *Global Spread*, pp. 11–13, 19.

33. For background on these efforts, see DoD, *Annual Report FY94*, pp. 43–45; *SIPRI Yearbook 1993*, pp. 566–70.

34. See Broad, "A Smuggling Boom Brings Calls for Tighter Nuclear Restraints."

35. For discussion, see OTA, *Proliferation of WMD*, pp. 104–109. For background on the CSCE, see ACDA, *Arms Control and Disarmament Agreements*, pp. 319–35.

36. Nolan, "Technology and Non-Proliferation," p. 432.

37. For background on NWFZs, see Jon Brook Wolfstahl, "Nuclear-Weapon–Free Zones: Coming of Age?" *Arms Control Today*, March 1993, pp. 3–9. For text and background of the Latin America accord, see ACDA, *Arms Control and Disarmament Agreements*, pp. 64–88.

38. For discussion of such measures, and their possible application to the Middle East, see Geoffrey Kemp, *The Control of the Middle East Arms Race* (Washington, D.C.: Carnegie Endowment for International Peace, 1992), pp. 119–46; Gerald M. Steinberg, "Middle East Arms Control and Regional Security," *Survival*, Spring 1994, pp. 126–41.

39. For discussion, see Stephen P. Cohen, "Solving Proliferation Problems in a Regional Context: South Asia," in Aspen Strategy Group, *New Threats*, pp. 163–95; Michael Klare, "The Next Great Arms Race," *Foreign Affairs* 72:3 (Summer 1993), pp. 136–52; James F. Leonard and Adam M. Scheinman, "Denuclearizing South Asia: Global Approaches to a Regional Problem," *Bulletin of the Atomic Scientists*, June 1993, pp. 17–22; Nolan, "Ballistic Missiles in the Third World," pp. 13–14.

40. Such activities, collectively called "peace operations" by the U.S. military, include both "peacekeeping," or the maintenance of a cease-fire or peace accord that has been agreed to by the parties involved, and "peace

enforcement," or the use of military force (under international auspices) to *impose* a peace plan that has been approved by the U.N. Security Council but is being opposed by some or all parties to the dispute. In a peacekeeping operation, international forces are present at the invitation of the warring parties; in peace enforcement, they may have to insinuate themselves in the face of armed opposition. Needless to say, there can be a great deal of overlap between the two, as visible in the U.N. peacekeeping mission in Somalia. For further discussion of these distinctions, see Boutros-Ghali, *An Agenda for Peace.*

41. For a detailed description of such a force (with cost estimates), see Morrison, Tsipis, and Wiesner, "The Future of American Defense," pp. 38–45.

42. "The most persuasive tool the nuclear-weapon states have to decrease the motivation of non-nuclear-weapon states to opt for nuclear weapons," proliferation experts Wolfgang K. H. Panofsky and George Bunn wrote in 1994, "is to *deemphasize the role of nuclear weapons as instruments of national policy*" (emphasis in the original). Wolfgang K. H. Panofsky and George Bunn, "The Doctrine of the Nuclear-Weapon States and the Future of Non-Proliferation," *Arms Control Today*, July/August 1994, p. 9.

Index